CUSTOMIZING THE BODY

CUSTOMIZING THE BODY

The Art and Culture of Tattooing

REVISED AND EXPANDED EDITION

Clinton R. Sanders
with D. Angus Vail

Temple University Press Philadelphia

Temple University Press
1601 North Broad Street
Philadelphia PA 19122
www.temple.edu/tempress

♾The paper used in this publication meets the requirements of the American National
Standard for Information Sciences—Permanence of Paper for Printed Library Materials,
ANSI Z39.48-1992

Library of Congress Cataloging-in-Publication Data
Sanders, Clinton.
Customizing the body : the art and culture of tattooing / Clinton R.
Sanders with D. Angus Vail.—Rev. and expanded ed.
    p. cm.
Includes bibliographical references and index.
ISBN-13: 978-1-59213-887-6   ISBN-10: 1-59213-887-X (cloth : alk. paper)
ISBN-13: 978-1-59213-888-3   ISBN-10: 1-59213-888-8 (pbk. : alk. paper)
1. Tattooing--Social aspects. 2. Tattoo artists. I. Vail, D. Angus. II.
Title.
  GT2345.S26 2008
  391.6'5--dc22
  2008001837

2 4 6 8 9 7 5 3 1

Contents

Preface to the Revised and Expanded Edition

In those days, a tattoo was still a souvenir—a keepsake to mark a journey, the love of your life, a heartbreak, a port of call. The body was like a photo album; the tattoos themselves didn't have to be good photographs. . . . And the old tattoos were always sentimental: you didn't mark yourself for life if you weren't sentimental (Irving, 2005: 74–75).

 Much has changed on the tattooing (and larger body alteration) landscape since *Customizing the Body* first appeared in the late 1980s. Perhaps the most important change has been the transformation of tattooing from the ostensibly "deviant" practice I discussed in the first edition to the popular cultural phenomenon it is today.

There are (at least) three criteria sociologists use to define an activity, perspective, or appearance as fitting into the category of "deviant." First, the phenomenon could be seen as constituting or causing some sort of social harm. Since much of what might be considered to be socially harmful rests on the values of the person or persons doing the defining, what is regarded as "bad" behavior, "disgusting" or "shocking" appearance, or "inappropriate" thoughts is largely a matter of taste (though sociologists tend to overlay their personal tastes with a legitimating patina of theory). A second way of understanding deviance is to see it simply as something that is relatively rare. This "statistical" orientation, of course, has some presumed relationship to the values/harm model since what is bad by definition is presumed to be appealing to only a relatively small number of twisted, misguided, or unfortunate people.

A third, and to my mind the most useful, way of thinking about social deviance is to see it as behavior, thoughts, or appearances that are widely regarded as "bad." Consequently, when those who engage in the bad behavior, think the bad thoughts, or publicly display their bad appearance come to the attention of some audience or another, they are subjected to punishment or some other kind of negative social reaction. This third orientation has the advantage of making a distinction between breaking rules and being "deviant" in that deviance is defined as that which is the focus of social reaction. A person might break rules and not be found out—he or she is a rule-breaker but not a deviant—or one could not break rules and still be "falsely accused" of being a violator—he or she is a deviant but not a rule-breaker. It is especially useful for understanding the shifting social definition of tattooing and other forms of permanent body modification in that this "labeling" perspective (deviance as a socially applied label) incorporates the central idea that defined deviance changes over time, from culture to culture, and depends on just who is doing the defining (see Becker, 1963; Goode, 2005: 86-93; Rubington and Weinberg, 2002).

Tattooing and, to a somewhat lesser degree, other modes of body alteration have been "de-deviantized" since the early 1990s in light of the last two definitions of deviance. Tattooing has become more widely practiced (that is, more popular) and has, therefore, come to be seen as less odd, unusual, rebellious, or otherwise deviant. In general, those things your friends do are significantly less likely to be negatively regarded than are those things strangers do.

Although I see it as wise to take the findings of survey research with considerable skepticism, polls conducted in the early– to mid–1990s suggested that somewhere between 3 and 10 percent of the general population were tattooed (Anderson, 1992; Armstrong and McConnell, 1994; Armstrong and Pace-Murphy, 1997). Recently, a study conducted by Anne Laumann, a dermatologist at Northwestern University, revealed that 24 percent of American adults between the ages of 18 and 50 are tattooed and one in seven had a body piercing somewhere other than the earlobe (nearly one-third of young adults between the ages of 18 and 29 said they were pierced) (Laumann and Derick, 2006).

The movement of tattooing into the realm of popular culture displays certain features of the contemporary culture industry and reveals how fad-like phenomena emerge. Culture producers, beset by the problem of "commercial uncertainty" (that is, what popular cultural products will or will not be successful [see Sanders, 1990]), are constantly on the lookout for new materials

Preface to the Revised and Expanded Edition

with potential commercial appeal. Typically, the producers keep
an eye on the interests, activities, and appearance of those outside the boundaries of social power. The tastes and entertainment
and material interests of minorities, teenagers, disaffected urban
residents, and other "outsiders" are filched by the culture industry, cleaned up and homogenized, avidly promoted as the latest
thing, and sold to the larger consumer market. In short, the major
source of innovation in popular culture is in the materials and
activities of the relatively poor and powerless; innovation flows up
the stream of power.

This process has impelled the movement of tattooing into popular culture. Beginning with the "tattoo renaissance" of the 1960s
(discussed in Chapter 1), musicians, movie actors, and other entertainment figures admired and followed by young people started acquiring and displaying tattoos. Similarly, sports figures—typically
from minority and/or impoverished backgrounds—were tattooed.
Despite the fact that most of the tattoos displayed by entertainers
and (especially) athletes look as if they were done by eight-year-
olds with magic markers, the fact that admired public figures were
tattooed gave tattooing a certain popular cultural cachet.

While exposure by key figures in the mediated popular culture
is an important factor in the rise and dissemination of cultural
interests and products, cultural innovation and the consumption
of particular materials also derive from people's immediate social
networks and contacts. As we see in Chapter 2, an important
factor in people's decisions to get tattooed is that their friends or
family members sport tattoos. Understandably then, as more
people are tattooed, more people have contact with those who are
tattooed, and more people see it as reasonable or desirable to
acquire a tattoo. Cultural popularity is a form of contagion.

As tattooing has inserted itself into mainstream popular culture
in the late twentieth and early twenty-first centuries, it has been
thematically assimilated into a variety of media materials. At this
writing, television viewers have access to such tattoo-themed
shows as "Miami Ink" on TLC, "Inked" on A&E, and "Tattoo Stories" on FUSE. Popular memoirs such as Emily Jenkins's *Tongue
First* (1998) and serious novels like John Irving's *Until I Find You*
(2005) and Sarah Hall's *Electric Michelangelo* (2005), a finalist for
2004's Man Booker Prize, feature tattooing and tattooists. Mass
market booksellers like Borders and Barnes & Noble have a vari-

ety of tattoo-oriented titles such as *International Tattoo Art, Skin & Ink,* and *Tattoo Magazine* on their magazine racks. Clearly, tattooing has moved out of the dark underground of the 1950s into the spotlight of mainstream commercial culture.

Given the "mainstreaming" of tattooing, the declining power of the tattoo to generate what I call (after Quentin Bell) "conspicuous outrage" becomes an interesting issue. When the traffic cop who stops you for speeding or the youth minister in your church sports a tattoo, the mark clearly has lost a considerable amount of stigma potential. The issue then becomes "How can those who fit into or aspire to the common social category of 'rebel' visibly demonstrate their divergent identities?" The question "What is next on the horizon of rebellious body alteration?" is commonly tossed at me by the journalists who still call me when they have been assigned filler stories for the leisure section of their papers. When I choose to catch the question, I usually make note of the rising popularity of full-body tattooing and multiple piercings and less frequently encountered, and usually startling, alterations such as extensive facial tattooing and surgical implants of horns, feline-like wire whiskers, and bladders that can be inflated or deflated for appearance-altering effect.

In addition to being incorporated into the lucrative world of popular culture, in the latter part of the twentieth century tattooing also became more firmly situated in the world of "serious" art. The general issue of what products constitute "art" and what factors increase or decrease the likelihood that an activity is deemed "artistic" and an actor is defined as an "artist," was the primary focus of Chapter 5 in the first edition of *Customizing the Body* and is an issue we touch upon again in the 2008 Epilogue. Continuing the trend detailed previously, tattooing has remained a focus of attention as academics have continued to produce "serious" analyses, museums and galleries have continued to mount shows of tattoo works, and specialty publishers have continued to produce pricey coffee-table books containing photos and discussions of tattoo works. Tattooing has even been incorporated into a particular "school" of art. Those like Herbert Gans (1999) who espouse an egalitarian view of art that rejects the hierarchical distinction between "high" (serious, real, traditional) art and "low" (popular, mass, "brutal") art commonly see avant garde art as resting on the border between the simple world of commercial popular culture and the complex aesthetic world of high art where materials are created by specialists ("artists"), evaluated by experts ("critics"), and consumed by monied "collectors." Since the early 1990s, this border space between popular culture and traditional art has been taken over by the expansive category of "lowbrow" art (whose representatives derogatorily refer to traditional fine art as "art-school art"). Grounded on the underground art of the 1960s, and in reaction to the arid, theory-heavy installations that dominated conventional artistic work in the 1980s and 1990s, lowbrow art (sometimes labeled "outlaw art" or "l'art de toilette" by adherents) is composed of such diverse types of products as graffiti art, car art, underground comix, limited-production toys and statuary, customized clothing, "art brut," record-album art, black-velvet paintings, pulp art, poster art, prison art, tiki art, anime and manga, pulp art, and tattooing. Inspired by the dadaists and surrealists of the 1920s and 1930s, advocates and practitioners of lowbrow art reject the constraints imposed by critics, mainstream gallery owners, and other central players in the conventional art world and create an art that is self-consciously representational, dismisses the baggage of art theory, and revels in the aesthetic tastes displayed in urban, street-level culture. Clearly, tattooing has found a home in an established, if somewhat unruly, segment of the larger art world.

Despite its rising popularity and tentative incursion into the world of (at least marginally) legitimate art, it is still reasonable, I would maintain, to regard tattooing (and other forms of permanent body alteration) through the conceptual lens provided by the sociology of deviance. Quite a bit of ink has been spilled recently over the issue of whether "deviance" continues to be a viable and useful analytic category (see, for example, Goode, 2002, 2003; Hendershott, 2002; Sumner, 1994). I have no desire to enter this debate other than to say that I find many of the arguments offered by those who celebrate the "death" of deviance to be unconvincing at best. Creating rules is an elemental feature of social life and, consequently, violating rules and reacting to those violations are of equal importance. Studying misbehavior has been, and continues to be, central to the sociological enterprise. Given its focus on the tattoo as a boundary-setting mark, a sign of subcultural membership, and a potentially stigmatizing identity enhancement and tattooing as a disvalued, officially regulated or prohibited, and secretive occupational practice, *Customizing the Body* was, and is, a study in the sociology of deviance.

Fortunately—or unfortunately, depending on one's perspective—body modification still retains some of its unconventional character and marks practitioners as "deviants." A writer to the advice columnist Amy Dickinson ("Ask Amy") recently complained:

> You mentioned in a recent column that many people between 18 and 29 have tattoos. Sorry, but when you see people with a tattoo or piercing you can't help but question what they were thinking or whether they were even in their right minds when getting it. If these people were forced to have these atrocities done to them, we'd never hear the end of it. But to think they are willingly defacing their God-given bodies in this way is deplorable and despicable! (*The Hartford Courant*, July 30, 2006, p. D5).

To her credit, Amy did not agree.

Additional evidence of the continuing negative definition of tattooing was seen in 2007 when the U.S. Marine Corps banned new, large, publically visible tattoos. The Marine Corps Commandant observed that some marines are "tattooing themselves to a point that it is contrary to our professional demeanor and the high standards America has come to expect from us" (*The Hartford Courant*, March 29, 2007, p. A15).

Many corporations and businesses have a similar orientation to "body art," at least when displayed on public skin. Major corporations such as Wal-Mart and Disney, for example, bar employees from having visible body decorations (*The Week*, July 20, 2007, p. 35) and a 1999 survey conducted by researchers at the University of California at Los Angeles found that 90 percent of campus recruiters disapprove of tattoos (Kang and Jones, 2007: 46). This negative response to tattooing has generated some understandable resistance as heavily tattooed people have begun to discuss their problems with employers as a form of discrimination and to talk about initiating legal action (Wessel, 2007).

Clearly then, tattooing retains some of its deviant baggage despite the cultural changes that have occurred since *Customizing the Body* first appeared. Employers still reject tattooed job applicants and parents still bemoan their children's decisions to get tattooed ("What breaks my heart is the inevitability that [my son] will suffer for this. Whether it's the pain of tattoo removal or, worse yet, the anguish of regret, he will suffer" [Desocio, 2007]). The medical, psycho-therapeutic, and public health industries continue to cast body alteration as a dangerous practice and/or indicative of underlying pathologies. And researchers have developed a tattoo ink (Freedom-2) that may be removed with just one laser treatment and, therefore, requires somewhat less commitment on the part of tattooees (*The Week*, July 13, 2007, p. 22). Given this continuing negative response to tattooing and tattooed people, it is reasonable to see the presentation of tattooing as a deviant occupational practice, the tattooed person as someone who runs the risk of being the focus of negative social reaction, and the "tattoo community" as a deviant subculture that follow to be instructive and worthwhile.

Although *Customizing the Body* turned out to be, I am told, a rousing success in the world of university presses, it enjoyed only moderate attention in the larger media universe. Getting in on the ground floor of a popular cultural phenomenon does generate a certain amount of media attention, and I soon found myself on the journalists' golden Rolodex. In the 1990s I was interviewed for stories in *The New York Times*, *The Wall Street Journal*, the *Chicago Tribune*, *The Boston Globe*, *Newsweek*, *Ladies' Home Journal*, *Esquire*, and a number of smaller publications. I also appeared in special tattoo segments on NBC, the Discovery Channel, TLC, and a variety of local programs. While I sometimes found my conversations with journalists and media figures to be relatively interesting, interviewers frequently asked the same basic questions ("Why does someone get a tattoo?" "Does it hurt?" "What would you tell a parent whose child wants to get a tattoo?"), and dealing with the media soon became rather tiresome. Unfortunately, once one's name gets attached to a particular "hot" cultural topic a kind of academic "role entrapment" occurs—until the topic cooled I was hounded for comments even long after my active research interest in the issue was over.

Less tiresome were the calls, letters, and, later, e-mails I received from everyday people who had read the book or seen my comments in the media. The most common communication was from people who had finally decided to get a first tattoo after reading *Customizing the Body*. Some personal tales of initial hesitance

and eventual identity transformation were quite touching and re-
inforced many of the basic ideas in the book. For example:

> I had wanted a tattoo since high school . . . but never had
> the mental courage to get one because of expected major
> disapproval of family, friends and colleagues. . . . [T]he desire
> was often suppressed because of little exposure to tattoos. . . .
> However, I found and enjoyed [biker magazines]. I envied the
> biker lifestyle image, was discontented by my rigid 9-to-5/8-to-
> 11 television lifestyle and pissed off at my fear of getting a
> tattoo. . . . Thus, at the age of about 48, I told my wife for
> about the fourth time, usually late at night, what I wanted to
> do, and, with a tiny amount of support, I went . . . and got a
> 6-inch tiger inked on my arm. My wife, surprisingly, after a
> few days said she liked it, but said not to get any more.
> Nevertheless, . . . I got an equal sized dragon [on the other
> arm]. Each time I see them in a mirror, I am amazed how . . .
> good they look and, bottom line, I am glad to have them.
> There is no mistaking I am now a tattooed person.

In addition to tales of tattoo decisions and experiences
(commonly accompanied by photographs), I received numerous
requests from students for help with papers, theses, or disserta-
tions; requests from tattoo artists to support their applications to
zoning boards reluctant to grant their applications to open shops;
a request to testify to the superiority of a newly developed laser
tattoo removal system (I declined); and a tentative request from
the editor of a popular tattoo publication that I consider writing a
column for the magazine (again, I declined).

Reviews for *Customizing the Body* were generally positive. For
example, *Kirkus Reviews* called it "the most intelligent book available to date on the modern aspects of an increasingly popular form
of body decoration" and *Choice* labeled it a "fascinating and well-
written study." Reviews directed at sociological or academic audiences (such as in *Contemporary Sociology*, the *Journal of Popular
Culture*, *Communications Research*, *Symbolic Interaction*, and the
Journal of Contemporary Ethnography) were similarly approving.

The book was also reviewed in specialized, non-academic publications such as *Tattoo Magazine*, *Body Art*, and *Piercing Fans
International Quarterly*. Somewhat to my surprise, these reviews

were also quite positive (for example, "the book is a wellspring for the novice fan seeking information about tattooing, and it will give even those who think they know all about tattooing a fresh look at many aspects of the art"). While some reviewers (in both academic and non-academic publications) praised my attempt to present tattooing in reasonably accessible prose, the responses of some commentators to the sociological content was not always entirely favorable. For example, after a fairly positive opening, one reviewer for a British body modification publication observed:

> [T]he book is not without its problems. In particular, Sanders' use of the sort of writing style which afflicts most academic sociologists will cause many a reader . . . to exclaim "What Bullshit!" and hurl the book across the room. . . . Nevertheless, I strongly urge anyone interested in this . . . occupational world to stick with it . . . because, despite its jargon, sociology does have a way of putting an interesting slant on things which will surprise even those who have been involved with tattoos all their lives. And . . . because the numerous quotes from tattooists and their customers are so often spot on and delightful.

It is sometimes difficult to tell the negative reviews from the positive ones.

The initial spurt and continuing dribble of media attention generated by *Customizing the Body* were moderately ego gratifying but the more significant personal consequences of writing the book had to do with my career as an academic sociologist. I received a number of requests from journals and other publications to write pieces on tattooing and body modification. At first, I was pathologically agreeable when confronted by these requests (see Sanders, 1991, 1998, 2000, 2001). As time went on and my research interests moved on to other things, I passed on the majority of these requests to younger (and more actively involved) colleagues.

One of the consequences of the appearance of my research on tattooing with which I am most pleased is that it helped legitimate academic research on purposive body alteration and prompted, to a greater or lesser degree, a number of young sociologists to explore the general topic. *Customizing the Body* laid the groundwork for later investigations by Angus Vail (1999a, 1999b), Katherine

Irwin (2001, 2003), Kim Hewitt (1997), Margo DeMello (2000), Michael Atkinson (2003) and other young social scientists. One of the best things to happen because of my book was that Angus Vail, the co-author of this edition, enrolled in the sociology graduate program at my university and began to work with me on his doctorate. As we discuss in the Epilogue, Angus moved beyond my interest in tattooing as a form of voluntary deviance and focused primarily on tattoo artists and serious collectors as interactants in an established art world, thus expanding the idea I proposed in 1989—that tattooing is an interesting issue that can be examined using the analytic tools offered by the sociology of art.

The relevance of *Customizing the Body* to the sociological analysis of art is, to my mind, the book's greatest virtue and its most important contribution. I rely on the view of art as a product created through cooperative activities of people interacting within the occupational network of an art world that was originally proposed by Howard Becker (1974) in a seminal article published in the *American Sociological Review*. Becker expanded on this perspective in his book *Art Worlds* (1982) where he emphasized that the work of creating art was not a unique activity and that products regarded as "art" were designated as such within a stratified occupational world organized around shared conventional understandings. In *Customizing the Body* I use the case of tattooing to explore which factors increase or decrease the likelihood that an activity will be defined as "artistic," its product defined as "art," and/or the worker producing it defined as an "artist."

Despite this central focus of the book—its expansion of the "institutional" perspective within the sociology of art—*Customizing the Body* has had little impact in that particular area of sociology. While often mentioned within the substantive context of the sociology of deviance or popular culture, the book has rarely, if ever, been referred to by sociologists working in the larger arena of artistic production. In my experience, sociologists who focus on the arts tend to be a somewhat elitist bunch and are inclined to study and discuss "established," conventional, or "fine" arts. These works tend to have an aesthetic and art-history spin to them (see, for example, Crane, 1987; Halle, 1993; Martorella, 1982; Zolberg, 1990) and it would be unlikely that many sociologists of the arts would pay much attention to an ethnography of such a plebeian practice as tattooing.

One need only to take in a couple of episodes of "Inked" or "Miami Ink" to recognize that much of what I wrote about tattooing in the late 1980s continues to be relevant. The occupational world of tattooing and the interactions that take place within the tattoo shop are essentially the same as I first described them. The impact of the tattoo on the recipient's personal and social identity and the symbolic meaning of the tattoo for the tattooee have not changed. What has changed, as I have mentioned, is that tattoo consumption has spread widely within Western culture, and simply wearing a tattoo no longer stigmatizes the tattooed person or acts to outrage members of conventional society. The fad-like spread of tattooing and its incorporation into popular culture have decreased its power to symbolize rebellion.

However, these changes have not made tattooing and other forms of permanent body modification any less sociologically interesting or significant. What Angus Vail and I have done in expanding and updating *Customizing the Body* is to provide an account of the changes that have occurred within the artistic and cultural world of tattooing and the larger world of body alteration in the past decade and a half. One change—and a fairly superficial one—is seen in the rise and decline in popularity of certain tattoo styles and images. As we emphasize in the Epilogue, innovations in the technology of tattooing are partially responsible for stylistic changes. More fundamental changes have occurred in the increased availability of specialized tattoo and body art publications and the related changes in the established organizations that mount tattoo conventions and compete for dominance in the larger tattoo world.

As the tattoo world has expanded, established tattooists and tattoo organizations at the local, national, and international levels have lost their ability to control entry into and knowledge of the "hidden" techniques of tattooing. This is another key issue we present in the Epilogue. The decline of the traditional apprenticeship structure discussed in Chapter 3 has "softened" the borders of tattooing practice and has led, as we emphasize, to an occupational world in which behavior previously seen as not permissible is now more common.

We also explore the central actors in the tattoo world—those who are serious and committed collectors, who spend considerable sums on their collections, who are most familiar with the aesthetic conventions of tattooing, and who patronize the most skilled practitioners of the art/craft. The conventions used by these committed collectors to plan and execute their collections are presented in some detail. We then explore the more extreme fringes to which body alteration has moved, due, in large part, to the desire of some (typically young) members of the society to outrage and to symbolically set themselves apart from mainstream society and its more conformist and conventional elements. Finally, we present the "serious" literature on tattooing and other forms of purposive body modification that has emerged since 1989. As seen in Chapter 2, prior to the publication of *Customizing the Body* there was only a very limited body of academic discussion. Apart from the anthropological discussions, most of this material emphasized the medical dangers of tattooing and the psycho-pathological factors that impelled people to permanently decorate their bodies. As we stress in the Epilogue, this sort of psycho-medical bias is still common in the literature. However, arguably prompted by the perspective offered in the first edition of *Customizing the Body*, much of the more recent literature on body alteration is less condemning and more appreciative.

Angus and I see ethnography as, most centrally, an attempt to reveal a world that is relatively unfamiliar to the reader. In encountering this unfamiliar world, the reader, we hope, will come to realize that the worlds and actors that may appear to be rather bizarre at first glance have ordinary interests and pursue ordinary goals just like the rest of us. As Erving Goffman (1961) so eloquently put it when introducing his ethnography of a mental institution:

> It . . . still is my belief that any group of persons—prisoners, primitives, pilots, or patients—develop a life of their own that becomes meaningful, reasonable, and normal once you get close to it and that a good way to learn about any of these worlds is to submit oneself in the company of the members to the daily round of petty contingencies to which they are subject (pp. ix–x).

In the following pages we hope to introduce you to a social world that is both exotic and ordinary, and we base our portrayal on years of being and interacting with tattooed people. We hope this exposure whets your curiosity and, with *Customizing the Body* as your tour guide, prompts you to venture out into the often mundane, sometimes bizarre, but always interesting, world of body modification on your own.

> *[T]he tattoo culture on display at Daughter Alice made Jack ashamed of his mother's "art." . . . The old maritime tattoos, the sentiments of sailors collecting souvenirs on their bodies, had been replaced by tasteless displays of hostility and violence and evil . . . skulls spurting blood, flames licking the corners of the skeletons' eye sockets. . . . Jack took Claudia aside and said to her: "Generally speaking, attractive people don't get tattooed." But this wasn't strictly true. . . .* (Irving, 2005: 339–340).

Preface to the First Edition

As is commonly the case for fieldworkers, I became involved in this project through personal experience. In the early seventies I had decided to symbolically commemorate the long-awaited receipt of my Ph.D. by piercing my left ear. While this minor body alteration had little impact on my interaction with the junkies, musicians, hippies, and high-school students with whom I lived and worked at the time, I did notice that "normal citizens" began to treat me even more coolly than usual. Here was a nice little sociological study—interview men with pierced ears about how they went about deciding to alter their bodies, how this affected their everyday interactions, and what steps they took to deal with untoward encounters.

I started collecting newspaper clippings about piercing and talking informally about the phenomenon with pierced acquaintances and the occasional person I would accost on the street. My return to academia and a contract to produce a deviance text forced me to put the study on a back burner. A few years later, a colleague to whom I had casually revealed my interest in stigmatizing body alteration passed along a copy of an obscure erotic magazine that contained an article on piercing and, a few months later, presented me with an early issue of *Piercing Fans International Quarterly*, the major (and, as far as I could tell, the only) publication directed specifically toward this subculture. The striking photos of ventilated genitalia and the text, which tended to rely heavily on quasi-anthropological legitimation of the practice ("They've been doing it for centuries in Africa so it can't be all that bad"), made me aware that here was a group practice ripe for sociological plucking. I soon realized, however, that I would have to move to Los Angeles in order to participate with the core members of the social world surrounding body piercing—a move that I decided was fraught with significant personal and professional drawbacks.

As I avidly consumed subsequent issues of *PFIQ* I noticed that most of the piercing devotees whose bodies were pictured and who professed their interest in meeting with like-minded individuals in the "personals" section (aptly called "Pin Pals") commonly bore extensive and exotic tattoos. Here, it seemed, was an eminently viable research alternative; a body alteration subculture that was both more accessible and (though I am somewhat chagrined to admit it) less personally off-putting.

And so, through this rather unlikely and serendipitous introduction, I came to partake in an experience that has resulted in the following account and has also indelibly altered my own body. In keeping with the symbolic interactionist perspective that provides the basic analytic context of this discussion, the concepts of *process* and *meaning* are consistently emphasized. I stress the typical stages actors spoke of moving through as they *became* tattooed, *developed* requisite tattooing skill, *negotiated* interactions and relationships, *learned* to cope with or avoid untoward consequences of their decisions, and so forth. Similarly, the basic typological categories employed—for example, kinds of tattooists, types of tattoo customers, defined tattoo functions—are founded on the meaning categories actors routinely presented and overtly used to make sense of their ongoing experience and to devise viable courses of action. As is conventional in "neo-Chicago school" ethnographies such as this, I make extensive use of specific descriptions recorded in my fieldnotes and extracts from actors' verbatim accounts to illustrate key points.

Chapter 1 opens with a general overview of body alteration and a brief historical and cross-cultural description of tattooing as a mode of symbolic communication. This material is followed by a discussion of the development of tattooing in western society from the eighteenth century to the present. The chapter concludes with a presentation of the "production of culture" perspective and a discussion of the basic social process by which produced objects come to be defined as "art" and undergo stylistic change. The following substantive chapters are grounded on this historical and conceptual framework. Chapter 2 focuses on the "career" of the tattooed person—especially the process by which he or she comes to be tattooed and the impact of this choice upon his or her self-definition, social identity, and interaction. The next chapter presents the other major actor in the tattoo exchange, the tattooist. The process of becoming a tattooist and the occupational rewards and tribulations are discussed in some detail. This chapter emphasizes the differences in perspective and occupational experience between commercially-oriented "street" tattooists and those tattoo "artists" who define themselves and their work within the larger legitimating context of the contemporary fine art world. The final substantive chapter focuses on the setting of the tattoo "studio" and the commercial exchange that takes place within it. I pay particular attention to the means by which the tattooee minimizes both the short-term and long-term risks inherent in tattoo consumption, and the techniques used by the tattooist to exercise control over the customer. The last chapter reprises the major conceptual issues and extends the discussions of institutional legitimation and the transformation of a deviant activity into an artistic practice. As has become conventional in sociological ethnographies, the methodological appendix offers the reader a relatively informal account of the various sources of data upon which the discussion is based and some of my own experiences during the course of the research.

Although not all of my colleagues and acquaintances have been entirely supportive of my interest in what one anonymous reviewer derogatorily referred to as the "wacko world of tattooing," those for whom I have the most respect realized that even the most ostensibly bizarre social world is, as Erving Goffman observed, "meaningful, reasonable, and normal once you get close to it." I am particularly grateful for the advice, criticism, and support offered by: Patricia Adler, Peter Adler, Howard Becker, Spencer Cahill, Derral Cheatwood, "Cloud," Robert Faulkner, Alan Govenar, Kenneth Hadden, Douglas Harper, Edward Kealy, Stephen Markson, Robert Prus, Arnold Rubin, Susan Spiggle, Priscilla Warner, and Joseph Zygmunt. For allowing me to hang around and ask all kinds of questions, I am indebted to Mike, Les, Jesse, Steve, Pat,

Frank, Patti, Don, Bill, Bob, Peter, P. J., Flo and the rest of the folks at the National Tattoo Association, Butch, Dana, Ed, and ·all of the other colorful members of the tattoo community I have had the pleasure of knowing. I especially appreciate the faith shown by Janet Francendese, Senior Acquisitions Editor at Temple University Press. She was willing to take the chance rather than simply sending me the standard letter telling me that it was all very "interesting" but did not "fit into our publishing program at this time." I am also grateful to Charles de Kay of Temple University Press for his consistent expressions of support and his careful editing. Shotsie Gorman's sage advice, consistent tolerance, and extensive knowledge played a major role in shaping this book. His unique artistic skills have transformed my body and his warm friendship has touched my heart.

Finally, I offer my deepest thanks to Eleanor Lyon. Throughout the course of this project her enthusiasm in talking about the research, her willingness to read what I wrote, and her ability to provide gentle criticism were immeasurably helpful in tightening the conceptualization and smoothing the style. I could not ask for a better colleague or partner.

Portions of this book are adapted from previously published articles:

"Marks of Mischief: Becoming and Being Tattooed," *Journal of Contemporary Ethnography* 16 (January 1988): 395–432, with the permission of Sage Publications.

"Tattoo Consumption: Risk and Regret in the Purchase of a Socially Marginal Service," from Elizabeth Hirschman and Morris Holbrook, eds., *Advances in Consumer Research*, Vol. XII (New York: Association for Consumer Research, 1985), pp. 17–22, with the permission of the Association for Consumer Research.

"Organizational Constraints on Tattoo Images: A Sociological Analysis of Artistic Style," from Ian Hodder, ed., *The Meaning of Things: Material Culture and Symbolic Expression* (London: Allen and Unwin, 1988), with the permission of Unwin, Hyman.

"Drill and Fill: Client Choice, Client Typologies, and Interactional Control in Commercial Tattoo Settings," from Arnold Rubin, ed., *Marks of Civilization: Artistic Transformations of the Human Body* (Los Angeles: UCLA Museum of Cultural History, 1988), with the permission of the UCLA Museum of Cultural History.

CUSTOMIZING THE BODY

Chapter 1

Introduction: Body Alteration, Artistic Production, and the Social World of Tattooing

A person's physical appearance affects his or her self-definition, identity, and interaction with others (Cooley, 1964 [1902]: 97–104, 175–178, 183; Stone, 1970; Zurcher, 1977: 44–45, 175–178). People use appearance to place each other into categories, which aid in the anticipation and interpretation of behavior, and to make decisions about how best to coordinate social activities.

How closely one meets the cultural criteria for beauty is of key social and personal import. The extensive research on attractiveness indicates that there is consensus about the physical factors that characterize beauty. When presented with series of photographs, experimental subjects are able to identify quickly and reliably those that show beautiful people and those that show ugly people (Farina et al, 1977; Walster et al., 1966).

Attractiveness has considerable impact on our social relationships. We think about attractive people more often, define them as being more healthy, express greater appreciation for their work, and find them to be more appealing interactants (Jones et al., 1984: 53–56). Attractive people are more adept at establishing relationships (Brislin and Lewis, 1968), and they enjoy more extensive and pleasant sexual interactions than do those who are not as physically appealing (Hatfield and Sprecher, 1986). Their chances of economic success are greater (Feldman, 1975), and they are consistently defined by others as being of high moral character (Needelman and Weiner, 1977).

Attractiveness, then, affects self-concept and social experience. Attractive people express more feelings of general happiness (Berscheid et al, 1973), have higher levels of self-esteem, and are less likely than the relatively unattractive to expect that they will suffer from mental illness in the future (Napoleon et al., 1980).

Deviation from and conformity to the societal norms surrounding attractiveness are, therefore, at the core of discussions of appearance and alterations of the physical self. Those who choose to modify their bodies in ways that violate appearance norms—or who reject culturally prescribed alterations—risk being defined as socially or morally inferior. Choosing to be a physical deviant symbolically demonstrates one's disregard for the prevailing norms. Public display of symbolic physical deviance, then, effectively communicates a wealth of information that shapes the social situation in which interaction takes place (Goffman, 1963b; Lofland, 1973: 79–80).

These issues of voluntary body alteration, deviation from appearance norms, and the social impact of purposive public stigmatization provide the central theme orienting this introductory material and the subsequent chapters on the social and occupational world of tattooing. In non-western tribal cultures, the dominant pattern is that certain modes of body alteration typically are deemed essential if one is to assume effectively the appropriate social role and enjoy comfortable social interactions. Failure to alter the physical self in culturally appropriate ways—for example, by wearing a particular costume, or by not having the body shaped or marked in a prescribed manner—labels one as deviant and, in turn, generates negative social reaction.

While the pattern shows considerable historical variability, in western societies purposive body alteration has been, and continues to be, primarily a mechanism for demonstrating one's disaffection from the mainstream. Tattooing, body piercing and, to a lesser degree, body sculpting are employed to proclaim publicly one's special attachment to deviant groups, certain activities, self-concepts, or primary associates.

This connection to unconventionality is the key to understanding the organization of and change within the social world surrounding contemporary tattooing in the United States. Like all deviant activities, tattooing is the focus of social conflict. The production world that revolves around commercial tattooing is shaped primarily by its historical connection to disvalued social groups and disreputable practices. On the other hand, this connection to deviance imbues the tattoo mark with significant power—it is an effective social mechanism for separating "us" from "them." At the same time, not all participants in this world have an interest in fostering the deviant reputation of tattooing. As we will see later in this chapter, those who define tattooing as an *artistic* practice are deeply involved in a process of collective legitimation. Like some photographers (Christopherson, 1974a, 1974b; Schwartz, 1986), potters (Sinha, 1979), recording engineers (Kealy, 1979), stained glass workers (Basirico, 1986), and others (for instance, Neapolitan, 1986), a growing number of tattoo producers are attempting to have their product accepted as art and the related activities of tattoo creation, collection, and appreciation defined as socially valuable. Unlike the craftworkers who have navigated this route to social acceptance before them, however, tattooists labor under a special handicap. Not only must tattoo "artists" broach the wall separating craft from art, they must also overcome widespread public distaste before they can achieve the certification so grudgingly bestowed by key agents of the mainstream art world. This is what makes the story that follows unique, exciting, and sociologically instructive.

In the remainder of this chapter I present a basic historical and cross-cultural account of body alteration. This is followed by a brief description of the production of culture perspective and the institutional theory of art. These orientations structure my view of the social process by which certain objects and activities are produced and come to be socially valued as legitimate art. Finally, I outline the general organization of the tattoo world with particular emphasis on the burgeoning social movement directed at changing the tarnished reputation of tattooing.

ALTERATIONS OF THE BODY AND PHYSICAL APPEARANCE

Clothing and Fashion

People construct their appearance in a wide variety of ways to control their social identities, self-definitions, and interactional prospects. At the simplest level, clothing and fashions are adopted in order to display symbolically gender, social status, role, life-style, values, personal interests, and other identity features (see, for example, Blumer, 1969; Bell, 1976; Lurie, 1983; Flugel, 1969). In modern societies powerful commercial interests focus significant resources in an effort to shape the meaning of clothing and market fashions to consumers.

Clothing style is of sufficient symbolic importance that it often is controlled through "sumptuary laws" that allow only members of specific (usually high status) groups to wear certain materials or fashions. In ancient Egypt, for example, only members of the upper class were allowed to wear sandals. Similarly, in eighteenth century Japan the lower-class citizens were forbidden to wear silks, brocades, and other forms of fine cloth.

Unconventional or alienated subcultures commonly use clothing as a mechanism of "conspicuous outrage" (Bell, 1976: 44–56). The flamboyant costumes adopted by hippies in the 1960s, the punk rocker's torn clothing held together by haphazardly placed safety pins (Anscombe, 1978; Hennessy, 1978), and the outlaw biker's leather jacket (Farren, 1985) and dirt encrusted "colors" (Watson, 1984) clearly symbolize disaffection with mainstream values and identification with those who are overtly discontented with the status quo. Fashion, like all other mechanisms of appearance alteration, is used symbolically to proclaim group membership and to signal voluntary exclusion from disvalued social categories.

Non-Permanent Body Alteration

One of the most common mechanisms people have used to identify themselves and enhance their beauty is through the use of body paint. Thevoz (1984) maintains that members of tribal cultures use paint to differentiate themselves from animals and human beings who do not belong to their tribe or clan. Paint marks one as human and signals social connections. Due to its lack of permanence, in the majority of cultures in which it is practiced, body painting is "event oriented"; it marks a break from the everyday activities of the group. The paint symbolically sets the decorated person apart from his or her everyday self.

5   Introduction

Body painting is ancient and geographically widespread. Excavations of European paleolithic burial sites have revealed implements and pigments used for body painting as well as pictorial representations of painted figures (Hambly, 1974 [1925]: 308–310; Thevoz, 1984: 9–21). There is considerable cross-cultural continuity in the basic colors employed and the symbolic meaning attached to them. Red (typically derived from iron-bearing clays) is commonly used to represent blood and symbolize fertility and mortality. White (from clay or ash) is associated with the supernatural and is ritually used as the color of mourning and purification. Black (from charcoal or berry juices) typically symbolizes impurity and evil (Vlahos, 1979: 22–32; Hambly, 1974 [1925]: 146–160; Thevoz, 1984: 54).

Whether one lives in contemporary America—where approximately $5 billion is spent each year on makeup and hair care products (Freedman, 1986: 43)—or among the Sharanahua of Peru—where a man commonly expresses his appreciation for a woman's beauty by saying, "Her paint was lovely" (Vlahos, 1979: 27)—body painting is used to enhance attractiveness. The Nuba of the Sudan, for example, have developed body painting as a major form of personal decoration. Nuba body art is primarily an aesthetic practice related to celebrating the human body, health, and physical strength. Young Nuban men create highly personal designs intended to accentuate their physical development. The use of color and form is a matter of personal creative choice rather than being dictated by tradition or ritual meaning. Body decorations are valued for their uniqueness, symmetry, and enhancement of physical characteristics. The Nuba are proud of the designs and intend them to be admired by and attract the attention of the opposite sex (Faris, 1972; Brain, 1979: 42–45).

Hair is another body element that is routinely shaped, cut, colored, removed, and otherwise used as a medium of aesthetic creativity and social communication. Male facial hair has, in various times and societies, symbolized either high rank or low status, callow youth or venerable age, adherence to convention or rebellion (see Guthrie, 1976; 25–37). For both males and females hair style consistently has been a semi-permanent way to demonstrate opinion of and connection to current popular taste, established authority, and mainstream values (Charles and DeAnfrasio, 1970; Freedman, 1986: 82–85; Brain, 1979: 116–120). Hair service workers in contemporary western societies commonly define hair as a medium of aesthetic expression and their personal service activities to be a minor art form (see Schroder, 1972; Terkel, 1972: 233–241; Bertoia, 1986).

Permanent Forms of Body Alteration

Like clothing, body painting and hair styling are mechanisms for altering appearance that have in common the relative ease with which one can change the social "vocabulary" as the message becomes outdated, undesirably stigmatizing, or otherwise worthy of reconsideration. They are modes of body alteration most commonly associated with transitional statuses or temporally limited social events. The major forms of permanent alteration—body sculpture, infibulation (piercing), cicatrization (scarification), and tattooing—are, on the other hand, typically connected to permanent statuses (for example, gender, maturity), life-long social connections (for example, clan or tribal membership), or conceptions of beauty that show considerable continuity from generation to generation (for example, head shaping among the Mangbetu of Central Africa or the Chinook of the American northwest coast). Permanent body alteration and non-permanent corporeal adornment in both tribal and modern cultures share the rigorous social support of the bearer's significant reference group. No matter what the overt purpose of the alteration—protection from supernatural forces, communication of sexual availability, demonstration of courage, symbolization of membership, or whatever—all types of body modification have a decorative function. The transformation makes the body aesthetically pleasing to the individual and the relevant reference group.

Body Sculpting • Reshaping the body so as to meet criteria of beauty is a common practice in many cultures. For centuries Chinese women's feet were bound to create the "lotus foot." The ideal three-inch foot (just the right size to fit into a man's palm) was not only a form of symbolic and actual social incapacitation, it was also considered to have erotic significance. The feet were erogenous zones and were fondled and licked by the attentive lover. Connoisseurs were even stimulated by the odor of putrification caused by restricted circulation in the properly bound foot. For women of the Chinese aristocracy, the unbound foot was a source of ostracism and significantly reduced the chance of marriage. Because of its erotic significance the lotus foot was also adopted by prostitutes, concubines, male homosexuals, and transvestites (see Brain, 1979: 88–89; Kunzle, 1982; Vlahos, 1979: 44–45).

In western societies body sculpting to attain beauty or to avoid identification with disvalued groups is a common practice. Hair is straightened, "ethnic" noses are reshaped through plastic surgery, diet and exercise reduce or enlarge the body in line with the current style.

The rise of the corset and tight-lacing in the mid to late nineteenth century was a particularly interesting western body-alteration phenomenon. In his detailed discussion of tight-lacing, Kunzle (1982) presents a somewhat different view of the practice from the conventional analysis that stresses the relationship between the "wasp-waist" aesthetic and male oppression of women. He maintains that tight-lacing was a symbolic protest against the constraints and expectations inherent in the conventional female role. Tight-lacers were defined as deviant. They were ridiculed in the popular media because their altered physique was associated with the "unwomanly" outdoor culture and because the drastic body alteration made them unfit for child-bearing.

Plastic surgery is the dominant form of permanent body sculpture practiced in contemporary western societies. While plastic surgery is regularly used to ease the stigma experienced by individuals who suffer from severe facial disfigurement (Mcgregor, 1974; Mcgregor et al., 1953), it is more commonly employed for aesthetic ends. Approximately 5 percent of the American population (some 200,000 individuals each year) has submitted to cosmetic reconstructions of the body to erase signs of aging, remove unwanted fatty tissue, increase or decrease breast size, or otherwise move the recipient into the currently approved range of physical beauty (Finn, 1984; Zarum, 1983; Lavell and Lewis, 1982; Hatfield and Sprecher, 1986: 351–363).

Piercing and Scarification • Piercing and scarification are two other forms of drastic body alteration regularly practiced in a wide variety of cultures. The primary function of infibulation in most societies appears to be decorative, though some tribal cultures use piercing to symbolize important social positions (especially for women) such as marital status or sexual maturity (see Fisher, 1984; Jonaitis, 1983). Among the Tchikrin of central Brazil, for example, the ears of both male and female infants are pierced at birth and large, cigar-shaped wooden earplugs are inserted. The male infant's lower lip is also pierced, and, after he is weaned, this hole is gradually enlarged and decorated with strings of beads. At puberty the Tchikrin boy participates in a ceremony in which he is given a penis sheath (symbolizing power and control), his hair is cut in the adult style, and his lip ornament is changed to that worn by grown men. As a mature adult the Tchikrin male may wear a lip disk four inches in diameter or larger (Vlahos, 1979: 41; Brain, 1979: 178–180).

In contemporary western society, limited body piercing—especially of women's ears—for decorative purposes is conventional. More extensive infibulation (of the nose, cheeks, nipples, genitals, and so on), however, is commonly viewed with disfavor—thereby making it a form of body alteration that is eminently suited for symbolizing disaffection from mainstream values.

Scarification is the major approach to decorative and symbolic permanent body modification used by dark-skinned peoples on whom tattooing would be ineffective. As employed by African tribal groups, scarification is a decorative form primarily intended to indicate one's position in the social structure. The basic cicatrization technique involves lifting and cutting the skin, followed by the application of an irritant preparation that inhibits healing and promotes the formation of a raised keloid scar. Nuba women, for example, undergo a series of scarification rituals related to their physiological development: cuts are made at puberty, the onset of menstruation, and after the woman's first child is weaned (Brain, 1979: 70–73). Scarification is used to indicate tribal membership, to symbolize passage into adult status, as a form of preventive medicine (for example, by the Bangwa of Cameroon), and to enhance the beauty of the body. Because cicatrization is quite painful, it is commonly part of rituals of passage designed to display the initiate's courage and endurance (for example, among the Kabre of Togo and Australian aborigines) (see Brain, 1979: 68–81; Vogel, 1983).

Tattooing in Ancient and Tribal Cultures • The most ancient and widely employed form of permanent body alteration is tattooing. Archeological evidence indicates that tattooing was probably practiced among peoples living during the late Stone Age. Carved figures from European sites dated 6,000 years b.c. and Egyptian figurines created some 2,000 years later show facial and body markings thought to represent tattoos. Proof of the antiquity of the practice is derived from the mummified body of a priestess of Hathor (dated 2,000 b.c.) that bears parallel line markings on the stomach thought to have had medicinal or fertility functions. Tattooing in ancient Egypt was confined to women, especially concubines, dancers, and priestesses. Mummified remains bear series of dots and geometric line patterns. Singers and other female entertainers were decorated with the symbol of the goddess Bes, the protectress of women in these roles (Paine, 1979; Levy et al., 1979; Hambly, 1974 [1925]: 105–108).

In 1948 archeologists working at Pazyrykin in Siberia discovered a burial mound constructed by Sythian nomads in the fifth century b.c. A number of well-preserved human remains were found encased by ice, some of which bore intricate black line markings on the arms, legs, and torso. The tattoos were sophisticated animal designs—fish, cats, goats, and sheep—and probably held totemic significance (Paine, 1979: 18; Thevoz, 1984: 21).

As early as 2,000 b.c. tattooing spread from the Mideast to the Pacific Islands by way of India, China, and Japan. Theories of how the diffusion of tattooing into Pacific Island cultures took place vary. It is most probable that the practice was carried by the Ainu, a nomadic caucasian group that now inhabits the northern island of Japan. Samoan explorers may have adopted tattooing after encountering it in their western travels, and introduced it into Fiji, Australia, New Zealand, and the Hawaiian Islands. An alternative explanation of the diffusion holds that the practice was carried to Polynesia and New Zealand by South American explorers in their western travels. It is certain that tattooing was a feature of Aztec, Inca, and Mayan culture. Extensively tattooed mummified remains dating from the first century A.D. have been found in Peruvian excavations.

Whatever its route of diffusion, tattooing was a well-established decorative form by 1,000 B.C. Arguably, the most sophisticated, decorative, and rank-symbolizing tattooing in tribal societies was (and, to a limited degree, still is) practiced by the Maoris of New Zealand. Both males and females were tattooed, but with different designs and in different degrees. Maori women usually received limited *moko* markings on the lip and chin area, while men carried extensive facial and body tattoos consisting primarily of whorls, geometric patterns, and other non-representational, ornamental designs. The designs were so individual that, following contact with Europeans, they were often used by members of the nobility as signatures on legal documents (see Simmons, 1986).

Moko designs were inscribed with a serrated bone or shell adze dipped in pigment made from the oily smoke of burning nut kernels. The design was literally chiseled one-eighth of an inch into the skin as the adze was struck with a mallet. The moko process was extremely painful and surrounded by extensive ritual. The recipient's social contact was severely limited and he or she was forbidden to touch food or items used for food preparation during the course of the process, which commonly lasted several days. Typically, one side of a man's face was decorated when he was young and completed a number of years later.

Considerable status was attached to those who were most heavily tattooed. Maori males routinely used mussel shells to shave and tweeze facial hair in order not to cover the moko designs. The tattooed heads ("pakipaki") of enemies killed in battle were removed, preserved, and proudly displayed by victorious warriors, while heads that did not carry moko were rudely discarded as "papateas" or "plain-faced ones" (Paine, 1979: 42).

The dominant function of tattooing in all tribal societies was to denote the bearer's status or social identity. Commonly, the painful tattoo process was part of the rite of passage to adult status. By stoically undergoing the tattoo ritual, recipients could demonstrate their bravery to the other members of the group. In Borneo, for example, Kayan women were given ornate leg and arm tattoos often depicting traditional, stylized dog designs. Covering the arm below the elbow was particularly important since an undecorated arm was seen as a sign of cowardice—the individual was unable to endure pain. Among the Shan of the Society Islands, untattooed young men were regarded as immature since they did not yet have the courage to withstand the painful process. Tattooists encouraged the young recipient to be brave with the admonition, "If you wriggle too much people will think you are only a little boy" (Hambly, 1974 [1925]: 204–205; cf. Vlahos, 1979: 182–196).

Tattooing typically also had religious or magical purposes, often providing a means of identification or protection in the afterlife. In Fiji, women who died without tattoos were believed to be beaten by spirits of other women and served as food for the gods (Hambly, 1974 [1925]: 55). The spirits of women of Long Glat in Borneo were assigned tasks after death based on the extensiveness of their tattooing. The most heavily tattooed could gather pearls in the heavenly river, while those who died with partial decorations could watch, and those who were untattooed were excluded altogether (Paine, 1979: 42). In addition to assuring immortality or improving one's chances of enjoying a pleasant afterlife, tattooing in tribal cultures was often believed to insure the bearer's good luck; to help charm members of the opposite sex; to protect one from accident; to preserve youth; and to bring good health. Women of nomadic tribes in Yemen and the Maghreb, for example, still practice facial and hand tattooing intended to have prophylactic or therapeutic functions. The markings protect the bearer from eye diseases, insure fertility, and bring good fortune (Thevoz, 1984: 69–70; see also Hambly, 1974 [1925]: 109–170).

As a decorative art form, tattooing was, and continues to be, practiced most beautifully and with greatest skill in Japan. Clay figurines (haniwa) found in a grave mound near Osaka and dated from the fifth century B.C. show clear facial marks believed to be tattoos that performed decorative, religious, or status-display functions. This early form of tattooing appears to have died out by the fifth century A.D. The practice revived in thirteenth century Japan largely as a means of marking criminals and other social undesirables. Criminals were tattooed with symbols indicating the nature and geographic location of their crime. Members of outcast groups—principally *hinin* who were entertainers or dealt with criminals, and *eta* who slaughtered animals and tanned leather—were also marked with stigmatizing tattoos. By the early seventeenth century a form of tattooing called *irebokuro* (from "ire" meaning "to inject" and "bokuro" meaning "beauty spot") enjoyed wide popularity. This form of non-pictorial tattooing demonstrated pledges of undying loyalty and love. It was common for people to have a loved one's name or a vow to Buddah inscribed on their skin. Irebokuro eventually died out as a decorative practice largely due to government suppression.

In the mid-eighteenth century (during the Edo period) a Chinese novel called the *Suikoden* became immensely popular among Japanese from all social strata. The *Suikoden* told of the adventures of a band of 108 brigands who, like Robin Hood and his merry men, devoted themselves to fighting against the wealthy and corrupt government bureaucrats. The most popular versions were heavily illustrated with *ukiyo-e* (wood block) prints by well-known artists of the time, especially the famed Kuniyoshi. Some of the most popular outlaw characters, such as Shishin, "the nine-dragon man," and Basho, who wore the image of a fierce tiger on his back, bore extensive full-body tattoos. Soon Japanese from all walks of life were patronizing ukiyo-e artists, who now specialized in tattooing, receiving ornate designs (now called *irezumi*) displaying heroic figures, gods, mythical creatures, and other traditional and popular images.

Irezumi flourished until the mid-nineteenth century when it was forbidden by the Emperor Meiji; he saw it as an immoral practice and was concerned that newly admitted western visitors might see it as a sign of barbarism. However, westerners were fascinated by Japanese tattooing; skilled artists—now called *hori* after the word meaning "to engrave"—decorated the bodies of European and American sailors, merchants, and visiting dignitaries. Following official prohibition, irezumi became an underground and disvalued decorative form among the Japanese. It was adopted predominantly by laborers, artisans, criminals, entertainers, and, especially, fire fighters. The practice continues to be favored by many members of the *yakuza*, the organized criminal underworld (Richie, 1973; Richie and Buruma, 1980: 11–33; Levy et al., 1979: 852–854; Rondinella, 1985: 49–53; Brain, 1979: 62–65; Fellman, 1986).

It is in Japan that non-western tattooing developed to its most ornate, complex, and colorful. Although it fell into official disfavor and is currently a stigmatized practice, the art of the Japanese hori is still practiced and a sizeable and active tattoo subculture flourishes. In addition to its importance as a traditional art form, Japanese tattooing is a significant modern phenomenon because of its major impact on the form and content of contemporary western body art.

The History of Contemporary Western Tattooing • The ancient tribal groups inhabiting the British Isles practiced extensive tattooing. The Picts were named for the iron implements they used to create tattoo designs; the term "Briton" is derived from a Breton word meaning "painted in various colors" (Paine, 1979: 19). Briton males were heavily decorated with animal designs intended to enhance their fearsome appearance. In his memoirs Julius Caesar noted that the Britons were colored blue and carried designs that made them "frightful to look upon in battle" (Oettermann, 1985: 11). This contact with invading Roman legions resulted in the adoption of tattooing by the occupying Roman soldiers. The practice became popular and continued to spread within the military until it was banned in the third century by the Christian Emperor Constantine who maintained that it violated God's handiwork.

Centuries later the Anglo-Saxons continued to practice this ancient form of decoration as members of the nobility bore tattoos that, most commonly, displayed pledges of devotion to loved ones or had religious significance. Following the Battle of Hastings, King Harold's mutilated body was identifiable only because he had "Edith" tattooed over his heart. From the eighth through the tenth centuries, western tattooing was again banned by the Church as a form of deviltry and because it disfigured the body created in God's image. During the campaigns to wrest control of the Holy Land from the Muslims, tattooing again became a frequent practice as crusaders had themselves marked with the crucifix or other religious images to insure a Christian burial should they die in a foreign land. Until the eighteenth century this form of religious tattooing was the only significant practice responsible for retaining tattooing within western culture. Tattooists in Jerusalem did a lively business among pilgrims who received religious images commemorating their journey and indicating their devotion to God. This practice continues to this day (see Govenar [1983]).

The modern history of western/European tattooing begins with the exploratory voyages of Captain James Cook and his encounters with tribal tattooing in the South Pacific. In July of 1769 Cook noted in the ship's journal:

Men and women [of Tahiti] paint their bodies. In their
language, this is known as ta-tu. They inject a black colour
under their skin, leaving a permanent trace. . . . Some have
ill-designed figures of men, birds or dogs; the women generally
have the figure Z simply on every joint of their fingers or toes.
The men have it likewise and both have other figures such as
circles, crescents, etc. which they have on their arms and legs.
In short, they are so various in the application of these figures
that both the quantity and situation of them seem to depend
entirely upon the humour of each individual. Yet all agree in
having all their buttocks covered with a deep black, over this
most have arches drawn one over another as high as their
short ribs which are near a quarter of an inch broad. These
arches seem to be their great pride as both men and women
show them with great pleasure (quoted in Thevoz, 1984:
39–40; Oettermann, 1985: 23).

Prior to this encounter with tattooing, the practice was called "pricking" in the west. Cook introduced the Tahitian word "ta-tu" meaning "to strike" or "to mark" and soon "tattoo" became the common term.

Officers and sailors of the *Endeavor* received tattoos from Tahitian artisans to commemorate their adventures and, on his second voyage to the Pacific, Captain Cook returned to England with a heavily tattooed Tahitian prince named Omai who was exhibited as an object of great curiosity to members of the British upper class.

Omai was one of the first of a series of tattooed people on display in western aristocratic circles at the end of the eighteenth century. The first tattooed European to be publicly exhibited was Jean Baptist Cabri, a French sailor who had jumped ship in the Marquesas in 1795 and was, according to his account, adopted by a tribe and tattooed on the face and body as a mark of honor (*Tattoo Historian*, No. 7, 1985: 4; Ebensten, 1953: 16). A few years later an Englishman named John Rutherford returned from a voyage to New Zealand. He told of being captured by the Maoris, forcibly tattooed, and compelled to marry a chieftain's daughter. After five years Rutherford escaped and returned to London where, in the early nineteenth century, he became the object of great public interest (Burchett and Leighton, 1958: 23–25). By the 1850s a number of heavily tattooed Europeans were making a living by exhibiting themselves to the public and to meetings of prestigious medical associations. Their often fanciful stories—printed in the popular media—as well as contact with irezumi—after Japan was opened to western merchants and travelers initiated a lively tattoo fad in Europe by the late nineteenth century.

For the most part, the European middle-class was not affected by the "tattoo rage" as it was dubbed by the press. The most avid tattoo consumers were sailors, craftsmen, the military, and members of the aristocracy. The most popular designs were South Sea and nautical images, identification marks (especially military and craft guild insignia), religious tattoos, marks of political allegiance, and love vows. It was the tattooing of the nobility, who commonly were tattooed in the course of travels in the orient, that drew the most public attention. Led by the *London World*, newspapers of the day carried lurid accounts of aristocrats' tattoo experiences. Among the famous tattooed personages were Czar Nicholas II of Russia, King George of Greece, King Oscar of Sweden, Kaiser Wilhelm of Germany, and most of the male members of the British royal family (Ebensten, 1953: 16–20; Parry, 1971 [1933]: 98; Richie, 1973; Oettermann, 1985: 12).

Soon the tattoo rage made its way across the Atlantic and began to affect the rich and powerful in America. On December 12, 1897, readers of the *New York Herald* were asked:

Have you had your monogram inscribed on your arm? Is your shoulder blade embellished with your crest? Do you wear your coat-of-arms graven in India ink on the cuticle of your elbow? No? Then, gracious madame and gentle sir, you cannot be *au courant* with society's very latest fad (quoted in Parry, 1971 [1933]: 103).

The first professional tattooist to practice in the United States was Martin Hildebrand. He claimed to have "marked thousands of soldiers and sailors" while travelling among both the Confederate and Union forces during the Civil war. By the 1890s Hildebrand had opened an atelier on Oak Street in New York and was continuing to ply his trade. Other well-known American artists practicing during this period in the Chatham Square area of New York were Samuel F. O'Reilly, "Professor" Charlie Wagner, Jack Hanley ("The World Famous Artist"), and Lewis ("Lew-the-Jew") Alberts. For the most part, the Bowery tattooists and their colleagues in other East Coast cities lacked formal artistic training and were, at best, only moderately talented. They devoted themselves to inscribing crude, badge-like marks on largely working-class patrons who populated the bars, pool halls, and barbershops located in run-down urban areas. For a brief time in the 1890s the Japanese master Hori Chyo was enticed by a $12,000 a year offer from a New York millionaire to practice in America and two other Japanese tattoo artists were brought to New York under the sponsorship of Samuel O'Reilly. These oriental tattooists were primarily responsible for the introduction of dragons, serpents, and other oriental designs into American folk tattoo imagery (Parry, 1971 [1933]: 101; Fried and Fried, 1978: 162–166).

Samuel O'Reilly's place in tattoo history was assured by the major part he played in the development of the electric tattoo machine. This technological innovation was significant because it increased the rate at which tattooing diffused in the society. Tattooing with the electric machine subjected the customer to less pain and necessitated far less skill and experience on the part of the tattooist. Consequently, the number of tattoo practitioners and clients increased dramatically during this period.

In 1876 Thomas Alva Edison patented an electric stencil pen device for making punctures on paper patterns used in sign painting and embroidery. Fifteen years later O'Reilly received the first American patent for an electromagnetic tattoo machine (which he called the "tattaugraph") which was, with only minor modifications, adapted from the Edison design. In 1904 Charlie Wagner was awarded a patent for a significantly improved tattoo machine with two electromagnetic coils set transversely to the tube and needle assembly rather than the rotating coil design of the O'Reilly instrument. The basic tattoo equipment used by contemporary tattooists has changed little since then (Eldridge, 1982; Fried and Fried, 1978: 159–166).

O'Reilly's colleague Lew Alberts, who was originally a wallpaper designer, became a prolific creator of tattoo patterns. His work is of particular importance to the course of western tattooing because he reproduced sheets of his designs and sold them to fellow tattooists. A large percentage of the highly conventionalized tattoo designs found on the wall "flash" of contemporary tattoo shops originated in the design charts created by "Lew-the-Jew" in the late nineteenth century (Fried and Fried, 1978: 166; Levy et al., 1979: 856).

Early in the twentieth century tattooing began to loose favor among the American elite and increasingly came to be seen as the vulgar affectation of the unsavory types who frequented the Bowery and similarly disreputable urban areas. Ward McAllister, a member of New York's Four Hundred, expressed the typical upper-class viewpoint when he stated to the press that tattooing was:

> certainly the most vulgar and barbarous habit the eccentric
> mind of fashion ever invented. It may do for an illiterate
> seaman, but hardly for an aristocrat. Society men in England
> were the victims of circumstances when the Prince of Wales
> had his body tattooed. Like a flock of sheep driven by their
> master, they had to follow suit (quoted in Parry, 1971 [1933]:
> 102).

Prompted by the overt distaste expressed by members of the American elite, media stories of venereal diseases contracted in unhygenic tattoo establishments, and the increased popularity of tattooing within socially marginal subcultures, tattooing fell into disrepute in the United States by the 1920s. Additionally, it came to be seen as a deviant practice because heavily tattooed men and women were commonly exhibited as curiosities in circuses and sideshows. P. T. Barnam displayed tattooed dwarfs, tattooed wrestlers, tattooed ladies, and entire tattooed families (most notably Frank and Annie Howard). The Depression spurred this definition of the tattooed-person-as-freak as unemployed men and women became heavily tattooed in order to find some means of earning a living (Parry, 1971 [1933]: 58–78; Fried and Fried, 1978: 159–165; Eldridge, 1981).

The Tattoo Renaissance ▪ Since the mid-nineteenth century western tattooing was practiced entirely outside the institutional constraints of a professional art world. Tattoo images tended to be relatively crude and highly conventionalized with death symbols (skulls, grim reapers, and so forth), certain animals (especially panthers, eagles, and snakes), pinup styled women, and military designs predominant. The traditional clientele consisted of young men from working-class backgrounds who tended to acquire a number of small, unrelated, badge-like designs with little thought to continuity of body placement (Rubin, 1983; Fried and Fried, 1978: 158–169; Fellowes, 1971). Practitioners were commonly from the same social background as their clients, unassociated with the larger art world and primarily motivated by economic gain. The basic skills involved in the tattoo craft were typically acquired through apprenticeship with established tattooists and the dominant occupational values emphasized technical skill rather than aesthetic qualities.

By the mid-twentieth century, tattooing was firmly established as a definedly deviant practice in the public mind. Despite the short-lived flirtation of European and American elites with tattooing, members of the middle class saw it as a decorative cultural product dispensed by largely unskilled and unhygienic practitioners from dingy shops in urban slums. Tattoo consumers, in turn, were typically seen as being drawn from marginal, rootless, and dangerously unconventional social groups. The tattoo was a symbolic poke-in-the-eye directed at those who were law-abiding, hard-working, family-oriented, and stable.

Since the mid-1960s, however, tattooing has undergone what some (for example, Hill, 1972; Tucker, 1981; Rubin, 1983) have called a "renaissance." Although a commercially-oriented craft structure continues to dominate contemporary tattooing and the general public continues to define it as a deviant activity, significant changes have been occurring during the last two decades. Younger tattooists, frequently with university or art school backgrounds and experience in traditional artistic media, have begun to explore tattooing as a form of expression. For many, this exploration has been motivated by dissatisfaction with the substance of conventional fine art forms and the career limitations presented by the insular socio-occupational world of artistic production. Unlike the traditional tattooist, the younger artists emphasize creative over economic values, specialize in custom designed— commonly large-scale—tattoos and are selective about the images they create and the clients with/on whom they will work. Congruent with their background and aesthetic orientations, the new tattoo artists draw images from diverse artistic sources. Fantasy/ science fiction illustration, traditional Japanese styles, tribal designs, portraiture, and abstract expressionism are major influences on contemporary, fine art tattooing (see Tucker, 1981; Rubin, 1983; Wroblewski, 1981). The new tattooists are also involved in technical innovation, experimenting with an expanded color spectrum, moving away from the traditional hard-edged black outline and employing single-needle techniques which produce highly detailed and fragile images.

As tattoo practitioners who define themselves as "artists" and present their products as "art" have become more prominent, the larger art world has begun to take notice of the medium. Tattooing is increasingly legitimated as the work is shown in museums and gallery shows and subjected to critical discussion by academics and critics/agents of the traditional art world. The tattooists, as a consequence, profit as their work comes to look like art, is displayed like art, is discussed like art, and is bought and sold as art. Their social and occupational status is enhanced, they enjoy greater control over their worklives, and they encounter a new client pool with sophisticated aesthetic tastes and sufficient disposable income to purchase extensive custom-designed art products.

As is the case with stylistic change within other media, new approaches to tattoo form and content derive from the process of cultural diffusion (cf., Bell, 1976: 96; Rosenblum, 1978: 112). The rich tradition of Japanese tattooing has had a major impact on contemporary fine art style. The use of stylized background elements (for example, wind and wave designs) to frame and tie together foreground images in a form of tattoo mural is a major consequence of this diffusion. In an interview an international-ly known tattoo artist explained his adoption of oriental style in this way:

> My own work has been . . . working toward this [use of existent imagery]. I seized on the Japanese thing early in my career because it was the first role model of some kind of articulated tattooing that had an impact because of its scale and because of the subject matter and fitting things to body contours as opposed to the badge motif of most Western tattooing—the hodgepodge collection. I approached the Japanese work and tried, as it were, to create a context for this to occur in the West.

Similarly, the traditional designs of tribal cultures have had some impact on contemporary western tattoo style. Drawn largely from the tattoo tradition of Hawaiian, Maori, Samoan, and other Pacific Island cultures, this "neo-tribal" stylistic form consists of solid black, commonly abstract, designs that closely follow body contours.

THE SOCIAL ORGANIZATION OF CULTURAL PRODUCTION

All of the forms of body alteration discussed above share a con-sciously constructed purpose for those who engage in them. They are mechanisms of social communication. Most basically, all forms of body modification involve some measure of decoration;

the corporeal changes move the recipient closer to the aesthetic ideal of the group—be it conventional or deviant—with which he or she identifies. Further, they have the function of providing symbolic information about the bearer's personal interests, social position, relationships, or self-definition.

Body alteration is culture; it is meaningful to the members of the society in which it occurs, and it is produced within complex webs of collective action. As seen above, cicatrization, body painting, infibulation, tattooing, and other forms of body alteration have, in most societies, clearly defined and broadly understood aesthetic meaning. Contemporary western tattooing—the primary focus of attention here—is of particular interest because its social definition is undergoing significant change. Tattooing is being moved away from its roots as a widely disvalued craft-like practice pursued by producers and consumers who are marginal to mainstream social groups. In turn, impelled by the purposive activities of a variety of committed individuals, it is coming to be defined as an art form centered in a "minor art world," which has a clear, if somewhat conflictual and marginal, relationship to the larger social world that revolves around accepted and valued artistic endeavors.

In the remainder of this chapter, I will briefly present the two dominant conceptual contexts used to orient this analysis. The *production of culture perspective* focuses on the process by which cultural materials are conceived, created, distributed, evaluated, and utilized. The *institutional theory of art* deals with the process by which objects and activities come to be socially labeled as art and the producers directly involved in the creative endeavors assume the social role of artist. Having laid this conceptual foundation, I will then move to the organization of the social world surrounding tattoo production, the structure of the market for tattooing, and the pattern of regulation by which agents of the larger society exercise control over tattoo production and impede its legitimation as an acceptable cultural phenomenon.

The Production of Culture

Analyses of art works, craft materials, items of popular culture, and so forth traditionally have focused primarily on the form and content of these cultural products. Recent work employing the "production of culture perspective" (for example, Peterson, 1976; Sanders, 1982; Tuchman, 1983; Jensen, 1984) emphasizes the importance of the social organization of art and media production systems as being the central factor shaping the form and content of cultural items and determining the social process by which they come into being. This perspective directs attention to the cooperative activities of social actors ("collective action") working together within production organizations to conceive, create, and distribute artistic materials (Becker, 1974). This interaction is importantly constrained by structural features such as the division of labor, available resources, technological developments, and distribution channels.

Within this structural context the collective action is coordinated through the use of "conventions"—shared understandings that specify the commonly accepted and expected form and content of the art product ("product conventions") and the usual relationships that constrain the interactions of production personnel ("production conventions"). (See Becker, 1982: 28–34; Burns, 1972; and Lewis, 1969 for more extensive discussions.) The content of cultural materials is derived from the product conventions that specify the appropriate materials employed, abstractions regularly used to convey central ideas, suitable dimensions of the work, and other form/content features (see Rosenblum, 1978; Gombrich, 1969: 291; Becker, 1982: 29). Product conventions are known to and expected by critics, collectors, producers, and the various other members of the world surrounding the cultural product. The response of the larger audience/consumer group and the commercial success of the product are directly related to the producer's compliance with or deviation from conventional expectations. Conventions imply an aesthetic, and creators who alter or ignore established expectations pay the price. Leaders of technical and stylistic revolutions affront the political status quo of the relevant production world and commonly find it more difficult to produce their work, gain acceptance, and market their product.

Functional analyses of deviance (for example, Merton, 1968; Durkheim, 1966 [1938]) emphasize the importance of deviance as a positive source of social change. This general principle is apparent within worlds of cultural production. In the absence of overt questioning and violation of convention, the cultural product becomes boring, repetitious, and, eventually, less marketable. From their perspective, cultural workers commonly chafe at the constraints of routine production. They explore modes of innovative deviance in order to enhance the quality of their worklife and to retain a "creative" self-definition. Through repetition certain unconventional approaches gain a measure of acceptance, lose their deviant impact, and come to be incorporated into the standard repertoire of conventional practice (Becker, 1982: 63–66, 303–310; Hauser, 1982: 409; Sanders, 1982: 68–69; Wilson, 1986: 126).

Stylistic features of cultural products are grounded in more than the conventions and ideologies within production systems. The conventions shaping the form and content of art works and related cultural products are also constrained by other aspects of the social organization surrounding production. The typical division of labor, the available technology, the political and economic characteristics of the larger social milieu in which the production world is imbedded, and other socio-structural features shape the product and constrain the process by which it is created, distributed, consumed, and evaluated (see Peterson, 1982). These factors also shape the process by which new modes of expression come to be included in the corpus of materials and activities that are socially defined as art.

The Institutional Theory of Art

A variety of creative endeavors—pottery, weaving, photography, and tattooing, for example—occupy the grey definitional area separating art from craft. Craftsmanship is conventionally characterized as involving an emphasis upon technical skill, client control over the production and content of the product, the creation of objects that are functional as well as decorative, and the dominance of an occupational orientation on the part of the craftworker (see Sinha, 1979; Christopherson, 1974a, 1974b; McCall, 1977: 39; Becker, 1978; Kealy, 1979).

Aestheticians have devoted a considerable amount of energy to isolating inherent product characteristics that can be used to differentiate between art and non-art. In contrast, the "institutional theory of art" regards art as an honorific label that comes to be applied to certain objects or activities by certain agents operating in the social world surrounding artistic production, marketing, consumption, and appreciation (see Dickie, 1974; Danto, 1964; Becker, 1976). From this perspective, art is a matter of constructing a consensual definition. Objects or activities that look like art, are discussed like art (especially with regard to some extant tradition and theoretical perspective), bought and sold like art, created by social actors who consider themselves to be artists, and presented for appreciation or sale in settings (for example, galleries and museums) in which art is typically displayed or marketed have the greatest likelihood of being defined as art. Central actors within the social world surrounding art—especially producers and marketers—have a vested interest in this definitional process. The honorific label significantly increases an object's market value, and the social role of "artist" carries with it the implication of talent and sensitivity. Further, successful aspirants to the status of artist commonly enjoy considerable control over both their worklives and the outcome of their productive activities.

A flexible, indistinct, and highly permeable boundary separates art from craft. Commercial artists and artist-craftsmen reside in this marginal space. The former utilize conventional artistic media in more-or-less conventional ways but, like craftsmen, are involved in a service activity directed predominantly by the needs and tastes of the client. Artist-craftsmen work with materials—clay, precious metals, fabrics, and so forth—that are typically shaped for functional or decorative purposes by those who are traditionally defined as craftworkers. However, they tend to emphasize the aesthetic features of their work (especially uniqueness and beauty), display their products in galleries and museums, and create objects which are the focus of "serious" appreciation and discussion. Artist-craftsmen, their products, and the conventions that surround them often come to be the center of "minor art worlds" (Becker, 1982: 276–281).

Contemporary tattooing is undergoing this transition from a (generally disvalued) craft to a (partially legitimated) art form. This process of definitional change has significant impact on— and is affected by—the organization of both the social structure surrounding tattoo production and consumption and the regulatory environment in which tattooing must operate.

CONTINUITY AND CHANGE IN TATTOO PRODUCTION AND CONTENT

The Production Structure and Producer Perspectives

Systems of commercial cultural production typically display a "craft" organization; the structure centers around the activities of a body of "creative professionals" who produce materials that are, in turn, evaluated by members of an administrative group that chooses which products will be marketed on the basis of their assumed commercial potential. At base, this is a conservative structure. Decision-makers at the managerial/administrative level are uncertain which features will assure success in the marketplace. This problem of "commercial uncertainty" is dealt with, in part, through a reliance on formulae. Products that have proven to be commercially successful in the past are reproduced with only minor variation (Hirsch, 1972; Gitlin, 1983). In addition, production systems that display centralized and oligopolistic organization are minimally inconvenienced by competition and tend to market materials characterized by stylistic homogeneity. In contrast, less centralized and bureaucratically organized production yields higher levels of competition and increases reliance upon the decisions made at the creative level. Creator autonomy generates innovation and product diversity (see Peterson and Berger, 1975; DiMaggio, 1977).

Tattooing is characterized by individual entrepreneurship, decentralization, local competition, and minimal interaction among primary creators. The relatively simple materials necessary for tattooing are available to anyone who gains access to equipment suppliers, and the basic techniques are easily acquired. Tattooists, therefore, tend to be individualistic, secretive, and competitive. Levels of technical skill vary widely. Given the apparent decentralized organizational structure of the socio-occupational world surrounding tattoo production, one would expect considerable stylistic heterogeneity. Why does this highly decentralized and competitive system not generate stylistic diversity, rather than the homogeneous, formulaic, and tradition-bound corpus of work that, until only recently, has typified contemporary tattooing? The majority of professional tattooists have consistently emphasized a commercial, rather than creative, occupational orientation. The desire to maximize profit required the tattooist to cede considerable control over his or her worklife and to attend primarily to the demands of the customer (cf., Sinha, 1979; Rosenblum, 1978: 63–86; Faulkner, 1983: 148–167). The typical clientele, in turn, had only limited experience with tattooing and defined the indelible images as having limited functional utility—principally, decoration and/or symbolization of personal association or self-identification. Tattoo customers most commonly chose to purchase images that were like those carried by friends, family members, or other primary associates. The tattooist was, in other words, subjected to limited market demands and felt little commercial pressure to engage in innovative or educational interactions with the client.

In addition to the dominant economic orientation of the producer and the narrow demands of a stylistically conservative clientele, tattooing has been highly formulaic due to the structural centrality of and power exercised by a few tattoo supply firms. Commonly run by ex-tattooists, these organizations provide most tattooists with the equipment and materials (pigments, standard design sheets, needles, acetate sheets for making templates, and so forth) they need to do business. Of equal importance is the fact that tattoo equipment suppliers have been (and continue to be) at the center of the organizational communications structure. Supply firms publish newsletters which contain interviews, photos of tattoos, and general gossip. They also are responsible for organizing yearly conventions attended by tattooists and tattoo enthusiasts. The work on display in the newsletters and at the conventions has continued to be overwhelmingly formulaic, although the technical quality varies considerably. (See Eldridge, 1986, for a history of tattoo suppliers.) Most tattooists and tattooees, therefore, have, until recently, had limited exposure to stylistic diversity; and evaluations of tattoo quality have emphasized the apparent technical skill rather than the innovativeness of design content.

These dominant perspectives and organizational features—limited client experience and taste, the prominence of a commercial orientation among primary producers, and the tight control over essential resources exercised by a small group of supply firms—have had a significant restraining effect on innovation within tattooing. The changes in style that have been occurring recently have been primarily the result of the incursion of a new breed of tattooist with a markedly different perspective, and the concurrent expansion of the client pool by collectors from diverse social backgrounds who have tastes and views of the functions met by the tattoo/product that are very much unlike those of the traditional tattoo consumer.

The new "fine art" tattooists value control, innovation, and aesthetic quality over commercial success. Commonly having had academic training and experience with a variety of traditional artistic media, they tend to view the larger art world as their primary reference group. Most tattoo artists focus their energies on the creation of large-scale, custom-designed pieces and typically turn down requests to inscribe traditional images. Like many professional artists, fine art tattooists experience conflict between the roles of creative artist and practical business person. Most deal with this role conflict by exercising some degree of guidance during their interaction with clients. Their position is typical of what Griff (1970: 156) refers to as the "compromise role" in his discussion of artistic socialization.

The "compromise role" is a mixture of both the traditional and the commercial roles. Like the commercial-role artists, those who assume the compromise role believe that they are instruments of the clients; however, they conceive of themselves as active, rather than as passive, agents. In carrying out this conception of themselves, they translate the demands of the client but at the same time attempt to persuade him to accept innovations, specifically the interjection of fine-arts symbols into their illustrations.

This orientation is well illustrated by the statement of a prominent East Coast tattoo artist.

(Clients usually) don't say, "I want this or I want that." They pick a design off the wall and I try to prompt them to think about it—what the tattoo means. . . . They pick a design which is reasonable. I mean, I only put designs on the wall that I feel are either valid aesthetically or have some kind of cultural context. I try to keep the designs within that range. . . . I always feel that I want to touch a bit—not physically. I just want to touch base and say, "I'm glad I can help you get through this point. Why don't you give me some feedback on your decision behind the tattoo—what you want to do. . . . " I become their hands—which is satisfying in that respect. I focus my entire energy on that tattoo to make it the most beautiful thing I can. I impose my own set of aesthetics and value judgments as to what beauty is and what it isn't in the context of the image that they choose. I feel that, through my life's experience, and studying the history of Western art, and being bombarded with the imagery and the evolution of beauty in our culture, I can manifest those qualities in a language that everyone can understand despite their education.

The fine art tattooist tends to drift (or be propelled) into tattooing out of dissatisfaction with the constraints and occupational limitations encountered in the traditional art world. Although they usually bring new aesthetic orientations and modes of evaluation to tattooing (cf. Kealy, 1979; Schroder, 1973: 294–310), tattoo artists consistently express appreciation for and connection to the history and tradition of western tattooing (cf. Bell, 1976: 101; Danto, 1964: 579). At the same time, they find much of the symbolic content of American folk-style tattooing to be boring, repetitious or, in some cases, morally and/or politically repugnant.

The Tattoo Market

As touched on above, the clientele is a central element of the organizational set which revolves around the process of cultural production. The client pool is, in essence, a "market" which is identified, defined, and targeted by system actors whose interests are primarily financial (Peterson, 1982: 146; DiMaggio, 1977).

The growth and changing character of the tattoo consumer pool in the past two decades has had considerable impact on tattoo style, the occupation of tattooing, and its redefinition as a legitimate form of artistic production. Coming from a higher socioeconomic background than the traditional tattooee, the new client commonly has more disposable income, emphasizes the decorative/aesthetic function of the tattoo over its affiliative/self-definitional function, and shares the tattoo artist's interest in the production of a uniquely creative and innovative custom-designed image. The fairly homogeneous "taste public" (Gans, 1974) traditionally centered around tattooing has given way to an enlarged and more diverse market that has, in turn, led to a correspondingly more heterogeneous repertoire of available styles. This key interaction between artists and a new client population which both drives and supports stylistic change is described by tattooist D. E. Hardy (1982: 47–48).

> The designs (value symbols) developed and plied as stock in trade over the last hundred years have become inadequate or antiquated to many portions of the society served. The growth of interest in this form of expression by a wider range of people has called for expanded imagery and more specialized stylists. . . . New people with ability and interest are changing the content of the field. Innovative forms arise from a thin creative segment of the crowd and disperse in diluted form to alter popular tastes. This is the result of original ideas commissioned by clients seeking something unique, filtered through a talented artist, the personal taste of a tattooer presenting new forms, or the adaptation of images from other media.

This relationship between a changing market and innovation in tattooing is a specific example of what has come to be a general understanding within the sociology of art: art product consumers are not passive receptors but act, both individually and collectively, to shape and constrain the style of art works (see Becker, 1982: 312–313; Watson, 1968; Henning, 1960; Rosenberg and Fliegel, 1970; Faulkner, 1983). This principle is particularly apparent in tattooing since few artistic relationships are as intimate and interactive as that between the tattooist and his or her client (Tucker, 1981: 44–47). Tattooing does not entail an impersonal and bureaucratized market system in which administrators, gallery directors, critics, and other "gatekeepers" are the primary audience used by the creative personnel to orient stylistic decisions. Instead, the tattoo artist works directly with the buyer in an association that, due to the significant control exercised by the client, is most accurately characterized as a cross between a service relationship and that that exists in a traditional patronage system.

The Regulatory Environment of Tattooing

All art worlds exist within a larger socio-legal environment that sets conditions to constrain the production, the form, and the content of artistic products. The state always displays considerable interest in the content of art works. Often, as in the case of propagandistic styles such as "socialist realism," it uses art to mobilize or inspire the populace for its own ends. Those in positions of constituted authority also have a vested interest in restricting art works that are seen as threatening the moral or political status quo, and in placing constraints upon production processes or cultural products that may negatively affect the public health (see Becker, 1982: 165–191; Peterson, 1982: 144–145).

As we have seen, tattooing has had a long history of association with socially disvalued groups. The negative social definition of tattooing is, however, largely derived from its voluntary use by members of deviant or marginal groups as a symbolic boundary-maintaining mechanism. Professional criminals, outlaw bikers, users of illegal drugs, prostitutes, those who identify with "punk" culture, and other members of counter-conventional subcultures commonly receive tattoos that symbolize their membership and demonstrate their indelible commitment to the group.

Few modes of cultural production are the focus of such extensive official regulation as is tattooing. (See Goldstein, 1979a, for an overview of the legal restrictions on tattooing in the United States.) While the impetus for these legal restrictions is primarily derived from the association of tattooing with ideological and behavioral disaffection from conventional norms, the official rationale usually employed emphasizes the protection of public health. Anecdotal evidence linking the tattoo process with the spread of communicable diseases such as hepatitis, herpes, and syphilis is typically presented to justify official regulation or outright prohibition. Recent legal attempts in the United States to define tattooing as an art form protected by Constitutional guarantees of free speech have, as yet, proved to be unsuccessful. For example, in the case of *Yurkew* v. *Sinclair* (495 F. Supp. 1248, 1255–56 [D. Minn. 1980]) the court found that the defendant was within his rights to deny rental space in the Minnesota State Fair to a tattoo artist because, while the tattoo product itself may be protected by the First Amendment,

> [the] process of tattooing is not sufficiently communicative so as to implicate the First Amendment as regards government regulation and licensing because not only is the tattoo itself more communicative than the process but unsuccessful applicant for tattoo booth at state fair failed to show content of images he created through the process and there was no suggestion that political or social thought was conveyed or that the observer or recipient would regard the process as communicative and, also, fact that sterile and sanitary conditions were essential for the undermined contention that tattooing was a First Amendment activity.

The association of tattooing with deviant groups and communicable disease, together with the dangerousness implied in its regulation by official agents of social control, has significant impact on the practice of tattooing. Its legitimation as a viable art form, its diffusion into more prestigious social segments, its adaptation as an artistic medium by creators, and the innovative expansion of its stylistic repertoire are impeded by negative definition. While legal regulation places limits on the legitimation and stylistic diversity of tattooing, it does not appear to be particularly effective in limiting the *availability* of tattooing. Even in those areas in which the practice is officially prohibited, the demand for tattooing remains high, and illegal tattooing by "bootleggers" is common. Traditional mechanisms of official control generally have been ineffective in decreasing the availability of tattooing for a variety of reasons. The cost of production is relatively low, the necessary technical skills are easily acquired, public advertising is not required in order to maintain an active market, the client pool is fairly homogeneous, and most tattooists are careful to avoid the official heat that would be generated were they to inscribe tattoos on "public" skin or underage customers (Best, 1981).

Where tattooing is officially regulated, established tattooists tend to support regulation. Licensing and other forms of legal restriction limit the incursion of competitors. In addition, the proprietors of licensed establishments use official sanction to symbolize the high quality of their service and enhance their status relative to underground competitors. It is common for licensed tattooists to prominently display signs attesting to their official legitimacy (for example, "Approved by the Board of Health") and to include these statements on the business cards provided to customers.

CONCLUSION: FROM DEVIANCE TO ART

As a world of cultural production, tattooing is in the midst of significant change; it is moving away from its historical roots as a disvalued craft while vying for the honorific position of being defined as a fine art form. The issues of status and control are central to the process by which objects and activities come to be valued as "art" and those that produce them given the label of "artist." The social role of artist affords cultural production workers significant control over their worklives—they have the advantage of being seen as creative people rather than technical instruments by which client demands are fulfilled.

This process of redefinition typically entails a variety of tactical maneuvers on the part of the central actors of the production world vying for artistic legitimacy. First, the activity is attached to an ongoing body of history and tradition encompassing an identifiable aesthetic. Second, the practice is identified with a body of practitioners who are innovative, uniquely skilled, and who, commonly, have earned artistic legitimacy through involvement in production activities (for example, painting or sculpture) that have previously been labeled as art. Third, the production process is presented as resulting in original and singular works rather than simply reproducing a mass of replicas of limited economic value.

The development of a body of knowledgeable clients is a fourth step in the process of artistic legitimation. These collectors—individuals and institutions—are intimately familiar with the product conventions that differentiate inferior items from those that display exceptional quality. They also have the economic resources necessary to commission and acquire the most exemplary products from the most skilled producers. Further, the chances of achieving artistic sanction are enhanced if the products are displayed in museums and galleries, the settings in which "real" art traditionally has been isolated from the ordinary, mass-produced, and aesthetically inferior objects of the everyday world. Finally, the creators, the medium in which they work, the production process itself, and the resultant product should be the focus of "serious"—usually academic—discussion. When the "candidate" medium comes to be the object of critical appraisal in academic conferences and influential communication organs within the art world, unique styles are differentiated, reputations are generated, evaluative conventions are refined, and inclusionary rationales are constructed. Abstracted academic discussion indicates the significance of the product (why else would academics spend time talking about it?) and helps to situate it within the legitimating boundaries that enclose artistic work (see Christopherson, 1974a, 1974b; Rosenblum, 1978; Kealy, 1979; Schwartz, 1986; Neapolitan, 1986).

The contemporary art world, which has "allowed"—although not without considerable conflict—the inclusion of such non-traditional products as conceptual art (Meyer, 1972), art based on the mass-produced materials of popular culture (Amaya, 1972), computer-generated images (Prueitt, 1984), "postal" art (Fish, 1986), and Dadaist satire (Richter, 1965), is ripe for the acceptance of fine art tattooing.

Lead by an increasingly influential group of practitioners, the isolated subcultural world of tattooing is laying siege to the walls surrounding the realm of institutional art. These "creative barbarians" typically have had formal academic training in art, have

worked in a variety of traditional media, display astonishing levels
of technical skill, and regard tattooing as a creative endeavor similar to that pursued by legitimated artistic workers. They aspire to
the status and control afforded by the role of artist. They concentrate on the production of unique and expensive "pieces" for an
upscale clientele that understands the relevant artistic rationales
and for whom tattooing has overtly aesthetic meaning. This "new
breed" of tattooist is working to expand the boundaries of tattooing by experimenting with photo-realistic portraiture, oriental
traditions, "fantastic art" illustration, nonrepresentational abstractions, and other innovative stylistic approaches. Chafing under the continuing public distaste for the tattoo medium, they
consistently refer to themselves as "tattoo artists" and their establishments as "studios." They take great pains to disassociate
themselves from "scratchers" who are technically unskilled and
"stencil men" who are incapable of doing creative custom work.

The recent appearance of specialized "serious" publications
dealing with tattooing is particularly important in the legitimation process. In 1982 tattooist Don Ed Hardy founded *Tattootime*,
a slickly illustrated annual containing scholarly articles about
conventional tattoo images, innovative stylistic developments,
body decoration in non-western cultures, and other issues of interest to academically inclined practitioners and enthusiasts.
Equally serious analyses of tattooing are available in Lyle Tuttle's
quarterly, *The Tattoo Historian*, and the various publications produced by C. W. Eldridge of the Tattoo Archive in Berkeley.

In turn, the larger art world has begun to take notice. Galleries
and museums are now exhibiting both photographic repro-
ductions and living samples of exemplary tattoo art. Mainstream
publishers are marketing expensive "coffee-table" books containing full-color photos and learned discussions by accepted art critics that situate tattooing within the larger context of western art
history (for example, Wroblewski, 1985; Rondinella, 1985; Richter,
1985; Thevoz, 1984). High culture periodicals now present articles on tattoo art (for example, Tucker, 1981; *New Yorker*, February 9, 1987: 28–31) while academicians meet to read papers
about tattooing and publish proceedings (for example, Rubin,
1988) that further help to identify the practice as a legitimate

artistic endeavor. In short, a significant segment of tattoo production is proceeding along the traditional route by which a variety of other "inferior" media have come to be sanctified as art.

While accounts of the collective action by which photography, print-making, pottery, weaving, and other marginal forms of cultural production have come to be defined as art are instructive, they do not mirror entirely the status transition of tattooing. These other creative practices were never saddled with the intense public distaste and ongoing association with social deviance that has surrounded, and continues to impede the legitimation of, tattooing. In many regards, the literature on social problem definition and the growth of social movements directed at prompting ameliorative public redefinion of certain actors and activities is equally relevant. Central participants in the tattoo subculture are engaged in a process of collective legitimation similar to that pursued by other disvalued social actors whose behavior is stereotypically defined by an "unknowledgeable" public as constituting a "social problem" (cf. Spector and Kitsuse, 1977). Like homosexuals, the mentally disordered, political radicals, recreational drug users, racial minorities, and other unconventional groups, tattoo artists and other key members of the tattoo world are attempting to publicly redefine tattooing and the tattoo mark as nonthreatening, unproblematic, and, even, admirable. To the extent that they are successful, tattooing will continue to expand as it comes to be more broadly defined as a legitimate art form, as it continues to be taken up by skilled practitioners who value creativity and stylistic innovation, and as the pool of collectors and enthusiasts becomes more heterogeneous and requests art products that are unique, aesthetically exciting, and socially relevant.

Chapter 2

Becoming and Being
a Tattooed Person

The disreputable connections of tattooing in the west (presented in the last chapter) lead conventional members of society to define people with tattoos negatively. In turn, discussions of tattooing and tattooed persons generated by psychiatric and criminological analysts reflect (and reinforce) these commonplace definitions.

Despite their ritualistic statements about the "objectivity of the scientific enterprise," social and behavioral scientists do not construct their analyses of human behavior in a vacuum. Instead, what analysts see and describe and the understandings they attempt to develop are shaped by factors often quite separate from the phenomenon of interest. Preexisting attitudes, personal experience (or lack thereof), and theoretical commitments, together with the methodological approaches utilized and the characteristics of the "subjects" upon whom attention is focused constrain the picture constructed by the researchers. Commonly, the result is a portrayal of behavior far removed from the actual phenomenon and the intimate, everyday understanding of the actors to whom it is most familiar. These problems are exacerbated when the phenomenon of interest is controversial, unusual, deviant, or otherwise outside of the immediate experience and comfortable world of conventional, academically oriented researchers.

Few social and behavioral scientists have personal experience with the tattoo process or have intimately involved themselves in the complex social world that revolves around tattooing. Researchers who have focused on the tattoo phenomenon usually employ structured techniques, which insulate them from intimate involvement with tattooed people, and chose institutionalized subjects who are "convenient to manage in their research situations" (Taylor, 1970: 87). It is hardly surprising, therefore, that psychiatrically trained researchers who study tattooed inmates of mental institutions discover a link between possession of tattoos and psychopathology, or that criminologists who study incarcerated tattooees commonly find a relationship between being tattooed and being inclined to engage in legally proscribed activities.

The serious (as opposed to fan-oriented or popular) literature on tattooing tends to present relatively simplistic and commonly monistic perspectives on the motives and character of tattooed persons. In part, this is due to methodological weaknesses—few studies make use of control groups, research subjects are drawn from highly selected populations, and there is an overreliance on standard psychological tests and official records. Researchers' conclusions commonly are subjective and value-laden (Taylor, 1970: 85–86). Further, the analyses are overdeterministic (Wrong, 1961). The decision to be tattooed is consistently presented as being driven by assumed internal malfunctions or externally generated socio-pathology rather than being due to the exercise of choice within the bounds of available behavioral alternatives as defined by the actor. The decision to be tattooed is rarely presented as having essentially "healthy," pro-social, self-affirming roots; most studies are premised on an assumption of pathology.

Psychiatric studies of tattooed persons focus almost exclusively on inmates of mental institutions.[1] Even a cursory review of the medical and psychiatric literature shows that researchers have a relatively low regard for "those persons who have their bodies painfully scarred" (Newman, 1982: 232) with tattoos. The tattooed person is variously described as "simple-minded," "immature," "hostile," "aggressive," "self-destructive," "untrustworthy," and "infantile" (Goldstein, 1979c: 883, 885; Zimmerman, 1979: 911). Being tattooed commonly is defined as symptomatic of psychopathology. Briggs (1958: 1039), for example, observes:

> The presence of a single meaningless tattoo mark suggests a prepsychotic or psychotic phenomena (sic) . . . the appearance of multiple tattoo marks which differ greatly in motivation,

which have no symmetry, and which have no apparent connection one with the other, is always diagnostic of a severe psychoneurosis. . . . The type of tattoo may be such that the type of psychoneurosis may be apparent. . . . A study of the tattooed individual, the designs and the obvious motivation behind each design is as valuable in determining the emotional pattern of an individual as is a multiphasic personality test or a Rorschach test.

In those studies in which the MMPI is delivered to institution-alized tattooed persons, the results show tattooees to score high on the psychopathic deviation scale (Kurtzberg et al., 1967) and the hypomania measures (Yamamoto et al., 1963).

The sexual symbolism of tattoo designs is of particular interest to psychiatric researchers. These analysts consistently define the possession of overtly heterosexual images (for example, nude women, "pornographic" phrases) as *actually* revealing the homo-sexual interests or hidden homosexual anxieties of the bearer (Ya-mamoto et al., 1963: 365; Post, 1968: 519; Grumet, 1983: 486–487; Haines and Huffman, 1958: 111; Kander and Kohn, 1943: 326–327; Parry, 1971 [1933]: 1–23). Much is made of the sexual symbolism of the tattoo process: "The very process of tattooing is essentially sexual. There are the long, sharp needles. There is the liquid poured into the pricked skin. There are the two partici-pants of the act, one active, the other passive. There is the curi-ous marriage of pleasure and pain" (Parry, 1971 [1933]: 1). Some commentators go even further, suggesting that tattoo artists are typically latent or overt homosexuals "who have chosen this occu-pation because it puts them in almost constant close proximity to the male body, which they can feel, stroke, and fondle without arousing suspicion" (Post, 1968: 519).[2]

In a somewhat more charitable vein, some psychiatrically ori-ented analysts see tattoos as having ego-protecting functions. Hamburger (1966), for example, hypothesizes that tattooees suffer from an "underdeveloped ego" and the tattoo is a mechanism by which the tattooed person copes with this inadequacy. In another relatively sympathetic discussion, Popplestone (1963) presents the tattoo as one of a variety of exoskeletal defenses—modifications of the body that protect the "psychological integrity" of the person in the face of perceived external threat.

There is considerable disagreement in the psychological litera- ture over the diagnostic value of tattoo possession or design con- tent. Haines and Huffman (1958: 112), for example, suggest the utility of viewing tattoos as indicators of the emotional maturity and personality characteristics of the wearer. More recently, Gru- met (1983) has advised clinicians to use interpretations of tattoo symbolism and discussions of tattoos with patients as part of the diagnostic process. He maintains that

> the tattoo can be viewed as a psychic crutch aimed to repair a crippled self-image, inspire hope, keep noxious emotions at bay, and reduce the discrepancy between the individual and his aspirations. . . . Like the dreaming process, tattoos condense, symbolize, and displace psychic energy to a meaningful image. . . . In some tattooed individuals such designs may provide the key to a nexus of psychopathological factors, while in others they merely enhance the verbal history (p. 491; cf. Ferguson-Rayport et al., 1955; Yamamoto et al., 1963).

In contrast, the literature that focuses on incarcerated tattooed persons or that posits a relationship between criminal behavior and tattoo possession tends to be less strident and condemnatory. It also is less likely to be oriented toward a pathology perspective and is based on more methodologically sound research than are the psychiatric studies (see especially Taylor, 1970, and Mosher et al., 1967). Persons incarcerated for criminal offenses are signifi- cantly more likely than psychiatric patients to be tattooed. Most studies indicate that from one-third to two-thirds of prison in- mates possess tattoos. Various analysts see being tattooed as in- dicating a penchant for violence (Newman, 1982), a tendency toward self-destructive behavior (Burma, 1965; Kurtzberg et al., 1967; Taylor, 1970), a pathological need for attention (Haines and Huffman, 1958), or a tendency to engage in certain forms of prop- erty crime (Haines and Huffman, 1958; Orten and Bell, 1974).[3] It is more common, however, for the research with incarcerated per-

sons to stress the importance of the tattoo as a symbolic affirma-
tion of valued associations and identities or as a response to the
prison experience itself.

In the prison population crude, nonprofessional, "jailhouse tattoos" predominate. These markings are often acquired early in the
individual's penal experience (Edgerton and Dingman, 1963:
145–146). Commonly, the new inmate receives a tattoo in order to
symbolize involvement with an inmate social network, which provides protection and support. Researchers who have studied incarcerated females find tattoo marks to most commonly be related
to intensely emotional lesbian relationships developed within the
institution (Burma, 1965; Agris, 1977; Fox, 1976). Other analysts
emphasize the inactivity and boredom that characterize the
prison experience. From this perspective, the tattoo activity is essentially something to do—either to the self or to one's intimates—in order to pass the time (Scutt and Gotch, 1974: 110;
Burma, 1965: 274).

The primary theme that runs through most of the studies of
tattooed prisoners is that being tattooed is a functional response
to the "identity stripping" experienced by all those thrust involuntarily into the depersonalized environment of the total institution.
Shorn of the personal effects which constitute his or her "identity-kit" (Goffman, 1961: 14–21), the inmate copes with this painful loss, in part, by acquiring identity symbols, which can not be
taken away by officials. Further, tattooing within the institution
is strongly proscribed by prison officials. Through the acquisition
of tattoos the inmate symbolically defies those who personify
authority (see Ross and McKay, 1979: 43–78). In other words, the
literature focused on the tattooed law violator presents tattooing
as an essentially rational, even healthy, means by which the individual copes with the "pains of imprisonment" (Sykes, 1966). It
presents one of various ways in which the prisoner affirms membership in a protective primary reference group, asserts independence from oppressive authority, and symbolically reestablishes
key aspects of an identity, which is ritually stripped during the
official initiation into the total institution.[4]

In contrast to much of the "scientific" literature on tattooing,
this chapter presents the phenomenon as a normal, symbolically

meaningful form of permanent body alteration in contemporary society. Choosing to mark one's body in this way changes the tattooee's experience of his or her physical self and has significant potential for altering social interaction.

Despite attempts by key members of the tattoo subculture to define tattooing as an honorable and acceptable form of personal and artistic expression, the tattoo continues to be seen as an indication of the bearer's alienation from mainstream norms and social networks. It is a voluntary stigma that symbolically isolates the bearer from "normals." Since tattooees are deemed to be responsible for their deviant physical condition, the mark is especially discrediting (Jones et al., 1984: 56–65).

Like most stigmatizing conditions, however, tattooing also has an affiliative effect; it identifies the bearer as a member of a select group. When publicly displayed the tattoo may act as a source of mutual accessibility (Goffman, 1963b: 131–139). Fellow tattooees commonly recognize and acknowledge their shared experience, decorative tastes, and relationship to conventional society. Tattooing also has affiliative impact in that it is routinely employed to demonstrate one's indelible connection to primary associates (for instance, name tattoos) or groups whose members share specialized interests and activities (for example, motorcycling, use of illegal drugs, or involvement with a specific youth gang).

THE PROCESS OF BECOMING
A TATTOOED PERSON

Deciding to Be Tattooed

Becoming tattooed is a highly social act. The decision to acquire a tattoo (and, as we will see in a later section, the image that is chosen) is motivated by how the recipient defines him or herself. The tattoo becomes an item in the tattooee's personal identity-kit (Goffman, 1961: 14–21) and, in turn, it is used by those with whom the individual interacts to place him or her into a particular, interaction-shaping social category (cf. Solomon, 1983; Csikszentmihalyi and Rochberg-Halton, 1981).

When asked to describe how they decided to get a tattoo, the vast majority of respondents made reference to another person or group. Family members, friends, business associates, and other people with whom they regularly interacted were described as being tattooed. Statements such as, "Everyone I knew was really into tattoos," "It was a peer decision," "Everyone had one so I wanted one," and "My father got one when he was in the war and I always wanted one, too," were typical. Entrance into the actual tattooing "event," however, has all of the characteristics of an impulse purchase. It typically is based on very little information or previous experience (58 percent of the questionnaire respondents reported never having been in a studio prior to the time they received their first tattoo). While tattooees commonly reported having "thought about getting (a tattoo) for a long time," they usually drifted into the actual experience when they "didn't have anything better to do," had sufficient money to devote to a nonessential purchase and were, most importantly, in the general vicinity of a tattoo establishment. The following accounts were fairly typical.

> We were up in Maine and a bunch of us were just talking about getting tattoos—me and my friends and my cousins. One time my cousin came back from the service with one and I liked it. . . . The only place I knew about was S——'s down in Providence. We were going right by there on our way back home so we stopped and all got them.

> My friends were goin' down there to get some work, you know. That was the only place I knew about anyway. My friends said there was a tattoo parlor down by the beach. Let's go! I checked it out and seen something I liked. I had some money on me so I said, "I'll get this little thing and check it out and see how it sticks." I thought if I got a tatty it might fade, you know. You never know what's goin' to happen. I don't want anything on my body that is goin' to look fucked up.

The act of getting the tattoo itself is usually, as seen in these quotes, a social event experienced with close associates. Sixty-nine percent of the interviewees (11 of 16) and 64 percent of the questionnaire sample reported having received their first tattoo in the company of family members or friends. These close associates act as "purchase pals" (Bell, 1967). They provide social support for the decision, help to pass anxiety-filled waiting time, offer opinions regarding the design and body location, and commiserate with or humorously ridicule the recipient during the tattoo experience (see Becker and Clark, 1979).

The tattoo event frequently involves a ritual commemoration of a significant transition in the life of the recipient (cf. Van Gennep, 1960; Ebin, 1979: 39–56; Brain, 1979: 174–184). The tattooee conceives of the mark as symbolizing change—especially, achieving maturity and symbolically separating the self from individuals or groups (parents, husbands, wives, employers, and so on) who have been exercising control over the individual's personal choices. A tattoo artist related his understanding of his clients' motivations in this way:

> I do see that many people get tattooed to find out again . . . to say, "Who was I before I got into this lost position?" It's almost like a tattoo pulls you back to a certain kind of reality about who you are as an individual. Either that or it transfers you to the next step in you life, the next plateau. A woman will come in and say, "Well, I just went through a really ugly divorce. My husband had control of my fucking body and now I have it again. I want a tattoo. I want a tattoo that says that I have the courage to get this, that I have the courage to take on the rest of my life. I'm going to do what I want to do and do what I have to do to survive as a person." That's a motivation that comes through the door a lot.

One interviewee expressed her initial reason for acquiring her first tattoo in almost exactly these terms:

> (My friend and I) both talked semi-seriously about getting (a tattoo). I mentioned it to my husband and he was adamantly opposed—only certain seedy types get tattoos. He didn't want someone else touching my body intimately, which is what a tattoo would involve . . . even if it was just my arm. He was against it, which made me even more for it . . . I finally really decided sometime last year when my marriage was coming apart. It started to be a symbol of taking my body back. I was thinking that about the time I got divorced would be a good time to do it.

Locating a Tattooist

Like the initial decision to get a tattoo, the tattooist one decides to patronize commonly is chosen through information provided by members of the individual's personal network. Fifty-eight percent of the questionnaire respondents located the shop in which they received their first tattoo through a recommendation provided by a friend or family member. Since, in most areas, establishments that dispense tattoos are not especially numerous, many first-time tattooees choose a studio on a very practical basis—it is the only one they know about or it is the studio that is closest to where they live (20 percent of the questionnaire sample chose the shop on the basis of location, 28 percent because it was the only one they knew about).[5]

Most first-time tattooees enter the tattoo setting with little information about the process or even about the relative skill of the artist. Rarely do recipients spend as much time and effort acquiring information about a process which is going to indelibly mark their bodies as they would were they preparing to purchase a TV set or other far less significant consumer item.

Consequently, tattooees usually enter the tattoo setting ill-informed and experiencing a considerable degree of anxiety. Their fears center around the anticipated pain of the process and the permanence of the tattoo. Here, for example, is an interaction (quoted from fieldnotes) that took place while a young man received his first tattoo.

> *Recipient*—Is this going to fade out much? There's this guy at work that has these tattoos all up and down his arms and he goes back to the guy that did them every couple of months and gets them recolored because they fade out.
> (General laughter)
> *Sanders*—Does this guy work in a shop or out of his house?
> *R*—He just does it on the side.
> *Tattooist*—He doesn't know what the fuck he's doing.
> *R*—This friend of mine told me that getting a tattoo really hurts. He said there would be guys in here hollering and bleeding all over the place.
> *S*—Does he have any tattoos?

R—No, but he says he wants to get some. . . . Hey, this really
doesn't hurt that much. It doesn't go in very deep, does it? It's
like picking a splinter out of your skin. I was going to get either
a unicorn or a pegasus. I had my sister draw one up because I
thought they just drew the picture on you or something. I
didn't know they did it this way (with an acetate stencil). I
guess this makes a lot more sense.

S—You ever been in a tattoo shop before this?

R—No, this is my first time. Another guy was going to come in
with me, but he chickened out.

As will be apparent in later chapters, tattooists, for the most
part, are quite patient about answering the questions clients ask
with numbing regularity (pain, price, and permanence). This
helps to put the recipient more at ease, smooths the service delivery interaction, and increases the chances that a satisfied customer—who will recommend the shop to his or her friends and
perhaps return again for additional work—will leave the establishment (see Govenar, 1977; Becker and Clark, 1979; St. Clair
and Govenar, 1981).

Choosing a Design and Body Location

Tattooees commonly described the basic reasons for deciding to
become tattooed in very general terms. Wearing a tattoo connected the person to significant others who were similarly
marked, made one unique by separating him or her from those
who were too convention-bound to so alter their bodies, symbolized freedom or self-control, and satisfied an aesthetic desire to
decorate the physical self.[6]

The image one chooses, on the other hand, is usually selected
for a specific reason. Typically, design choice is related to the person's connection to other people, his or her definition of self or,
especially in the case of women, the desire to enhance and beau-
tify the body.

One of the most common responses to my question, "How did
you go about deciding on this particular tattoo?" was a reference
to a personal associate with whom they had a close emotional relationship. Some chose a particular tattoo because it was like that

worn by a close friend or a member of their family. Others chose a design that incorporated the name of their boy friend, girl friend, spouse, or child or a design associated with that person (for example, zodiac signs).

> I had this homemade cross and skull here and I needed a coverup. [The tattooist] couldn't just do anything so I thought to myself, "My daughter was born in May and that's the Bull." I'm leaving the rest of this arm clean because it is just for my daughter. If I ever get married I'll put something here [on the other arm]. I'll get a rose or something for my wife.

> This tattoo is a symbol of friendship. Me and my best friend—I've known him since I could walk—came in together and we both got bluebirds to have a symbol that when we do part we will remember each other by it.

The ongoing popularity of "vow tattoos" such as the traditional heart with "MOM" or flowers with a ribbon on which the loved one's name is written attests to the importance of tattooing as a way of symbolically expressing love and commitment (Hardy, 1982a).

Similarly, tattoos are used to demonstrate connection and commitment to a group. For example, military personnel pick tattoos that relate to their particular service, motorcycle gang members choose club insignia, and members of sports teams enter a shop en masse and all receive the same design.

Tattoos are also employed as symbolic representations of how one conceives of the self, or interests and activities that are key features of self-definition. Tattooees commonly choose their birth sign or have their name or nickname inscribed on their bodies. Others choose more abstract symbols of the self.

> I put a lot of thought into this tattoo. I'm an English lit major and I thought that the medieval castle had a lot of significance. I'm an idealist and I thought that that was well expressed by a castle with clouds. Plus, I'm blond and I wanted something blue.

> [Quote from fieldnotes] Two guys in their twenties come in and look at the flash. After looking around for a while one of the guys come over to me and asks if we have any bees. I tell him to look through the book (of small designs) because I have seen

some bees in there. I ask, "Why do you want a bee? I don't think I have ever seen anyone come in here for one." He replies, "I'm allergic to bees. If I get stung by one again I'm going to die. So I thought I'd come in here and have a big, mean-looking bee put on. I want one that has this long stinger and these long teeth and is coming in to land. With that, any bee would think twice about messing with me."

Tattooees commonly represent the self by choosing designs that symbolize important personal involvements, hobbies, occupational activities, and so forth. In most street shops, the winged insignia of Harley-Davidson motorcycles and variants on that theme are the most frequently requested images. During one particularly busy week in the major shop in which I was observing, a rabbit breeder acquired a rabbit tattoo, a young man requested a cartoon frog because the Little League team he coached was named the "frogs," a fireman received a fire fighter's cross insignia surrounded by flame, and an optician chose a flaming eye.

No matter what the associational or self-definitional meaning of the chosen tattoo, the recipient commonly is aware of the decorative/aesthetic function of the design. When I asked tattooees to explain how they went about choosing a particular design, they routinely made reference to aesthetic criteria—they "like the colors" or they "thought it was pretty."

(I didn't get this tattoo) because of being bad or cool or anything like that. It's like a picture. You see a picture you like and you put it in your room or your house or something like that. It's just a piece of work that you like. I like the art work they do here. I like the color (on my tattoo). It really brings it out—the orange and the green. I like that—the colors.[7]

A number of factors shape the tattooee's decision about where on the body the tattoo will be located. The vast majority of male tattooees choose to have their work placed on the arm. In his study of the tattoos carried by 2000 members of the Royal Navy, Scutt found that 98 percent had received their tattoo(s) on the arm (Scutt and Gotch, 1974: 96). In my own research, 55 percent of the questionnaire respondents received their first tattoo on the arm or hand (71 percent of the males and 19 percent of the females). The sixteen interviewees had, all together, thirty-five tattoos, twenty-seven of which were carried by the ten males. Eighty-one percent (twenty-two) of the mens' tattoos were on their arms (of the remainder two were on hips, one was on the back, one on the face, and one on the recipient's chest). The six women interviewees possessed eight tattoos—three on the back or the shoulder area, three on the breast, one on an arm, and one on the lower back. Thirty-five percent of female questionnaire respondents received their first tattoo on the breast, 13 percent on the back or shoulder, and 10 percent on the hip (see Figure 1).

Clearly, there is a definite convention affecting the decision to place the tattoo on a particular part of the body—men, for the most part, choose the arm while women choose the breast, hip, lower abdomen, back, or shoulder. To some degree the tendency for male tattooees to have the tattoo placed on the arm is determined by technical features of the tattoo process. Tattooing is a two-handed operation. The tattooist must stretch the skin with one hand while inscribing the design with the other. This operation is most easily accomplished when the tattoo is being applied to an extremity. Tattooing the torso is more difficult and, commonly, tattooists have an assistant who stretches the client's skin when work is being done on that area of the body. Technical difficulty, in turn, affects price. Most tattooists charge 10 to 25 percent more for tattoos placed on body parts other than the arm or leg. The additional cost factor probably has some effect on the client's choice of body location.

Pain is another factor shaping the tattooee's decision. The tattoo machine contains needle groups that superficially pierce the skin at high speed, leaving small amounts of pigment in the tiny punctures. Obviously, this process will cause more or less pain depending on the sensitivity of the area being tattooed. In general, tattooing arms or legs generates less pain than marking body areas with a higher concentration of nerve endings or parts of the body where the bones are not cushioned with muscle tissue.[8]

The sex-based conventions regarding choice of body site are largely determined by the different symbolic functions of the tattoo for men and women. Women tend to regard the tattoo (com-

Figure 1: Body Location of First Tattoo (N = 163)

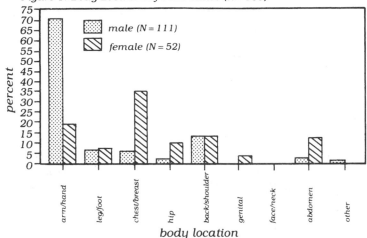

body location

monly a small, delicate design) as a permanent body decoration
primarily intended for personal pleasure and the enjoyment of
those with whom they are most intimate. The chosen tattoos are,
therefore, placed on parts of the body most commonly seen by
those with whom women have primary relationships. Since tattoos on women are especially stigmatizing, placement on private
parts of the body allows women to retain unsullied identities
when in contact with casual associates or strangers (see Goffman,
1963a: 53–55, 73–91). Here, for example, is a portion of a brief
conversation with a young woman who carried an unconventional
design (a snake coiled around a large rose) on what is, for women,
an unconventional body location (her right bicep).

Sanders—How did you decide on that particular design?
Woman—I wanted something really different and I'd never seen
a tattoo like this on a woman before. I really like it, but
sometimes I look at it and wish I didn't have it.
S—That's interesting. When do you wish you didn't have it?
W—When I'm getting real dressed up in a sleeveless dress and
I want to look . . . uh, prissy and feminine. People look at a
tattoo and think you're real bad . . . a loose person. But I'm
not.

Another interviewee described the decision-making process she had gone through in choosing to acquire a small rose design on her shoulder, emphasizing aesthetic issues and stigma control.

> The only other place that I knew of that women got tattoos was on the breast. I didn't want it on the front of my chest because I figured if I was at work and had an open blouse or a scoop neck, then half would show and half wouldn't. I wanted to be able to control when I wanted it to show and when I didn't. If I go for a job interview I don't want a tattoo on my breast. I didn't want it, like, on my thigh or on the lower part of my stomach. I didn't like how they look there. I just thought it would look pretty on my shoulder. . . . The main reason is that I can cover it up if I want to.

Men, on the other hand, typically are less inclined than women to define the tattoo primarily as a decorative and intimate addition to the body. Instead, the male tattoo is an identity symbol—a more public display of interests, associations, separation from the normative constraints of conventional society, and, most generally, masculinity. The designs chosen by men are usually larger than those favored by women and, rather than employing the gentle imagery of nature and mythology (flowers, birds, butterflies, unicorns, and so forth), they frequently symbolize more violent impulses. Snakes, bloody daggers, skulls, dragons, grim reapers, black panthers, and birds of prey are dominant images in the conventional repertoire of tattoo designs chosen by men. Placement of the image on the arm allows both casual public display and, should the male tattooee anticipate a critical judgment from someone whose negative reaction could have untoward consequences (most commonly, an employer), easy concealment with clothing. One male interviewee spoke about the public meaning of tattoos and expressed his understanding of the difference between male and female tattoos as follows:

> You fit into a style. People recognize you by your hair-style or by your tattoo. People look at you in public and say, "Hey, they got a tattoo. They must be a particular kind of person," or, "He's got his hair cropped short (so) he must be a different kind of

person." The person with a tattoo is telling people that he is free enough to do what he wants to do. He says, "I don't care who you think I am. I'm doing what I want to do." (The tattoo) symbolizes freedom. It says something about your personality. If a girl has a skull on her arm—it's not feminine at all—that would symbolize vengeance. If a woman gets a woman's tattoo, that's normal. If she gets a man's tattoo symbolizing vengeance or whatever, I feel that is too far over the boards. A woman should act like a woman and keep her tattoos feminine. Those vengeance designs say, "Look out." People see danger in them.

THE INTRAPERSONAL AND INTERPERSONAL EXPERIENCE OF WEARING A TATTOO

Impact on Self-Definition

As indicated in the foregoing presentation of the initial motives that prompt the decision to acquire a tattoo, tattooees consistently conceive of the tattoo as having impact on their definition of self and demonstrating to others information about their unique interests and social connections. Interviewees commonly expressed liking their tattoos because they made him or her "different" or "special" (see Goffman, 1963a: 56–62).

Having a tattoo changes how you see yourself. It is a way of choosing to change your body. I enjoy that. I enjoy having a tattoo because it makes me different from other people. There is no one in the whole world who has a right arm that looks anything like mine. I've always valued being different from other people. Tattooing is a way of expressing that difference. It is a way of saying, "I am unique."

In describing his own understanding of his clients' motives, one tattoo artist employed the analogy of the customized car.

Tattooing is really just a form of personal adornment. Why does someone get a new car and get all of the paint stripped off of it and paint it candy-apple red? Why spend $10,000 on a car and then spend another $20,000 to make it look different from the car you bought? I associate it with ownership. Your body is one of the things you indisputably own. There is a tendency to adorn things that you own to make them especially yours.

Interviewees also spoke of the pleasure they got from the tattoo as related to having gone through the mysterious and moderately painful process of being tattooed. The tattoo demonstrated courage to the self ("for some people it means that they lived through it and weren't afraid"). One woman, when asked whether she intended to acquire other tattoos in the future, spoke of the excitement of the experience as the potential motivator of additional work.

(Do you think you will have more work done after you add something to the one you have now?) Oh God! I don't know why, but my initial reaction is, "I hope I don't, but I think I'm going to." I think getting a tattoo is so exciting and I've always been kind of addicted to excitement. It's fun. While it hurt and stuff it was a new experience and it wasn't that horrible for me. It was new and different.

In a poignant statement, another woman spoke similarly of the tattoo as memorializing significant aspects of her past experience. "In the future when I'm sitting around and bored with my life and I wonder if I was ever young once and did exciting things, I can look at the tattoo and remember."

Interactional Consequences

In general, tattooees' observations concerning the effect on their self-definitions of having a tattoo and the process of being tattooed were rather basic and off-hand. In contrast, all interviewees spoke at some length about their social experiences with others and how the tattoo affected their identities and interactions. Some stressed the affiliational consequences of being tattooed—the mark identified them as belonging to a special group.

I got tattooed because I had an interest in it. My husband is a chef and our friends tend to be bikers, so it gets me accepted more into that community. They all think of me as "the college girl" and I'm really not. So this (tattoo) kind of brings the door open more. . . . The typical biker would tell you that you almost have to have tattoos to be part of the group.

Most took pleasure in the way the tattoo enhanced their identities by demonstrating their affiliation with a somewhat more diverse group—tattooed people.

> Having a tattoo is like belonging to a club. I love seeing tattoos on other people. I go up and talk with other people with tattoos. It gives me an excuse because I'm not just going up to talk with them. I can say, "I have one, too." I think maybe subconsciously I got (the tattoo) to be part of that special club.

> Having tattoos in some ways does affect me positively because people will stop me on the street and say, "Those are really nice tattoos," and show me theirs. We kind of . . . it is a way of having positive contact with strangers. We have something very much in common. We can talk about where we got them and the process of getting them and that sort of thing.

Given the symbolic meaning carried by tattoos in conventional social circles, all tattooees have the experience of being the focus of attention because of the mark they carry. The positive responses of others are, of course, the source of the most direct pleasure.

> People seem to notice you more when you walk around with technicolor arms. I don't think that everyone who gets tattooed is basically an exhibitionist, someone that walks down the street and says, "Hey, look at me," you know. But it does draw attention to yourself. (How do people respond when they see your tattoos?) Well, yesterday we were sitting in a bar and the lady brings a beer over and she says, "That's gorgeous," and she's looking at the wizard and she's touching them and picking up my shirt. Everyone in the bar was looking and it didn't bother me a bit.

Not all casual encounters are as positive as this one. Revelation of the tattoo is also the source of negative attention when defined by others as a stigmatizing mark.

> Sometimes at these parties the conversation will turn to tattoos and I'll mention that I have some. A lot of people don't believe it, but if I'm feeling loose enough I'll roll up my sleeve and show my work. What really aggravates me is that there will

almost always be someone who reacts with a show of disgust. "How could you do that to yourself?" No wonder I usually feel more relaxed and at home with bikers and other tattooed people.

I think tattoos look sharp. I walk down the beach and people look at my tattoos. Usually then don't say anything. (When they do) I wish they would say it to my face . . . like, "Tattoos are ugly." But, when they say something behind my back. . . . "Isn't that gross." Hey, keep your comments to yourself! If you don't like it, you don't like it. I went to the beach with my father and I said, "Hey, let's walk down the beach," and he said, "No, I don't feel like it." What are you, embarrassed to walk with me?

Given the negative responses that tattooees encounter with some frequency when casual associates or strangers become aware of their body decorations, most are selective about to whom they reveal their tattoos. This is particularly the case when the "other" is in a position to exercise control over the tattooee.

Usually I'm fairly careful about who I show my tattoos to. I don't show them to people at work unless they are really close friends of mine and I know I won't get any kind of hassle because of them. I routinely hide my tattoos . . . I generally hide them from people who wouldn't understand or people who could potentially cause me trouble. I hide them from my boss and from a lot of the people I work with because there is no reason for them to know.

Tattooees commonly use the reactions of casual associates or relative strangers as a means of categorizing them. A positive reaction to the tattoo indicates social and cultural compatibility, while a negatively judgmental response is seen as signifying a narrow and convention-bound perspective.

I get more positive reactions than I do negative reactions. The negative reactions come from people who aren't like me—who have never done anything astray. It is the straight-laced, conservative person who really doesn't believe that this is acceptable in their set of norms. It seems as though I can actually tell how I'm going to get along with people, and vice-versa, by the way they react to my tattoo. It's more or less expressive of the unconventional side of my character right up front. Most of the people who seem to like me really dig the tattoo too (quoted in Hill, 1972: 249).

While it is fairly easy to selectively reveal the tattoo in public settings when interacting with strangers or casual associates, hiding the fact that one is tattooed, thereby avoiding negative social response, is difficult when the "other" is a person with whom the tattooee is intimately associated. The majority of those interviewed recounted incidents in which parents, friends, and, especially for the women, lovers and spouses reacted badly when they initially became aware of the tattoo.

(What did your husband say when he saw your tattoo?) He said he almost threw up. It grossed him out. I had asked him years ago, "What would you think if . . . ," and he didn't like the idea. So, I decided not to tell him. It seemed a smart thing to do. He just looked rather grossed out by the whole thing; didn't like it. Now it is accepted, but I don't think he would go for another one.

Another woman interviewee recounted a similar post-tattoo experience with her parents and boyfriend.

My family was devastated. I didn't tell them for a long time. My mother and I were on a train to New York City and I said to her, "Mom, I want to tell you something but I don't want you to get upset." She said, "You're pregnant!" I said, "No." She says, "You're getting married!" I said, "God, no!" It was downhill from there. When I said, "I got a tattoo," it was like, "Thank God! That's all it is." It wasn't that horrible. My father's reaction was just one of disgust because women who get tattoos to him are . . . I don't know . . . they just aren't nice girls. They aren't the type of girl he wants his daughter to be. He let me know that. He let me have it right between the eyes. He said, "Do you know what kind of girls get tattoos?" and just walked out of the room. That was enough. He thought tramps get tattoos or girls that ride on the back seats of motorcycles,

Figure 2: Extent and Source of Tattooee Regret (N = 163)

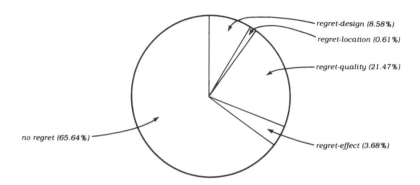

regret-design (8.58%)

regret-location (0.61%)

regret-quality (21.47%)

no regret (65.64%)

regret-effect (3.68%)

you know. I got a strange reaction from my boyfriend. We had a family outing to go to and there was going to be swimming and tennis and all this stuff and I was real excited about going. He said, "Are you going to go swimming?" I said, "Yeah." I was psyched because I love to swim. He looked at me and said, "You know, your tattoo is going to show if you go swimming." Probably. He didn't want me to go swimming because he didn't want his parents to know that I had a tattoo. Lucky for him it was cloudy that day and nobody swam. I told him, "I'm sorry but I know your parents can handle this kind of news." To boot, he's got a shamrock on his butt! So he has a tattoo—a real double standard there. He didn't say anything for a while after I first got it. It was subtle. He let me know he didn't like it but that, because it was on me, he could excuse it. He's got adjusted to it though. He just let me know that he's never dated a girl who's got a tattoo before. He would prefer that I didn't have it, but there isn't much he can do about that now.

Given the negative social reaction often precipitated by tattoos, it would be reasonable to expect that tattooees who regretted their decision would have emphasized the unpleasant interactional consequences of the tattoo. Interviewees and questionnaire respondents rarely expressed any doubts about their decision to acquire a tattoo. Those that did indicate regret, however, usually did not focus on the stigmatizing effect of the tattoo. Instead, regretful tattooees most commonly were dissatisfied with the technical quality of the tattoo they purchased (see Figure 2).[9]

CONCLUSION: TATTOOING, STIGMA, SELF, AND IDENTITY

When potential tattooees begin to think about altering their bodies in this manner, they devise an understanding of what the tattoo will signify to themselves and others through contact with tattooed associates or by attending media presentations of tattooing and tattooed people (cf. Cohen, 1973; Matza, 1969). In general, they define that tattoo as a mark of affiliation—demonstrating connection to significant groups, primary associates, or those who share specific interests—or as an isolative symbol of unconventionality, or unique personal decoration. Having come to conceive of themselves as tattooed, potential recipients locate a tattoo establishment and acquire the mark.

When revealed to others, the newly acquired corporeal embellishment affects interactions and relationships. Positive responses from co-interactants tend to reinforce social connections, certify tattooees' positive evaluations of self and the tattoo acquisition decision, and increase the likelihood that tattooees will expend the universe of situations in which they choose to reveal their unconventional body decorations.

If being tattooed leads to negative social and self-definitional consequences, regretful tattooees are faced with various alternatives. When met with disapproval tattooees may negatively evaluate the disapproving other and subsequently become more selective in disclosing the fact that they bear a tattoo (see Goffman, 1963a: 11). If regretful tattooees focus the responsibility for the negative consequences of having acquired the tattoo upon themselves, they can deny responsibility for the decision or take steps to obliterate the tattoo. Since negative evaluations of the tattoo decision are most commonly due to the perceived inferior quality of the work, regretful tattooees often have the offending mark covered or reworked by another, more skilled (one hopes), tattooist (see Figure 3).

The central factor shaping this process—from initial stages of interest through dealing with the consequences of being a tattooed person—is that the tattoo is conventionally regarded as a stigma symbol (Goffman, 1963a: 43). The decision to acquire a tattoo is not only a decision to alter one's physical appearance; it is a choice to change how the person experiences his or her self and, in turn, how he or she will be defined and treated by others.

Definitions of tattoos and tattooees, held by both the general culture and the "scientific community," are predominantly negative. Tattoos are defined as being symptomatic of the psychological or social deviance of the bearer. Conventional repulsion imbues tattooing with significant power and appeal. For some tattooees the act of acquiring a tattoo marks them as being involved in an exotic social world centered around the pleasurable flaunting of authority and convention (cf. Lofland, 1969: 106).

(Why do you think you initially wanted to put the tattoo someplace that is well hidden?) I guess I thought that someone would think it was creepy. It would have connotations of loose women or being foolish. Like kids don't think through the consequences of stuff. They do things impetuously. I thought that people might think I just ran down there in a fit of glee. (Actually) a tattoo is not serious. I think that is part of the pleasure of it. When I was first thinking about it it was, "Oh boy, let's do this!" It was sort of a gleeful thing. It is like being a little bit bad.

I can't think of one nice compact reason (I got a tattoo). They are pretty. But most of all they are a poke in the eye to people who don't have them—people who are straights or whatever.

The tattoo acts as more than simply a "mark of disaffiliation" (Goffman, 1963a: 143–147). It may also demonstrate connection to unconventional social groups. In some cases, it symbolizes

Figure 3. The Tattoo as Social Symbol: Acquisitional Process and Self-Definitional/Identity Consequences

decisional antecedents ⟶ *locate tattoo site*

1. contact w/tattooed other (as model or source of overt pressure)
2. contact with/exposure to tattoo setting (exotic place/culture)
3. media contact (learn "meaning" of tattoo and nature of tattooees)

tattoo meaning
A. Affiliative
   1. masculinity
   2. connection to significant other (e.g., vow)
   3. symbolization of group connection
   4. symbolization of shared interest/activity
B. Isolative/Individuating
   1. display of unconventionality
   2. personal decoration/beauty accessory

1. social/personal contact
2. media information, advertisements, Yellow Pages
3. encountering physical site

acquire tattoo
1. pleasure of place (exotic contact, new experience)
2. ritual (social display of courage, self-assertion, control, etc.)
3. alter self-definition (self as more beautiful, courageous, unique, connected, belonging, etc.)

revelation

social/personal response
A. Positive Response (admiration, praise, etc.)
   1. reinforce connection to positive responder and/or symbolized other (eg., vow)
   2. reinforce positive self definition
   3. increase likelihood of acquiring additional tattoos
   4. increase likelihood of further tattoo display/disclosure

increase likelihood of negative response

avoidance

reestablish positive self definition (disavowal of responsibility/intent—e.g., drunkenness, excessive peer pressure

B. Negative Response (disgust, avoidance, etc.)
   1. negatively define source of negative response
   2. negatively define self
   3. avoid future disclosure (secrecy, selectivity)
   4. obliteration (self or surgical removal)
   5. cover or rework tattoo (if regret due to technical dissatisfaction)

passing

regain non-deviant self

regain positive sense of choice, appearance (decrease cognitive dissonance)

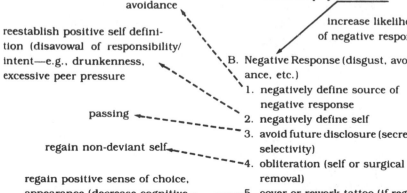

membership in subcultures (for example, outlaw motorcyclists, youth gangs) centered around socially disvalued or law-violating interests and activities.[10]

The stigmatized social definition of tattooing and the negative response tattooees commonly experience when "normals" are aware of their stigma may also precipitate identification with a subculture in which the tattoo is of primary significance. Within the informal "tattoo community" consisting of those tattooees who positively define their unconventional mark, the tattoo acts as a source of "mutual openness" (Goffman, 1963b: 131–139), providing opportunities for spontaneous appreciative interaction with others who are also tattooed (Pfuhl, 1986: 168–188; Goffman, 1963a: 23–25).[11]

As is commonly the case with subcultural groups bound together by the problems associated with possession of a physical stigma, the tattoo world has developed an organized core. More-or-less formal groups such as the National Tattoo Association hold regular meetings and provide practioners with technical information, legal assistance, access to the latest equipment and supplies, and other essential occupational resources. Serious tattoo "enthusiasts" and collectors are also active in this organized world. Tattoo conventions provide them with an opportunity to display their work, enlarge their collections, and associate with other tattooees in situations in which they are normal. Understandably, a major focus of organizational activity is the public redefinition of tattooing as a legitimate form of artistic production.

Contemporary commercial culture provides a variety of products (t-shirts, bumper stickers, buttons, and so forth) by which people may announce their perspectives, personal interests, and social attachments. Clothing, jewelry, hair style, and other aspects of personal decoration are used to demonstrate aesthetic taste. These modes of self-symbolization are, however, relatively safe and transitory expressions. For some, these conventional mechanisms are inadequate. Typically impelled by personal association with others who have chosen a more drastic and symbolically powerful approach, tattooees purchase what is, as yet, a "tarnished" cultural product (Shover, 1975). In so doing, tattooed people voluntarily shape their social identities and enhance their definitions of self. Drawn by both the affiliational and individuating consequences of their choice and despite the potential for disrupted interactions, tattooees choose to mark their bodies with indelible symbols of what they see themselves to be.

Chapter 3

The Tattooist: Tattooing as a Career and an Occupation

The career of the tattooist is similar to that seen in other work activities that involve providing a skilled service with marginally artistic features (cf. Schroder, 1973; Boles and Garbin, 1974; Fine, 1985). In general, the tattooist's career path is relatively simple and offers little opportunity for significant vertical mobility. Occupational entrance is typically somewhat serendipitous and the career is truncated—the tattooist commonly achieves an occupational position early in his or her career and tends to remain at that level. For most tattooists career mobility is horizontal, entailing the movement from shop to shop with little increase in status or income. Recognizing their limited mobility options, tattooists emphasize independence as the primary career value and goal. They have a skill that can be "put in the pocket." The ability to tattoo allows one to earn a living in a variety of situations while not being tied to a particular shop, boss, or locality. For most, making it as a tattooist means fully developing one's artistic and technical skills, achieving a reputation for skilled work in the tattoo world, and gaining the freedom to turn down unsavory, uncreative, or otherwise undesirable client requests.

OCCUPATIONAL CHOICE AND ENTRY

It is rare that a person focuses on becoming a tattooist and systematically goes about seeking to achieve that occupational goal. Instead, entry is typically "adventitious" (Katz and Martin, 1962). Rather than purposefully setting out to become a tattoo artist, the individual drifts from job to job before, almost accidentally, encountering tattooing and coming to define it as a viable occupational alternative. Entry is relatively spontaneous and impelled by a variety of situational contingencies.

Tattooists base their initial decision to pursue tattooing as an occupation on the perception that they possess some measure of artistic talent. While growing up the potential tattooist has commonly been involved in artistic activities and his or her talent has been recognized and employed by family members, peers, and, especially, high-school teachers (cf. Griff, 1970).

> I mean, like, I could draw. I never went to art school or nothing. In high school I never did anything I was told. I just drew. Some of my teachers loved it 'cause they were, like, throwbacks from the sixties. The ones that weren't used to tell me what to draw and stuff. They always let kids, like, draw and paint on the walls at school. They never let me do that. They, like, wanted me to paint football players and stuff like that for the school. I went back to my old high school the other day and I told my art teacher that I finally got a job that involves my art talent and she flipped.

When recounting how they had become involved with tattooing, all of the interviewees reported experiencing some form of occupational dissatisfaction at the time they began to realize that tattooing was a viable career alternative. Most of the tattooists—especially those from working-class backgrounds—were employed in routine, laboring jobs when they encountered tattooing.[1] The fine art tattooists, on the other hand, typically were pursuing commercial art careers or were attempting to "succeed" as serious artists. They saw themselves as being creatively stifled or as having limited chances of success in the highly competitive fine art world.

> The more I looked at art in the contemporary culture, the more I got involved in the business of art in America, the more I realized I was like the monkey on the end of the organ grinder's string. I really felt desperate about that because art had always

been my safe place, my private world, my own comfortable place. So I had to turn around and try to market that part of me. I started to feel really desperate. It was like walking through the streets and having people throw stones at you or something. The first time you go out to a gallery and try to market those things that are so intimately tied to your psyche it is a very scary experience. I don't know if all artists go through that in trying to make it in the art market, but I sure did. After the first bunch of rejections I just crawled back to my studio and didn't go back out for another year until I thought I had something that really had balls. I learned a lot about professionalism in terms of making art. But the more I tried to satisfy the criteria for exhibition the less it became my work and the more it became satisfying certain criteria. So I really felt desperate, depressed and very disturbed about the fact . . . I felt that I just couldn't make it as an artist in our culture.

The realization that tattooing presents a viable career alternative is most commonly initiated through direct contact with a working tattooist.[2] Often, recognition of the possibility of working in tattooing is precipitated by dissatisfaction with the work the individual sees being done by his or her personal tattoo artist. The following account by a commercially oriented tattooist is typical of the way interviewees described this early entry stage:

I did a lot of work on motorcycles from the time I was fifteen or so. I was taking a lot of trips to upstate New York. When I finally turned eighteen I was asking a guy up there if there were any tattoo shops around there. I was driving all around the city looking for them. I found out it was illegal in the city. This guy said that he had heard of a place up in N——. I asked a few questions when I got into town and got steered to them. I got to talking to the guy, an old carnival worker. He travels all over the place; he's there in the winter time and the rest of the time he's out on the road. This was early '71. I talked to him and I wanted to get a tattoo of an Indian motorcycle. I had a '48 and a '37. I drew up the design of the motorcycle I wanted and went back up there and had him put it on. I thought that it might be a mistake, man, I saw this guy's hand shaking. . . .

He must have been in his late sixties or so. He had a lot of
Charlie Wagner's work all over him. I started to watch him
going out of the lines and everything and I made the mistake of
letting him do a second one on me. He said, "I'm not used to
this design" and this and that. So I let him do this skull and
crossbones on me. The motorcycle has been redone a couple of
times. When this was healing up it swelled up like I had an egg
under the skin. A while after that I went up again and he was
asking me if I wanted to buy any equipment because he had
something set up for a guy, couple of machines and this and
that, needle bars, and some flash—110 bucks. That was high
dollar to me back then. I was working for [a factory] at the time
then I left there and was working at a construction warehouse.
I said, "Nah" and kind of let it go at that. When I seen how
crummy these were coming along, I went back up there and
said, "Can you just sell me part of it, I don't want to buy the
whole thing. I just want to do a little work on myself." So he
gave me one machine and a little toy train transformer, a
couple of old brass tubes, some brass needle bars, a couple of
packets of needles. That was 45 bucks.

Personal contact with a tattooist is, therefore, a key step in the
process of becoming a tattooist. Personal contact provides knowledge of the financial and creative opportunities offered by tattooing, a source of information about the technical aspects of the
tattoo process, and a source of the basic equipment needed to create a tattoo (cf. Boles and Garbin, 1974).[3] In some cases the tattooist acts directly as a recruiting agent.

(My friend) was much into pursuing the Japanese form as a
style for himself. Of course I presented him with a rather rare
opportunity for someone who hadn't been tattooing for more
than a year to get into a large scale tattoo. Little did I know
that I gave him much too much play. I had faith in his creative
and artistic ability but, after having been in the tattoo
business now for five years, I realize now that it takes two,
three, even four years before even a skilled draftsman becomes
skilled at tattooing. The transition from the traditional forms
to tattooing is a considerable transition not only emotionally

and psychologically but technically. So I gave up this large area of my body and got this tattoo and about three quarters of the way through the tattoo (he) asked me if I wanted to learn to tattoo. I never asked him to teach me. The thought that I wanted to learn to tattoo really didn't come into my consciousness until he said, "Would you like to learn to tattoo?" I said, "Certainly, I'd love to learn to tattoo."

Another tattooist spoke of the criteria he used in selecting his own apprentice.

(My apprentice) started coming in here to get tattooed. He got a small piece and we got to be friends and then he started realizing that he had crummy work and he wanted it covered. He started getting heavy work done. I could see that he was really interested in tattooing. He couldn't draw a straight line but that didn't matter to me. I knew I needed someone to help me in here because I was turning business away. You know, I have to have a day off and stuff. So I knew from experience if I got another artist to come around here who is already an established tattooist . . . that's hard to do because if someone has their shit together and is really good, they don't need to go work for someone else. So I could go out and get some young kid who is a good artist and teach him how to tattoo and as soon as he knows what he's doing—after a year, year and a half—he's going to say, "What the hell do I need this guy for?" He might even turn out better than me. I wanted first of all someone who was responsible and who I could trust that is not going to move next year. Then I wanted someone I thought could handle it. (My apprentice) doesn't draw but he's a carpenter, he races motorcycles, he's an achiever. He didn't just want to do things. He did them. I figure if you can master one craft you can master the craft of tattooing.

Interviewees provided fairly straightforward accounts of the factors that prompted them to become tattooists. All stated that they had had a long-term interest in or "fascination" with tattoos. Many said they had played with tattoos as youngsters—collecting "lick and stick" tattoos from bubblegum packs, marking themselves and friends with ballpoint pens, and doing homemade tattoos with india ink and sewing needles stuck in pencil erasers. As they grew older and had contact with commercial tattooing, fascination with the atmosphere of the shop and the social world revolving around tattooing acted as an additional motivation.

> I was sixteen years old and gently ran away from home by joining the Navy. As all young Navy men do, I ran out on my first leave and got a tattoo. Mine was a traditional Navy tattoo put on by a fellow in Jacksonville Beach, Florida. I walked into that other world—a dingy old shop, very exotic, erotic, very mystifying. I became consumed with it. I couldn't stay out of the shop. I spent every day there. He began to teach me how to tattoo.

The "street" tattooists were typically drawn to tattooing by the income potential and occupational independence.

> I had a teaching degree and there weren't any jobs for art teachers. I was working in a factory and at that time I heard that there was a tattoo shop open in Connecticut. So I went down to see it. It looked like a fairly good business and I didn't think that the people running it had any more talent than I did. So I decided to try it.

"Fine art" tattooists, in contrast, commonly were drawn by their desire to pursue an art form that offered a creative outlet.

> The first female I ever saw with a tattoo was a friend of mine. I had no idea that she had a tattoo. At the time I was into natural health food and that whole hippie scene. Pure and natural. And to me bleaching my hair or putting a mark on my body was not OK. I was taken aback. I wasn't shocked or revolted by it. I was amazed that it wasn't the image of a skull with a dagger coming out of the eye. It was just flowers on her shoulder and the colors were beautiful. They just popped right out. The whole image of it looked like a piece of art work instead of the idea we usually project onto a tattoo. It got me to thinking. I was already involved in the arts and I thought I could do tattooing (cf. Griff, 1970: 155–157).

Few tattooists make a total commitment to tattooing once they are introduced to it as an occupational alternative. Instead, they commonly pursue a line of "phased commitment," continuing their current job for a time while amassing experience and making the necessary contacts in the tattoo world.

At this time I was working ten hour days welding. I got out of work and got cleaned up and had appointments from 6 o'clock on. I'd usually end up working to 10 at night or 2 in the morning. Then I'd be up at 6 to get to work. That was really crazy. Then (this tattooist) calls me up and says that things ain't working out with his brother and wanted to know if I still wanted to come down. This was great. I was into trying to learn. He was showing me quite a bit as I was getting work done. A couple of times when things got busy I just would grab one of his machines and start working too. It gave me some money to pay for what I was getting. I gave my notice at work and started working down there just on weekends. During the week I was doing work up here. I wasn't doing a lot of big pieces but there were four or five people I had work started on. A month after that I was working down there full time. Kept the place going like seven days a week.

My wife's friend's husband wanted the tattoo of a bass. He was a great bass fisherman. So he brought me a picture. After I had done two tattoos I was doing as good work as was coming out of tattoo studios. They were doing pretty bad work. I looked for a place to rent and I rented a small shop in the worst section of T——. It was rundown but busy. Populated by all the dregs of humanity . . . crazies and pimps and whores and dope addicts. Just about every kind of degenerate that was around was right there. So the rent was cheap. I rented this place from the bar next door and it was extremely cheap. I'd work at the factory during the day and I'd work in the tattoo shop at night. I drew most of the flash that I had. I had pretty good success. It got to be such a good business and gradually my income from the tattoo shop surpassed my income from the factory so I got rid of the factory job and went into the tattoo business full-time.

ACQUIRING EQUIPMENT

The equipment necessary for engaging in the creative activity is the essential resource within any art/craft form. Not only does the equipment allow one to pursue the production process, it is also symbolic. Possession of these necessary materials certifies that one is seriously involved in the creative activity. Further, learning to use the central resources involves learning the conventions that are key elements in the shared understanding of those who are actively engaged in the production work (Becker, 1982: 57).

The machines, pigments, needles, needle bars, and other equipment necessary to tattooing are not readily available to most people. The primary means of acquiring tattooing equipment for those seeking to enter the occupation is through personal contact, usually with practicing tattoo artists. The second major source of equipment is through advertisements in the classified sections of magazines directed at subcultural groups with some interest in tattooing. Commercial suppliers (especially Spaulding and Rogers of Voorheesville, New York) regularly advertise tattoo equipment in *Easyrider*, *Outlaw Biker*, and other magazines read by those who might be potential customers.

I tried to find out where I could buy equipment. That is something that other tattoo artists are rather secretive about. There's only one supplier that advertises. It used to be different when I was a kid. There were a lot of advertisements like in *Popular Mechanics*. This friend of mine happened to see an ad in *Easyrider* and I drove out there to Long Island and talked to the guys and bought some equipment. They let me know what I needed and they sold me a couple of machines and a power unit, colors, and so forth.

(I wanted) to find out about the equipment and to seriously consider it. I looked in the phonebook and if you look there you won't find tattoo equipment, you'll find tattooists. A friend of mine found an ad in the back of *Rolling Stone* magazine and gave it to me. I had looked for the information for close to three years. It didn't dawn on me to go to another tattooist and ask them. I had heard stories through the grapevine that certain people in the business did an apprenticeship and then opened up around the corner from the teacher and I'm sure that there were already three tattoo shops in this area and I was sure that I wouldn't get any information that way. I should have tried but I thought I could find out the information on my own. The ad in *Rolling Stone* was from Spaulding and Rogers which advertises in many magazines. I finally got the money together and bought the equipment. It was a pretty big step for me to make an investment in something I knew nothing about. I was supposed to go in on the equipment with some other people and they never came through. So there I was the first day with the equipment in my apartment and I was thrilled. It was like getting a Christmas present. But what was I to do?

LEARNING TO TATTOO

There is little available literature providing specific instruction about the technical aspects of tattooing.[4] Most tattooists acquire the necessary skills and are socialized into the role and perspective of the tattooist either through some form of apprenticeship relationship or through a piecemeal process of trial-and-error experience.

Tattooists have a reputation for being extremely secretive with regard to the technical aspects of tattooing. For the most part, their secretiveness derives from their desire to restrict competition in what is, at best, a limited market. Some tattooists refuse to take on apprentices out of fear of future competition. One tattooist interviewed required his apprentices to sign a statement that, should they leave his employment, they would not open a tattoo establishment within a twenty-mile radius of his studio (see Scutt and Gotch, 1974: 60–61; Shover, 1975: 482).[5]

There are three forms of apprenticeship in tattooing. Some established tattooists accept a few "students" who pay sizable sums of money (often as much as four thousand dollars) to learn the basic technical skills. One female respondent recounted her experience in a contractual apprenticeship that she entered in an effort to find a means of self-support following her divorce.

I started to become a tattoo artist when I was 20. I was in Newport and, at the time, it was something we all went and did. I had these tattoos and I was looking for something to do for a living when my marriage broke up. I was turned onto a man in Florida named S—— who agreed to teach me. What it was was that I lived in his house for three years and I had to complete 6800 hours of time in the shop. It started out that he gave me a panful of dirty tubes and a Q-tip and he said, "You clean 100 of these and then tell me if you still want to tattoo." I got that done and I said, "OK what's next? Let's go." So after three years I was doing pretty good and I went back to my hometown and opened up a business. Every night I would think, "Am I doing the right thing?" I really was because there was nothing else in my life. I had done a lot of things with the public. I love people. So I have no fear of working on another human. Some people have the fear of close contact with other people. I don't. Actually I apprenticed with S—— in Florida for 2 years. I started out shaving people. That was it. That was my main job. We went to Bike Week in Daytona and that was my first chance to really draw stencils—it was hectograph at the time—and start out doing the basic things. I couldn't have asked for a better man to train me. S—— is a very hard man to work for. He'd get me out of bed at 2 o'clock in the morning and he would make me sit there on this little stool next to him while he shaded. All he did was the shade work. His wife did all the lining. I'd sit there some nights and he would make me so mad I'd want to cry. But it made me a better person because he wouldn't just skip over something. He'd get it out and say this is the way you do it. He had four women apprenticing with him at the time and I completed 1600 hours in 9 months because I elected to work 7 days a week 12 hours a day to get everything I could because I wanted to get back home. I wanted to prove a point. When I left I had nothing and I wanted to go back and show I could do it.

The other two common means of acquiring tattooing skill through personal interaction with an established tattooist are less formal. The novice may be hired by the tattooist to do basic janitorial and shop maintenance work in return for occasional tattooing instruction or the initiate may simply be allowed to "hang out" in the studio, picking up basic knowledge by observing the tattooist.[6]

Whether involved in a formal or informal apprenticeship arrangement, all initiates are expected to take a major hand in the "dirty-work" of the tattoo establishment. Tattooing involves a considerable amount of backstage preparation that is not readily apparent to clientele. In addition to doing the basic sweeping and cleaning that takes place in any retail establishment, tattooist initiates commonly spend considerable time soldering needles to the needle bars used in the tattoo machines, cutting acetate stencils used to place standard designs on the client's skin, mixing dry pigment with liquid solvents (usually isopropyl alcohol, water, and glycerine), and sterilizing tattoo equipment and stencils. More experienced novices commonly are involved in shaving and sterilizing clients' skin, helping during the application process by stretching the skin being tattooed, applying antiseptic salve, and bandaging the completed tattoo (cf., Schroder, 1973: 154–162; Rosenblum, 1978: 26).

Everett Hughes (1971b: 317) could well have been referring specifically to the apprentice tattooist when he observed:

> In occupations in which mistakes are fateful and in which
> repetition on living or valuable material is necessary to learn
> the skills, it is obvious that there is a special set of problems of
> apprenticeship and of access to the situations in which the
> learning may be done. Later on, when the neophyte is at his
> work, there arises the problem of his seeming always to have
> known how, since the very appearance of being a learner is
> frightening.

The indelibility of the tattoo and the necessity of having, at least, some limited degree of technical expertise in order to effectively mark the skin necessitate that apprentice tattooists commonly practice on various skin substitutes before being allowed to work on a living tattooee. Novices typically practice on chicken carcasses, potatoes, melons, and various other fruits and vegetables in order to acquire the basic ability to line, shade, and color a tattoo. One respondent described this early practice stage and reported having discovered a unique skin substitute:

(The tattoo artist) gave me my first piece of tattoo equipment and said that I should go out and purchase the rest of the equipment and begin to practice on grapefruits. So that's what I did. I purchased a set of equipment from Spaulding and Rogers Manufacturers and proceeded to tattoo every goddamn grapefruit in sight. I had a lot of smelly grapefruits lying around the house for weeks. I tattooed bananas and cantaloupes and all sorts of other dishes. I discovered a technique myself somewhat later that was very rewarding . . . that was tattooing paper plates. I practiced tattooing a paper plate without puncturing through the paper so I could learn to control depth, penetration, speed. I got some understanding of dot patterns and speed with the machine. I did that mostly all on my own.[7]

The ready availability of one's own skin is tempting to the novice. Initiates commonly inscribe their first "live" tattoo on their own bodies. Because tattooing requires the skin to be stretched and is, therefore, a two-handed procedure, novices usually do this first tattoo on their legs. The outcome of this trial self-marking often is not altogether satisfactory.

(Do you remember the first tattoo you did?) The first tattoo I did was a needle job on myself here. It's covered up—a lightning bolt—a traditional sorcerer's sign of power. I tried it a couple of times and it just kept messing up 'cause we were using the wrong kind of ink. I tried it on someone else 'cause he showed me how. We were just doing it with needles. Then I found out that if you wrap the string around three needles that holds the ink inside. But it gave too thick of a line so I just went back to using a sharper needle. My old man didn't like the idea. I showed him this one (cross with "Dad") . . . the first one I did with the machine . . . and he said, "You asshole." But he was smiling when he said it. All my friends—no matter how bad it looked they wanted it. (So you started working on your friends when you got the machine?) I did it mostly on myself. On my friends I did a couple of nice ones that I could work with. That's easier than doing it on yourself 'cause all of the skin moves.

The next stage in the learning process typically involves the apprentice doing a limited amount of work on one of the host tattooist's clients. Since it presents fewer opportunities for irremediable error, the novice is usually allowed to color in part of a design that has already been outlined. A fine art oriented tattooist described how he trains initiates.

If you were my apprentice you would not do a tattoo. Let's say I felt you knew everything there was to know about the machine and now it's time for you to actually make a mark on human skin. Ok, here's a leaf. I do the outline, I do the shading. Now it's time to color. I do most of the coloring except for a little patch nowhere near the edge and then I might let you do a little piece of this. After you learn this I might let you color in the whole leaf. So it would be so gradual that you would never be in the position to hurt the client. It would be a very slow, gradual orientation. If you were an apprentice I would take a pen or a pencil and put it in a machine rather than a tube. Ok, now we put a piece of paper on the bottom of a table. Now, draw a picture there using the machine so you get used to the weight and get used to working in odd areas. When you can do things like that and the tattoo machine becomes an extension of your own hand then we will talk about skin. Tattooing grapefruit and things like that doesn't teach you anything because you aren't developing the feel. It's not real skin. I was talking to one guy and I told him . . . he owned a few machines . . . get up in the morning on a Sunday when you don't have to go to work and put that tattoo machine in your hand and keep it in your hand for the rest of the day. Whether your watching TV, whatever you're doing, learn to flip it around. When you can use it with ease and confidence, when you have developed the muscles in your hand—now go draw a picture with it. If I gave you a pencil with a fine tip and taped on half a pound of rock on the back of the pencil you would find it very difficult to control, to twist in your fingers, to work upside down or around corners—very uncomfortable.

Once the tattooist is satisfied that the novice has achieved some modest level of technical expertise, he or she is allowed to do a complete tattoo. In the tattooing settings I observed the novice tattooist was assigned to the most undemanding or least desirable clients. The novice tattooed over needle marks on heroin addicts; covered up crude, homemade ("poke and joke") marks clients had done on themselves; and attempted to improve the amateurish work some individuals had received while incarcerated. Since the marks being covered or improved were so disfiguring or socially stigmatizing, the practice subject was usually quite pleased with even the relatively unskilled efforts of the novice—particularly since the service was commonly provided gratis or at a greatly reduced price.[8]

Learning the technical aspects of a skilled activity provides considerable information about the aesthetics of that activity (Fine, 1985). This linkage between technique and aesthetics is particularly apparent in the process of learning to be a tattooist. Tattooists define the quality of a tattoo primarily on the basis of the technical skill apparent in its execution rather than on the content of the design. A "good" tattoo has clear, unbroken lines; displays symmetry; contains shading that imparts an appropriate dimensionality; and has bright, solid coloring. Further, the tattoo should be appropriately placed on the recipient's body, neither too large or too small for the body area and positioned so as to fit harmoniously with the musculature. Finally, the work should be done with enough technical competence that the area tattooed is not "overworked" or traumatized by the tattoo process (Richie and Buruma, 1980: 98; Bear, 1987). All of the interviewed tattooists emphasized the importance of technical skill over artistry.

> There's two distinct parts to being a real tattoo artist. One is the technical side of it and the other is the artistic side. For example, someone can be a fantastic artist but if they don't understand the technical aspects of tattooing then they aren't going to be able to translate their artwork into reality. It's just going to stick up in their head. Then, on the other hand, you have people who master the technical aspects of tattooing and they have no artistic ability and they never get beyond the stencil. But at least they are doing it properly and they aren't scarring people up . . . the lines are solid, the colors are bright.

But the ideal person is someone who is a real good artist and understands tattooing technique. For me, before something can be art I have to see craftsmanship. If I see something that I, or anybody, can do and it doesn't show that craftsmanship then I can't respect it as art. To me tattooing is a skilled craft and an art at times. Generally it's not art. It's just the reproduction of simple designs. It's usually not like a fine painting on the skin. There's nothing artistic about copying Yosemite Sam five hundred times. The important thing is to do it right. If they want Yosemite Sam they are going to get something that looks like Yosemite Sam—the lines are sharp and clear, the colors are bright and solid, it heals within a few days and they got what they paid for. That's the most important part. [Tattooist/friend] said, "First master the craft and the art will come on its own." Once I got over the hurdle of getting decent equipment and learning something about using it, the art started to develop (cf. Christopherson, 1974b; Sinha, 1979).

Independent trial-and-error experience is another common route by which one acquires tattoo skill.[9] This approach has clear liabilities. Commonly, the unaffiliated novice is unfamiliar with the most rudimentary workings of the tattoo machine and must engage in considerable experimentation to discover the right "stroke" and penetration of the needles in order to even begin to inject pigment under the skin. As a consequence, the novice's initial work is generally technically inferior to that produced under the supervision of a knowledgeable tattooist.

In addition to having surreptitiously observed tattooists while being tattooed or while posing as a potential client, the tattooists also reported having sought information from tattoo equipment suppliers early in the learning stage of their careers.

There was this guy in the factory where I was working that had a homemade tattoo, very large, his whole bicep. He wanted it covered and said that anything was better than the homemade tattoo. He said that he would let me cover it if I did it for nothing. So I drew up this huge dragon. I needed a place to do it so the woman I was going with at the time said I could do it in her kitchen. Everytime I got into some situation I didn't know about I would call long distance to the supplier in New York. These guys would tell me what I was doing wrong. When you first start you don't know how fast to run the machine or how far the needles should stick out. Greens and blues don't go in as readily as the reds do and you wonder why, things like that. One of the machines wouldn't run because a wire was shorted out on the frame and the guy told me that happened all the time. I blew a fuse on the power unit and we had to run down to a truck stop and buy a fuse for a CB radio. It was a Sunday and nothing else was open. Numerous things like that would happen. All in all it came out pretty well. This guy had drunk quite a bit and smoked quite a bit and he was half out when I was doing this anyway. It was kind of funny when I look back on it. I didn't realize what a mess the pigments make. I didn't know how to wash the pigment off his arm or anything. There was pigment all over the kitchen. It was a horror show, a real mess. I didn't have the opportunity to go through a traditional apprenticeship. It would have been nice. I usually had to phone long distance to someone who was in the tattooing industry. There was another supplier in California that I started to do business with who was rather helpful.

My idea with tattooing was not just doing it but getting my own designs out there. All that I had seen at that point were the traditional designs—skulls and little red devils. And I looked at those designs and said, "Yuck. Come on, there is so much more you could probably do." So my first tattoo was a little demon in space. It was sort of a gargoyle kind of face. We put it on (my friend's) leg. The outline went down fine. When it came to putting in the color, I went over and over it and it just wouldn't go in. I couldn't understand what was wrong. Then I started to get upset. Here I was with the machine and a problem and I had no one to ask. So I took a ride up to Spaulding and Rogers, laid my equipment out on the counter and said to (the owner), "It doesn't want to work." So he asked me to do what I do and I set up the machine and he told me I had the needles in backwards.

DEVELOPING SOCIAL SKILLS

The social relationship that develops between the tattooist and his or her client is of primary importance. If the novice tattooist is to be moderately successful as a service deliverer and/or a commercial artist, it is necessary to gain skill in defining client needs and devising tactics by which those needs can be both shaped and met. The street tattooist's basic goal in this regard is maximizing financial rewards while maintaining interactional control during the tattoo process. Learning to tattoo, therefore, involves learning how to structure the ritual performance that is central to building client trust (cf. Hughes, 1971b: 321–323; Rosenblum, 1978: 77; Schroder, 1973: 198–218; Henslin, 1968).

Fostering client trust is of particular importance in tattooing. Customers typically feel some degree of anxiety when entering the tattoo studio. The major source of this apprehension is the anticipation of pain. Unfamiliarity with those commercial settings in which tattoos are applied is another source of anxiety since most tattoo customers have never been in a tattoo studio prior to entering one to be tattooed for the first time.

The interactional skills fostered by the tattooist are more than ways to maximize income while minimizing conflict. The ability to "read" the client and shape his or her needs have another practical function. Simply complying with the customer's requests may result in a product that will have negative consequences for the tattooist, the client and/or the reputation of tattooing. Most tattooists routinely refuse to place tattoos on "public skin" (usually defined as above the neck and below the wrist) or to inscribe overtly anti-social or racist symbols on their customers. Tattooists understandably see their trade as being defined by the general public as, at best, of marginal propriety. The creation of permanent stigmatizing marks could well generate increased public outcry and intensified efforts at legal repression.

The desire to become skilled at defining client needs and controlling the commercial outcome also derives from an ethical concern for the impact of the tattoo on the social and psychological well-being of the client. In a particularly moving account one fine art tattooist described an encounter with a client early in his ca-

reer which strongly impressed upon him the necessity of maintaining an ethical stance.

I'll tell you where the lesson came from. I was tattooing for
[well-known East Coast tattooist] and he was there this one
day. The girl came in and she said she wanted—a really stupid
name—"Larry Joe Vitelli" tattooed around her nipple on her
breast. This girl was extremely fragile. I sensed that
immediately. She was not, in the American sense of the word, a
beautiful girl. She was sort of very plain, didn't have huge
breasts, was kind of boyish in figure, and dressed real clumsily,
and carried herself kind of clunky. She wanted this "Larry Joe
Vitelli" tattooed on her nipple. So I spent about 20 minutes
trying to talk her out of getting this guy's name tattooed on her
because I just don't think it is a good idea . . . although I will
do vow tattooing because I think it is a valid tattoo image. I do
my best not to do it, first. Then I realize that it is futile to try
to talk them out of it—love has its way of blinding the logical
person. So I didn't want to do this tattoo and [artist/proprietor]
comes out because this girl is protesting because she wants
this tattoo. He says, "You're going to do this tattoo because that
is what I hired you to do and that is what she wants. So you do
it." Ok. So I thought, "Here I am in a moral dilemma. I don't
want to do this tattoo because I know that this girl has
problems emotionally and I'm forced into it or I'm going to blow
my position here." So I decided I'll do the tattoo. So I start to
do the tattoo and I'm half way through it—I got "Larry Joe" on
there—and she starts making passes at me . . . sexual sort of
come on things. Here I am writing "Larry Joe Vitelli" on her
and she wants to get sexually involved with me. So I said to
her, "Well, you and Larry must have quite a relationship to do
something like this. I mean, this is a really intimate kind of
thing—having your breast tattooed with this guy's name. You'll
never be able to jump in bed with anyone else without them
seeing "Larry Joe Vitelli" written there." I said, "You must have
quite a relationship; you must really care about each other."
She goes, "Yeah, I really love him but I have no idea how he
feels about me." I'm in the middle of tattooing this on her. I

didn't trust my own intuition, I didn't follow my own
standards. I compromised. I didn't want to do the tattoo. And
when she came out and told me that, "I really love Larry Joe
Vitelli but I have no idea how he feels about me," I knew that
she had built up this totally unreal expectation that that tattoo
was going to win Larry Joe Vitelli. Obviously Larry Joe Vitelli
would consider her pathetic at that point because obviously he
wasn't the least bit interested in her. So what is that going to
do to the psyche of this girl? Either she just is totally apathetic
about it or is potentially going to be self-destructive. She was
self-destructive in getting the tattoo to begin with. I shuddered.
I really did, I felt sick, nauseous. I went home and I couldn't
sleep that night. I came back the next day and I told (the
owner), "You can fire me right now but the next time somebody
comes through the door and wants a tattoo and I don't want to
do it, I'm not going to do it. You want to take the responsibility,
you want to be the one to do that then you do it." So he
respected that. I should have done that right then and there. I
should have taken that stand before I carved that fucking
name in that girl. I'll never do anything like that again! That
was a real lesson for me.

Through contact with customers the tattooist learns how to
handle recurrent interactional situations and to control the definition of the tattoo situation held by clients—an issue that will be
discussed in some detail in the following chapter. Personal styles
of dealing with clients vary considerably, but all tattooists, of necessity, devise ways of easing interaction with and controlling
their customers.

Potential tattooees tend to ask fairly standard questions—by far
the most common being, "does it hurt?"—and tattooists develop
standard responses to these questions. Sometimes the responses
are humorous and designed to break the tension ("Did you ever
beat off with a handful of barbed wire?"). More commonly, tattooists attempt to project a serious and helpful demeanor and answer
standard questions simply and directly.

(What is the most common question that people ask you?)
"How much does that cost?" "Does it really hurt?" "How bad

does it hurt?" "Come on, tell me the truth. Does it really hurt?" So I tell them it does. I'm not going to bullshit people. I tell them it hurts. How much does it hurt? Well, how much do you hurt? I say, "You tell me what pain feels like." My personal feeling is that some places it hurts worse than others but it is mostly an irritating kind of feeling, a burning kind of a sensation. It burns. How much does it burn? I don't know. How do you feel burning? It's back to the same thing again, a little circle. So I tell them, "Look, here's the situation. If you want the tattoo I'm going to give you my honest opinion. It doesn't hurt that much that you wouldn't be able to take it. It hurts and some places will probably push you to the test. You'll have to deal with it. But if you really want it then you'll do it." I say, "If you have any second thoughts then don't even come in. Don't even bother to try it."

Tattooists, who see themselves as being motivated by more than commercial interest and feel some responsibility to both tattooing and the client, maintain that education is a central facet of their interaction with the customer. They reflect what Griff (1970: 156) describes as the "compromise role" in his discussion of commercial artists.

Those who assume the compromise role believe that they are instruments of the clients; however, they conceive of themselves as active, rather than passive agents. In carrying out this conception of themselves, they translate the demands of the client but at the same time attempt to persuade him to accept innovations, specifically the interjection of fine-arts symbols into their illustrations. Thus, many feel that they are involved in a crusade for better art. They believe that by raising the standards of their clients' art, they are at the same time raising the level of taste of the public.

A tattooist who predominantly did custom work stressed the importance of this educational, status-enhancing, client-oriented approach to in-shop interaction.

If the decision to get a tattoo is made on an intelligent or intellectual level by the public . . . if the public is uninformed or misinformed and then you just give them whatever they say they want and they are not enlightened enough to make the right decision, you are part of the problem and not part of the solution. What I mean is . . . Dad came home from World War II with some garish anchor and some eagle that today looks like some ball of shit—you have to have someone point out all the elements before you can even recognize what it is. Cousin Charlie came back from the Korean war with something very similar—maybe a rose with a dagger. Your brother Henry came back from Vietnam with a skull with a dagger going through it with "death before dishonor" or some other garish shit. If this is all you have ever seen then you have the tendency to think that this is all that is available. Now if the tattooist—I don't use the words "tattoo artist"—does not inform the public that things have changed, that there is a renaissance, he is a part of the problem. My job is to tattoo people but it is also to inform them, to give them choices, to help them make an intelligent decision. As long as there are people scratching, doing low quality work, that don't have a regard for the public, tattooing will always remain somewhat underground. Your mother would never ever think of getting a tattoo. But if it were socially acceptable, if it were part and parcel with the local beauty salon, if Nancy Reagan could go public and sport a tattoo—or Princess Di—then your mother might consider it.

While presentations such as this are indeed noble, the social skills developed by the tattooist have, for the most part, an eminently practical function. As emphasized in the following chapter, the tattooist's major goal is to control the interaction within the shop in order to ease his or her worklife and increase the profitability of the commercial operation. Studies of other types of service interactions clearly indicate that client satisfaction is based primarily on the experienced quality of the relationship with the service deliverer (see, for example, Ben-Sira, 1976; Greenley and Schoenherr, 1981; Zeithaml, 1984). Since the vast majority of tattoo customers are drawn by word-of-mouth recommendations from personal associates (cf. Schroder, 1973: 207–210), the satisfied client is the source of new business as well as a potential returnee should he or she desire additional work.[10]

THE TATTOOIST'S CAREER GOALS

Most tattooists are involved in a relatively simple, independently organized work activity within a nonbureaucratized and noncentralized occupational world. As a consequence, their career goals are rather narrowly conceived and few see themselves as being on a career path in which indicators of advancement are clearly demarcated. When asked to project the future of their careers the tattooists most commonly said that their primary goal was to gain more technical and artistic skill or to develop a unique personal style. Given the mediocre quality of most traditional tattooing, both street and fine art tattooists saw the prospect of doing better-than-average work to be a limited and reasonably attainable career goal. When asked what he would most like to change about his job, a street tattooist replied:

> I don't think I would change anything about the way I'm tattooing now. I just want to get to be a competent tattooist where I can put out a nice tattoo and make a comfortable living. I don't have any overwhelming desire to own a large home or a fleet of Cadillacs or anything like that. I just want to make a decent living and do better-than-average work. I know I will never be an [well-known fine art tattooist] but, at the same time, I'm already better after a few years of work than many people are after twenty or thirty. They had a whole career of tattooing and they never were any good. But they made a living and people bought their product.

Gaining visibility and status within the tattoo subculture is another goal pursued by tattooists. As in other art/craft worlds, one's reputation is based primarily on the evaluation of other practitioners (Becker, 1982: 351–371). Information about the quality of one's work is passed by word-of-mouth as tattooists travel from shop to shop and discuss business. One may also acquire a reputation through the display of photographs of his or her work in the major tattoo publications. The tattooing world tends to be fragmented into various factions centering around equipment suppliers and a few influential artists. Suppliers and key artists ˅re primarily responsible for producing tattoo magazines or news- ˙ters and interviewees consistently expressed dissatisfaction

with the apparent lack of evenhandedness in the choice of published photographs showing exemplary work. Tattooists strongly suspected that the choices are made on the basis of membership in personal networks or regional chauvinism (especially East Coast versus West Coast) rather than the quality of the represented work.

A third potential means of reputation building is through winning competitions held as part of the annual conventions sponsored by tattoo organizations such as the National Tattoo Association. However, only a small proportion of practicing tattooists attend these conventions and, as with tattoo publications, there is general suspicion among tattooists that prizes are awarded on personal grounds rather than on the grounds of an objective evaluation of technical and artistic merit.

Tattooists aspire to reputational status not only for its own rewards. Gaining a reputation for quality work also allows one to exercise significantly more control over one's work life and leads—at least potentially—to increased income. As is the case in most craft and art activities, the product's market value is determined on the basis of the reputation of the creator as well as its technical and aesthetic quality (cf., Sinha, 1979: 19). More importantly, however, acquiring a reputation allows the tattooist to be more selective in deciding to accede to some client requests while rejecting others. Specifically, accomplished and well-known tattooists can concentrate on doing custom work while turning down requests to apply the mundane and routine traditional designs (for example, black panthers, grim reapers, cartoon figures, Harley-Davidson insignia, snakes, and daggers) that are the bread-and-butter of the street shop (cf. Faulkner, 1983: 24; Sinha, 1979: 11; Richie and Buruma, 1980: 85–88). One fine art tattooist with an established reputation presented his decisions to refuse certain client requests in political as well as aesthetic terms.

I refuse to put down business logos, company imagery. To me that is the most repulsive shit in the world. Here they are totally crushed by the corporate structure in America— the wheel. They're complaining about their inabili*
effectual in the culture, totally apathetic. And *

me to tattoo the badge of the very forces that are holding them down. They want me to do *Playboy* bunnies. Now what does *Playboy Magazine* have to do with being a man in our culture? Nothing! It just manufactures this phoney fucking concept about life. What does the Rolling Stones tongue have to do with your life? Its a marketing image. They package the concept and they simplify it in the most simple terms and they pound it into their heads. So every dime that they make in their empty positions they spend on these products. They are just void consumers. You are getting caught up in the future and that doesn't have anything to do with getting Yosemite Sam tattooed on your body. Yosemite Sam is just a left over kind of image. If you want an icon let's search for one that has some meaning for you. So I don't do company logos. I don't do anarchist kind of social slogans like "fuck the world"—I usually consider that to be connected to the fascist right-wing bikers life-style forces which I don't deal with at all. Included in that business logo stuff is Harley-Davidson signs which I won't do. I won't tattoo someone, regardless of the choice of the tattoo, if I feel that that person has totally unrealistic expectations. If they think that that tattoo is going to make them fly when they walk out of here I'm not going to do that tattoo. I've been caught up in situations and I feel that—I don't know if this is egotistical or not—I feel that I'm really perceptive about people. I know when a fragile person walks through the door. Sometimes they don't have to say anything at all but they just speak loudly about the fragility of their emotional self. So what I do with them is I'll sit down and talk. I explain all of the social problems behind getting a tattoo—what kind of social ramifications there are, that people will reject you as a result of the tattoo, people will consider you to be a certain kind of person because of the tattoo. Then I'll say to them, "If you really want the tattoo come back in about three or four days." They never come back.

Another interviewee whose work largely consisted of standard designs taken from commercial flash saw selectivity as enviable but economically unfeasible for someone at his reputational level.

Turning down work because it's just not artistic enough is ok if you're a S—— or F—— [two well-known artists]. But I run a business here. If I turned down all the Harley wings or panthers I'd never make any money. . . . You like to do artistic work, and you like to do things that will enhance your reputation, but it is still a business, and you have to make a living, and you have to pay expenses. The landlady will not accept the excuse that the only work that came in was things that you didn't want to do because they weren't really that artistic.

Rising to the position of being able to concentrate solely on producing custom designed tattoos is valued over and above the fact that it allows the tattooist to escape the monotony of standardized and routine production. Most tattooists aspire to the honorific status of "artist." A unique "piece" custom designed for an individual client/patron is, almost by definition, a work of art. A design selected from wall flash and reproduced time after time for anonymous customers is, in contrast, a craft item despite the fact that it may exhibit the same or superior technical skill. Being in the position to do custom work exclusively, therefore, allows the tattooist to define him or herself as an artist involved in providing clients with a uniquely creative service and product (cf. Becker, 1982: 279–281).

Now, all of your life you make the purchase of these items that came off an assembly line and now you are going to buy a tattoo. You tend to be satisfied with what is put in front of you—no choice. You go into every shop and you see the same flash, you see the same panther hanging there on people's arms. Your brother has one, your cousin has one. You see them in all the shops so you tend to think that that is the state of the art. We just aren't used to buying individual personal service, certainly not traveling very far for it. People don't even know how to go about purchasing individual personal service. This is buying art. You have to wear it rather than framing it and putting it on your wall. That's the ideal—work with a tattooist, develop a design, wear it, and then take the original design and destroy it. I do a lot of that.

Finally, being the proprietor of one's own studio/shop, either as the sole practitioner or—ideally—as an employer of others, is a goal sought after by most tattooists (cf. Schroder, 1973: 263–299).[11] Working solo affords independence from the demands of a boss and allows one to choose his or her own work schedule.

> I like working for myself. That's a big part of it. I like living an independent life-style. Tattoo artists probably have this personality trait where they aren't good at taking orders from someone else. Most people I know in this business are independent. It's nice to be making a decent piece of change without having to work in a factory or something. I'm not getting rich by any means but I'm keeping my sanity and feeding my family. Everytime I start getting pissed off or bored with it I think, "It sure beats working on the loading docks and it sure beats not working at all and it sure beats punching in at 7:30 at (local factory)."

Most of the interviewees who were employees expressed the desire to have their own studio. However, these tattooists also recognized that owning one's own shop is not without its liabilities.

> I have the fantasy of having a nice comfortable living. I'm not out to make a million. If I had a chance to apprentice under a well-known artist like H—— I'd be crazy not to do it. They made it and they made it starting out not knowing anything and working their way up. My goal is to have my own shop. I see the money pass through my hands. I make 20 cents on the dollar. I would like to make 85 or 95 (cents) on the dollar. But I don't have the headaches or the overhead now. I come out at 10 o'clock and get in my car. If the place burns down (the owner) is the one that has to account for it.

Similarly, the one employee/tattooist who explicitly stated that he did not aspire to ownership (and who defined himself as a competent "stencil man" rather than a tattoo "artist") expressed satisfaction with his position.

> I guess I will stay in the business, at least until it is modernized enough so I can't stand it . . . like little franchises

like Burger King . . . little Tattoo Huts. If it comes to that I'll get out of it and do something else. I don't know if I'll ever work for myself again. It is too easy to work for somebody else if you can stand giving up a large portion of the money you make. Working for somebody else is fine. Let them have the headaches of being in business. You just sit there and do your shift and whatever else you have to do and that's it. Being a small business today is a pain in the ass.

THE TATTOOIST'S OCCUPATIONAL REWARDS

Tattooists, as we have seen, are drawn to the occupational activity by the independence, creativity, and income it offers. Depending upon the tattooist's orientation to tattooing, the occupational rewards of reliable income and creative opportunity are weighted differentially. Street tattooists define themselves as involved in a predominantly commercial enterprise that has the advantage of affording some degree of creativity (see Scutt and Gotch, 1974: 60). Fine art tattooists who specialize in custom designs emphasize the creative opportunities of the work but are also pleased that tattooing provides the financial security lacking in many artistic endeavors. One tattoo artist put it this way:

So tattooing suddenly appeared in my life and I realized that there was that opportunity to do that thing I always wanted to do so badly my entire life. That was to communicate on some indescribable level with each individual person that came through the door. At the same time I was making art and communicating, I was making a living. . . . Right from the first I decided I really wanted to tattoo as an alternative art form. It really gave me a chance to explore a fresh new place. I still believe this—tattooing is the only visual art form available that is totally without pretension.

This artist touches on a feature of the tattooing occupation that was most commonly cited as the major ongoing reward by experienced tattooists. Interacting with clients, ascertaining their needs, developing trust, fulfilling their desires, and vicariously feeling their pleasure were rewarding. The positive social experiences contained within the client relationship came to be defined as the dominant rewards of tattooing for a living.[12]

As with all service occupations, the relationship with the client is of central importance in tattooing. The client not only consumes the service/product, but also interacts with the service deliverer to shape and define the characteristics of the service outcome (see Spiggle and Sanders, 1984; Schroder, 1973: 8–15). Consequently, interaction with clients is central to the tattooist's experience of the rewards—and, as we will see later, the problems—afforded by his or her occupation.

One tattooist spoke of the pleasure of interacting with people who were, like him, "renegades."

> I am in (tattooing) because I love the people. It isn't what most people think. I don't tattoo strictly bikers and criminals. I tattoo everyone—doctors, lawyers, musicians, psychologists. But most people who get tattoos listen to the beat of a different drum and they are interesting, forceful people. They are making serious statements about themselves. It is interaction with artists. My customers are artists because they are creating right along with me through their choice of tattoo, where they put it, and how they wear it.

Tattooing is unique in that it is an art/craft service in which the client is not only a member of the practitioner's "public," but is also a central resource in another sense. The tattooee is, in essence, the tattooist's canvas. No other creative product involves the intimacy and indelibility of the tattoo. The tattooist creates an object/service that is a part of the client's "self" and his or her appreciation (or, in some cases, regret) is of paramount importance. Interviewees consistently expressed vicarious pleasure over the initial joy experienced by their creatively altered clients.

> Let's assume the person is reasonably intelligent and isn't getting the tattoo just to prove a point. Let's assume it was done when the person was cold sober and that the person who was working on him is as interested in making art as he is interested in making a day's pay. The tattooist has worked with

the individual to discuss the design, the placement, the color, and then the person gets the tattoo. The first effect is the person feels an incredible sense of accomplishment. I see it all the time. As soon as I finish a tattoo I send the person to the mirror. I don't look at the tattoo, I look at the guy's face. You see a smile break across the person's face. "Fuck it, I did it. I overcame all of the obstacles—what my mother, my rabbi, my priest said. I'm happy. I did it." The first experience is the exhilaration of having accomplished something.

Another interviewee, a part-time tattooist, who worked at a commercial art job during the day, expressed the pleasure he experienced when his skills were appreciated.

I'm supposed to do about twenty ads a day and they never get appreciated. The boss is always on my ass—more, more, more. All she wants is production. It is very rare that I can be creative in my work. I never get patted on my back so, being a tattoo artist, every time I do one the person that gets it usually really likes it. They always tell me, "Fred, that's great! Jesus, fabulous! Wow, look at that guy draw!" (The client) comes with something in his mind and I put it down on paper and he really likes it. That's what I think I'm there for. I really like the appreciation.

Not all tattooees are joyful and appreciative. As discussed in the preceding chapter, regretful tattoo clients are dissatisfied with the technical quality of the work and/or the design chosen. Medical removal of tattoos is expensive, painful, and rarely results in an entirely satisfactory (that is, unscarred) outcome (see Goldstein et al., 1979). Other than simply learning to live with the unsatisfactory mark, the regretful tattooee has the alternative of having the piece covered up with another tattoo or redone by a (one hopes) more competent artist/craftperson. Interviewees estimated that between forty and sixty percent of their work involved covering or redoing the tattoos of regretful tattooees. This was the work activity that the tattooists defined as most technically challenging and socially rewarding. In creatively altering or obliterating the offending mark the tattooist became the object of rewarding appreciation—he or she was responsible for renewing the client's positive experience of his or her physical self.

> The best part of being a tattooist is when someone comes in with a tattoo that is less than nice and you can fix that up or do something with it to make them happy with what they've got. I like that part a lot. Reworking some old crude piece of trash tattoo that they have gotten somewhere along the line and making it into something as nice as you can. That makes them happy and it makes me feel as if I've really accomplished something as far as helping the person out. Plus, you get a moment's glory because that particular customer thinks you are really a tremendous tattooist because you have made a silk purse out of a sow's ear. [13]

THE TATTOOIST'S OCCUPATIONAL PROBLEMS

Along with the advantages and rewards of any occupation come a variety of problems. The most basic problem for all workers, especially those involved in craftwork (Sinha, 1979) or the provision of a service (Mennerick, 1974), centers around the issue of exerting control over the daily routine of one's worklife. Some occupational problems may be due to idiosyncratic or personal factors such as a critical and demanding boss or an unruly and lazy employee. However, the most continuously troublesome difficulties are aspects of the worker's "occupational situation" (Kriesberg, 1952). The problems are seen as being endemic to the recurrent work activities and relationships that characterize the occupation.

For the tattooist the overriding problem inherent in his or her occupational situation revolves around the public's continuing negative definition of tattooing, tattooists, and tattooed persons. This "occupational stigma" is seen in the efforts of legislators and state regulators to exercise control over or entirely prohibit tattooing, as well as various forms of unofficial discrimination directed at tattooists.

Tattooists also have problems with the organization of their worklife, especially the time and energy constraints and the boredom that results from routine maintenance activities and the clients who request the same few conventional images with numbing regularity. Finally, tattooists experience a problem that is central to all service work. They find the daily process of relating to and exerting control over their clientele to be continuously problematic.

Problems of Occupational Stigma

Tattooing continues to carry the disreputable reputation acquired early in its history. As discussed in the first chapter, this image of disrepute was derived from the low status of the social segments from which early western tattooists typically drew their clients. The general public saw, and continues to see, the tattoo establishment as patronized largely by criminals, marginal laborers, drug abusers, members of motorcycle gangs, prostitutes, and other disvalued social types (Richie and Buruma, 1980: 11–33; Scutt and Gotch, 1974: 108–119, 179–184; Sanders, 1987). In short, tattooing is publicly defined as a tarnished occupational activity involving the creation of a service/product that symbolizes the "blemished character" of its clientele (Shover, 1975).

The negative image of tattooing also comes from its "dirty work" features (Hughes, 1971a). The tattooist routinely induces pain, handles the nude bodies of strangers, and is stained with blood and other body fluids. He or she is, however, not insulated from the stigma of unclean work by a medical degree, membership in a publicly legitimated professional association, or the assistance of a coterie of underlings who perform the most unsavory service activities.

The established tattooists interviewed[14] did not see themselves as being responsible for the continued negative public image of tattooing. Instead, they focused blame on the most marginal members of the occupation. Tattooing equipment was too cheap and available and any individuals, no matter how untalented or inexperienced, could call themselves tattooists and begin "marking people up." Driven largely by greed and feeling no concern for the public reputation of tattooing, these "bootleggers" or "scratchers" turned out work that was technically incompetent, marked public skin with anti-social symbols, and threatened the physical well-being of their unsuspecting and unsophisticated customer/victims with their unsanitary equipment and work practices.

A lot of the people who just get their *Easyrider* tattoo kits are just into it for the money. For everyone that is coming up and trying to improve themselves and better things, there are probably half a dozen more that are just tearing down what other people are doing. I'm learning all the time and getting more aware. It gets spooky—I'm trying to build up my business and all of these people out here who are bootlegging are just making it worse for everyone else. A lot of people might start coming down with diseases or they're going to be tattooing people that aren't of age, getting people in an uproar. Maybe they'll try and close everything down now.

Because of the stigma surrounding their occupation, tattooists are the focus of both formal and informal efforts to constrain or, in some cases, prohibit their activities.[15] Tattooists frequently recounted tales of legal difficulties, police harassment, unannounced visits from health department inspectors, and other forms of negative official attention. One interviewee, for example, described his experience in trying to open a studio in the New York metropolitan area:

[Established artist] was interested in starting a business and asked me if I was interested in going in as a partner in the business. So we began doing some research into [city] as a potential location. So we were trying to find out from the health department if they had any ordinances bearing on tattooing. I told him that I had friends that probably could do the research without stirring up a lot of snakes so that we could find out exactly what the story was. So I was in the process of putting out all of the feelers I had trying to find out that information. He went ahead and called up the health department and just blatantly asked them if they had any ordinances on tattooing. They said, "Well, we'll call you back tomorrow and let you know." So they called him back the next day and said, "Yes, we have an ordinance against tattooing." He said, "Well, could you send me a copy of it." They said, "Certainly." So they put it in the mail and when we received it it was dated the day after he called. So they had an emergency meeting of the city council, the mayor signed it and there was their ordinance banning tattooing.

Another tattooist spoke of the legal restraints on tattooing in his state as being the responsibility of a few legislators who were prejudiced against tattooing.

The legal thing is funny. In Massachusetts it's illegal. In Oklahoma it's illegal to do tattoos. You feel that laws that prohibit things should prohibit things that are bad for the public. Why is tattooing bad for the public in Massachusetts or Oklahoma but it is O.K. for the public in California? It's bad for the people in New York City but it is good for the people in the rest of the state. There's no other answer than what is being turned into laws is the personal preferences of the people who are making the laws at the time. If there were people in the legislature who did like tattooing at the time the laws would be much different. What it usually is is a couple of people who don't like it and the rest of them don't give a damn one way or the other. You don't get many votes saying, "I'm for tattooing." It's the personal whims of a few people who happen to be in power.

A third interviewee expressed a colorfully negative view of officialdom but, at the same time, recognized the financial advantages he enjoyed because tattooing was legally prohibited in an adjacent state.

Tattoo artists are the most discriminated against group in the country. They aren't allowed to discriminate against the Jews or the niggers anymore so they have to get us. You can go right down the street here and get any kind of porno and that's O.K. because it is free expression. You can fuck somebody in the ass or suck their cock and that's O.K. because it is among consenting adults. You can go to this abortion mill and kill your baby because that is allowing the woman to control her body. But you can't set up a shop where people can freely choose to get a tattoo without the bastards fucking with you. Right after we opened up here the first thing that happened was that the police came in here and arrested [tattooist/employee]. The local councilman saw us and·he told the police to come in here and harass us. He only did that because he couldn't come in here and kill us. If he had his way he would just as soon come in and beat the shit out of us. The assholes just want someone to beat on and they think we're just outlaws. They couldn't do it if we were organized, but this is such a cutthroat business you can't get anyone to work together. Everyone is just out for themselves. I can see why. I don't want tattooing legal everywhere. I'd loose a lot of business if tattooing was legal in Massachusetts. If it were legal everywhere then there would be a tattoo studio on every corner and nobody would be making any money.

As members of a stigmatized occupational minority, tattoo artists see themselves as having little recourse to mechanisms by which they can effectively combat legal or interpersonal discrimination. All of those interviewed saw themselves as doing what they could to personally alter the negative public image of tattooing. They took some pains to structure the shop environment so it was clean, bright, and entirely unlike the "bucket of blood" image in the public mind. Tattooists also attempted to combat their unsavory reputation by creating tattoos that were technically accomplished, avoiding the inscription of socially inflammatory images, and turning down client requests to tattoo overtly public skin. The fine art oriented tattooists, in particular, saw their concentration on custom designed, nontraditional images as being a step towards redefining tattooing as a legitimate, and thereby, publicly acceptable, art form.

If the person who is going to wear the tattoo has the choice and they want a heart with 'Mom'—"Oh, I didn't know I could have this also. Gee, now I can make an intelligent choice." If the person who is going to wear the tattoo is offered a choice— skulls and daggers—it's fine. As long as the person realizes that there is a choice and makes an intelligent decision based on what is available. But if somebody opens up a shop, puts up traditional flash and does not give the public a choice, doesn't do custom work—is incapable of doing custom work—he is not giving people a choice and he is perpetuating the image of tattooing your mother or Aunt Margaret have. (That is) that all tattooists are real scummy people, all tattoo shops are located on the waterfront, patronized by pimps and prostitutes—a real bucket of blood that is about one inch ahead of the law.

The established tattooists had few concrete ideas about how to engage in more collective responses to the problem of low occupational status. Occasionally, they suggested forming a national professional organization that would set standards for tattoo practice, certify qualified tattooists, exert pressure on supply companies to limit the availability of equipment, and engage in public relations. Given the fragmentation, individualism, greed, and conflict that tend to characterize the tattoo world, no one was particularly optimistic about the possibilities of forming a viable organization of this sort.

There has been talk over the past years of the tattooists all forming a union or getting together in some national organization. But there is so much backbiting, back stabbing, huge ego conflicts, that you can never get the entire tattoo community together. I don't know why they waste their time trying. A union certainly wouldn't work. I heard one proposal for a union in which they said everybody should charge the same prices across the country. But that's crazy. Why should some hack doing pitiful work charge the same amount as an art school graduate doing the finest work in the country? It wouldn't work. You can't get the tattoo community together. There are too many factions. This group hates that group. The groups are usually sided with some supplier and, of course, they don't get along. So there will always be this attitude of, "Well, I'm the best. That guy across the river is just a jerk. He can't do anything right. I taught him. I'm the best, he's nothing." Blah, blah, blah, blah.

There are so many factions and groups and suppliers. There should be one big club in my opinion. It should be like the AMA. Who's to go and say that the AMA is wrong. They got their schooling behind them, internship, and they band together and they are their own association. They know what is right and what is wrong in what they do. If I wanted to go in there and disprove the AMA, what credentials do I have? I don't know what the hell I'm talking about unless I studied medicine. Same thing with tattooing. These groups need to make the public aware. There's this urgency to make everybody aware of what is going on. As an artist you have to make sure that everyone is working clean. It would be good to have one tattoo artist's society. Illustrators have a society; graphic artists have a society. Tattoo artists should get together in the same way. I don't know if it could ever come off.

Interviewees did, however, see slow but positive changes occurring in their public reputation. More tattooists were doing higher quality work that was coming to public attention and the clientele was becoming more diverse as people with wealth, social status, and education acquired tattoos. One tattooist saw the general process of increasing tolerance for diversity as helping to create a social climate in which tattooing was more acceptable.

Tattooing has become more socially acceptable. It's because of the publicity. Everything has become more socially acceptable. Things that outraged people a while back don't outrage them anymore. The whole society has become more tolerant of everything. I don't necessarily think it is for the better but it has brought other things along with it. It's good for those people that do tattoos or get tattoos.

Problems of Worklife Organization

How much control a person exercises over his or her work and the flexibility or constraint that characterize the ongoing flow of work activity are central issues for all workers. For those involved in service activities the problem of controlling one's worklife revolves around contact with clients (Becker, 1970: 245). As described above, tattooists, like other artisans, experience considerable tension as they attempt to control their work activity in the face of client demands (cf. Becker, 1951; Sanders, 1974; Christopherson, 1974b: 134–138; Sinha, 1979: 16–19; Rosenblum, 1978: 122–127; Faulkner, 1983: 120–145).

Entrepreneurial or free-lance service deliverers also experience problems around the issue of independence versus insecurity. For the tattooist, being free from the conventional, hierarchical work situation carries significant disadvantages along with its rewards. Interviewees who were proprietors of their own studios regularly complained about the problems of feeling responsible and being "tied to the job." Because tattooing is a service that is, of necessity, provided during the evenings or on weekends when the clients are not working, tattooists are troubled by the effect of their occupational schedule on their family life.

> I don't like the hours. Plus, you're tied to your business. It's not really a business you can leave in someone else's hands. If you were selling something from behind a counter it wouldn't really matter who sold it. It would be the same product. But it would be different if someone came into the shop and you tattooed them or I tattooed them. They would not be going out with the same product. If you are a tattooist and you are trying to build up a good reputation for your shop and you do employ anybody, it has to be someone who is very skilled also and does good work on their own. It doesn't necessarily have to be your style but people will have to be satisfied. If they are dissatisfied with the work that comes out of the shop your reputation suffers also. So I don't like the fact that I have to do it all myself or I have to be there and supervise it. So you don't get the chance to see your family that most people normally do. You don't come home at five o'clock and have dinner with the wife and kids. When you do come home they go to bed shortly thereafter and you're up by yourself watching the TV. So you don't see your family as much as you might want to. But at least you're feeding them. You aren't having dinner with them but at least there is dinner.

The demand for the tattoo service tends to fluctuate with the season (summers are commonly busy while demand drops precipitously in the winter), the local economic situation (the tattoo is a luxury item, so demand decreases during economic downturns), and other factors beyond the tattooist's control. The sporadic and often unpredictable pattern of client flow is a key problem in the tattooist's worklife organization. Work is characterized by alternate periods of feast and famine.

I hate the waiting . . . the winter months. You aren't working by appointment. Walk-in only. You have to wait for your people to come in. There are days when you sit for 8 hours and tell jokes and look at each other and there are some days when you want to come in and shut the door and not look at anybody. I like it busy . . . an even pace. I don't like to work on twenty-five people in a day but I like an average of eight or ten people a day over ten hours.

I don't think anyone gets into tattooing that doesn't like tattoos. But there are some people in it with no talent for art at all. It looks so easy to do and it looks so lucrative. The amount you get for a tattoo for the time you put into it is quite high. I would probably make as much money as a dentist when I am working. The dentist, however, has half-hour appointments and he works steadily through the day, whereas I sometimes spend all day in the shop and not do anything. Sometimes you'll spend a day in the shop and do ten tattoos. It's very sporadic. If you did have a constant flow like a dentist you would make that kind of money.

As a consequence, tattooists face considerable uncertainty when trying to organize their economic lives.

I like least the uncertainty of not knowing whether I'm going to make a living or not. I'm getting over that. No matter how bad things have gotten I've always managed to get by. I generally can count on enough business to make ends meet. Some parts of the year you're making fifteen hundred bucks a week and then another time of year you're lucky if you make a hundred and fifty. Those kinds of adjustments are sometimes hard to make. You're making fifteen hundred a week and you're living that way and when you're making one fifty you don't have any money in your pocket.

Requiring clients to make appointments (and provide deposits) is the primary mechanism by which tattooists attempt to order the flow of their work. This approach is, however, not without its own liabilities. Clients routinely do not show up at the appointed time and walk-in customers are often annoyed when clients with appointments force them to wait for service.

This guy called me up and wanted to come in this week. I told him that if he wanted an appointment he would have to come up and leave a deposit and we would set something up. I said I could work on him Saturday if he got here half an hour early. I was expecting him Saturday and here he is on Monday knocking on my door. I used to work only by appointment. I'd say 80 percent of the people will show up. The people that usually break their appointment are people that you know. It is a problem. I had appointment slips made up. I just want to protect myself. I hang around half the day waiting for the appointment to show up and the day is shot. People show up two hours late and you're leaving and they say, "Hey, I had an appointment today." People are usually discouraged about leaving a twenty dollar deposit. I figure for a twenty dollar bill they are going to show up.

All work entails a certain amount of routine. The ratio of routine to novel activities encountered in a job is of central importance to the worker's feelings of satisfaction with the organization of his or her worklife. This is a particularly salient issue for tattooists or other artisans since creativity is a key element of their self-definition. Inflexible and boring work activities and the production of items that display routine characteristics are incompatible with the role of the creative artist (cf. Sinha, 1979).

The most onerous aspect of the tattooist's daily worklife involves having to engage in the time-consuming and uncreative activities surrounding technical preparation and the routine maintenance work encountered in any establishment that caters to a public. Cleaning, sterilizing, cutting stencils, coloring flash, soldering needles, and other repetitive preparatory and janitorial tasks are viewed with considerable distaste.

> When you are a professional tattooist you are almost married to it because it is almost a 24 hour-a-day thing. You work five or six days a week and then you have to put in at least one work day behind the scenes building needles, sterilizing, cleaning up, vacuuming the floor, drawing flash, cutting stencils . . . stuff that the public never sees you do. They think that you are just sitting there on your shift marking up people. That is the part that I like least about tattooing—like building needles. It is boring, monotonous work that goes on constantly.

Novel work routines and the creation of unique objects are seen, by both the general public and aspiring artists, as key features of artistic activity (Becker, 1982: 279–281). However, few art-like products are as conventionalized as is the traditional tattoo. Clients commonly enter the tattoo studio, spend a few minutes looking at the designs displayed on the walls and then choose a standard image with remarkable regularity.[16]

The street tattooist takes these routine requests for roses, butterflies, panthers, skulls, daggers, eagles, and other standard designs in stride. He or she is primarily a businessperson making a living by fulfilling the requests of customers (within certain boundaries) while not making overt value judgments about their taste or good sense. The commercial tattooist is, as one interviewee put it, the "silent tool" of the client.

In contrast, the steady flow of routine requests for traditional designs is especially problematic for the fine art tattooist. Early in their careers tattoo artists are more willing to compromise their artistic principles and apply standard designs because this provides opportunities to gain technical experience and helps build a reputation. Once they have established a "name" and have acquired expertise, the fine art tattooist takes a more active role in educating clients or shaping their wants so that the products are artistically unique. In this way the customer's associational and "totemic" desires are satisfied at the same time the tattooist's creative self-definition is maintained.

(Customers say,) "I thought I'd get a tattoo because I've always wanted one and because my uncle had one and my grandfather had one. I'd really like to have that tattoo (they had). Do you have that girl in the martini glass or whatever the thing is." I say, "Look, that was a particular tattoo that was important to your uncle or your grandfather or whoever but what does it have to do with you right now? What's going on in your life? What are you doing? What do you want? What do you see? What do you feel?" That's what I am interested in. Then I can turn around . . . sometimes it comes to me like a lightning flash . . . I know exactly what they think or what image they want. It has that feel that there is just real clear contact with their kind of visual vocabulary. I try to synthesize those ideas into the kind of image that will satisfy them and will be somewhat conventional.

Problems with Clients

Because direct interaction with a client is central to service work, this relationship is, as discussed above, a major source of satisfaction and, as will be emphasized further in the following chapter, a generator of occupational problems. A variety of studies of client work involving the sale of artistic skills or products with artistic features demonstrate that arts/crafts workers frequently have a rather negative view of their clientele (for example, Rosenblum, 1978: 79; Faulkner, 1983: 125, 146; Schroder, 1973: 188; Fine, 1985: 25–27; Becker, 1951; Rosenberg and Fliegel, 1970: 502–508).

The problems tattooists experience in their interaction with clients stem from a variety of sources. Some problems—extreme sensitivity to pain, fainting and other untoward reactions to the tattooing process, and inferior skin quality, for example—are due to factors that are not under the voluntary control of the client (these problematic characteristics and the tactics employed by tattooists to deal with them will be discussed in the following chapter). Because they are not deemed to be the client's responsibility, tattooists, as we will see, simply attempt to do the best they can. They try to provide the best service possible by working around these problems or by being prepared to deal directly with them should they arise. The client problems that are most troublesome for and annoying to tattooists are those over which the customers can exercise overt control. Clients who choose to be disrespectful of the tattooist's expertise, refuse to abide by the rules of the house, are obviously intoxicated or high on drugs, or who do not display a minimal level of care for their personal hygiene are the source of the major problems tattooists encounter in their occupational lives.

Like many workers who provide an expert service, tattooists chafe under the problem of having to deal with clients who are ignorant but demanding and who evidence little respect for their hard-won skills. One tattooist became quite agitated when he spoke of a particularly pushy and critical client who was seen as having attacked his artistic skills and self-defined expertise.

> You have these morons who have absolutely no idea of what is artistic . . . to have them sitting there telling you how things ought to be done. . . . Nothing galls me more than to be putting a piece on and have them look at it and say, "'That's enough shading." I've done years in art school. If it shouldn't really be that way I wouldn't have been doing it that way. One kid came in last weekend and wanted a Tasmanian devil. It was on a t-shirt and when you reduced it it didn't look right. So I added some shading to give it this three dimensional look. There's nothing like having a seventeen-year-old kid standing there and saying, "Well, should this really be there?" Of course it should be there, fool!

Another tattooist expressed his annoyance for problematic customers who displayed disrespect for his other clients, as well as the physical setting, and his own authority.

> (I have problems with) people who come in and are really belligerent. They don't respect, first of all, the situation . . . the situation being the front of the studio, being the open area where people can move in and out freely. The books are

available to them . . . it's a public area. But that public area should also be respected. So that putting your cigarettes out on the rug, coming in and eating a sandwich and throwing your shit on the floor, spilling beer all over everything—I don't tolerate that. But I don't go out there and just throw them out. I come out and remind them that this is the situation that you're in. Don't throw your shit around, don't put your cigarettes out on the floor. Act like a decent person here. Don't be hassling the other customers. Sometimes I have guys and there will be a girl in there and they will be all over her. "Hey baby, you going to get a tattoo on your tits?" Then I have to go out there and lay down the law. The law is that this is an opportunity for you to express yourself in terms of a visual form. I would be glad to help you do that. But if you want to come in here and hassle people and don't know how to behave socially in this context, then you are going to have to leave. That's it. So then if they come up to me and they say, "Well, I want you to do this." I say, "Look at the designs, take your time, think about what you want to do." "Well, I don't care, man. Get this guy out of here and take care of me." That kind of belligerent stuff. I just tell them, "Look, I'm not going to tattoo you. I don't have to deal with you. Go someplace else." So I just nix it off before it even gets started. Although I have been caught up in situations where people have gotten to the next stage which is getting through (the next) door. I have thrown people out of here for not stopping at that door. That's the portal; the territorial limit.

Clients who enter the tattoo establishment while intoxicated or stoned also violate the practical rules imposed by the tattooist and are defined as problematic. Not only do these customers tend to be belligerent and disrespectful, but they also are difficult to tattoo because of their inability to maintain the "appropriate receiving demeanor" demanded by tattooists. They move about, talk incessantly, jerk away in reaction to pain, spew vomit on the tattooist and his or her equipment, and generally make the tattooist's work more difficult and unpleasant.

There is a common perception among the general public that many of the people who receive tattoos do so because they are drunk and pressured into it by similarly intoxicated associates. Actually, most tattooists are extremely careful to avoid working on people who are obviously under the influence of alcohol (or other drugs). Drunken clients tend to generate conflict in the shop, and tattooists are aware that tattooing someone who is not entirely free to choose the procedure has the potential for causing trouble. In a business that continues to labor under the reputation of being on the margins of respectability, at best, this is to be avoided. Most shops have a prominently located sign that states the cardinal rules of the establishment—"PAY IN CASH, NO TATTOOING OF DRUNKS OR MINORS." While most intoxicated clients use alcohol as an analgesic in anticipation of a painful process rather than a deinhibiting motivator,they are roundly disliked by tattooists and are often the object of humorous disdain. The following exchange is drawn from my fieldnotes:

[Quote from fieldnotes] the artists get into talking about how
hard it is to work on drunks.
Mitch:—These fuckers come in here drunk and they're no good
at all. You can't get them to stay still. They just keep on falling
over.
Bob:—When I was working down in Georgia this guy came in
real drunk and wanted a pattern put on. I got him shaved and
put the stencil on and the guy got up, looked at it in the
mirror, paid his forty bucks and left. (Laughter.)
M—The other day I was working on this guy and he was
drinking soda. But he was getting loaded—he had booze in the
can. Finally he started to fall of the stool and his brother had
to come over and we leaned him up against the wall. His
brother was real pissed. Apologized all over the place.

Some clients are defined as troublesome because they do not exercise an acceptable level of care over their personal hygiene. Working in close physical proximity with the client's body, the tattooist demands a certain minimal degree of cleanliness.

I refused a guy last night because he was too dirty. It was about
100 degrees out and he works in a body shop all day and he
comes in straight from work and he was filthy. I just told him,
"Look, I don't give baths here. Go home and clean up and come
back. I'm not working on you like that." The other day there
was this guy in here getting a coverup, and he was filthy and
sitting here farting. A real pig. That was real obnoxious. I was
about ready to tell him to leave and go take care of his gas
problem.

I don't like it when people come in here and you spray their
arm with alcohol and all this dirt comes off like they never took
a bath before. You think about going to the doctor . . . most
people I know shower before they come in.

Finally, customers who shop for tattoos solely on the basis of
price ("What can I get for $25?"), complain about the cost of the
piece they select, or attempt to bargain with the tattooist for a
lower price are also negatively defined. These clients are seen as
not being respectful of the tattooist's expertise ("You wouldn't bargain with your dentist about how much he charges for fixing your
teeth") or as not displaying sufficient commitment to tattooing
("They don't want a tattoo, they just want to be tattooed").

It pisses me off when someone doesn't even understand what I
am doing. I draw something for someone that is highly
detailed, intelligently colored, a very exciting piece, real
nut-busting type of work and I give him a price—say eighty
bucks or whatever—and the guy rolls up his sleeve and he
says, "That's too fuckin' high because I got this in the
Philippines for thirty cents in 1952." How do you combat that?
Look jerk, don't you see that there is a difference. There is a
difference between 1952 and 1985. In those days it was a dime
for a bottle of beer and now it is a buck and a quarter. When
people are so blind that they don't know that there is a
difference I find it very frustrating. All I can tell them is to go
back to the Philippines and go back to 1952. I don't ask people
to agree with me—just to understand.

CONCLUSION

The tattooist is, on the one hand, a commercial artist, a worker involved in exercising (ideally) a unique skill while creating (again, ideally) for profit a product that contains elements of beauty—however that is defined by the various interactants in the commercial exchange. Understanding the problems and rewards encountered by the tattooist as he or she moves through the career process aids in understanding the experience of commercial artists generally. At the same time, the tattooist is involved in providing a decorative service; his or her occupational activity is, to a large degree, shaped by subordination to the demands of a particular clientele. The tattooist's ability to ascertain client characteristics, define client needs, develop viable commercial relationships, and control clients' demands is similar to that encountered in a wide variety of service work from providing medical care to supplying janitorial services.

While examining the work and experience of the tattooist helps to enlarge our general understanding of commercial art activities and service work, the unique features of tattooing imbue it with a special sociological interest. Tattooing is, in Hughes's (1971c) term, a "bastard institution" supplying what is still a semi-legitimate service/product to a limited but increasingly diverse "taste public." A diachronic analysis of tattooing demonstrates that services and products have social careers. Distinct stages and factors can be identified—alterations in the cultural context, the incursion of producers with established social legitimacy, changes in the status of the members of the consuming group, and so forth—that characterize and shape the product's career. In its movement from being widely regarded as a tarnished good (Shover, 1975) to becoming a marginally accepted form of artistic decoration, the tattoo and the social world that surrounds its creation and consumption have undergone significant change. Support personnel have arisen, technological innovations have been made, practioner/merchants have organized, various aesthetic perspectives and related "schools" have coalesced, and agents of social control have altered or, in some cases, abandoned their regulatory efforts.

This change in the cultural and organizational context has been paralleled by significant alterations in the careers and occupational experience of tattooists. An enlarged and diversified client pool has increased tattooists' occupational opportunities and enhanced their financial security. As tattooing has begun to enjoy a modest level of legitimacy within the larger art world, tattooists' positive self-definitions as creative artists and/or skilled technicians have been bolstered and enhanced. In turn, the technical and artistic quality of the tattoos being produced has risen significantly.

The previous chapter examined the tattoo experience of the consumer while this discussion has focused on the career and occupational experience of the tattoo practioner. We turn now to enter the tattoo studio, the immediate interactional setting in which the major actors meet and the tattoo encounter takes place. It is here that the tattooist employs his or her acquired social skills, places customers into definitional categories, and attempts to exercise control over the commercial and creative exchange. In turn, the tattooee attempts to communicate his or her desires and construct an understanding of the unfamiliar and often anxiety-producing situation. Like all social settings in which the collective action of cultural production is played out in a structure of unequal power and knowledge, the situated interaction of the tattoo event displays as much conflict as it does cooperation. This is what makes it especially interesting and sociologically significant.

Traditional "vow" tattoo with name in ribbon, rose, and bluebird by
Mike Nicholson. *(Photo by Mike Nicholson)*

left: Black panther with bloody claws by Mike Nicholson. One of the most conventional designs for men, it is typically placed on the upper arm.
(Photo by Mike Nicholson)

Tattoo by Filip Leu. In large tattoos, artists often use the posture of the collector to help in stretching the skin.
(Photo by D. Angus Vail)

facing page, top right: The Leu Family's Family Iron. Tattoo artists' work stations demystify the tattooing process by showing all of the materials of the trade to the customer. In this case, the stainless steel sink and white surfaces reinforce the appearance of cleanliness and the assortment of colors shows the artist's capacity for working in a variety of styles. *(Photo by D. Angus Vail)*

above: Flash by Mike Nicholson. Tattooists who work in Street Shops often rely fairly heavily on stock designs called "flash."

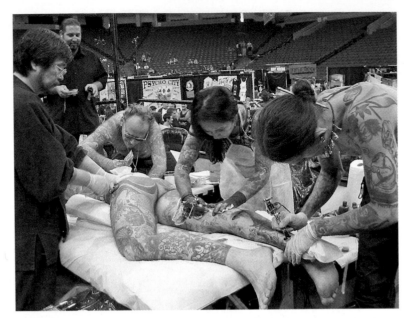

Collaborative tattoo by (l-r) Horitoshi, Bill Salmon, Junii, and Filip Leu, at Tattoo The Earth, Oakland, CA. Serious collectors value the skills of those who are capable of, and experienced with, working in the full body scale. *(Photo by D. Angus Vail)*

above: Tattoo by Filip Leu, The Leu Family's Family Iron. The Hanya mask is a common tattoo design in the Japanese canon. Hanya simultaneously incorporates the three faces of a jealous woman (anger, joy, and fear) and in so doing confuses demons or spirits who mean harm to the person who wears the tattoo. Because she watches the wearer's back, Hanya is a common design for backpieces. *(Photo by Maren R. Nelson)*

left: Tattoo by Filip Leu, The Leu Family's Family Iron. Western style backpieces often end at the belt line, but all backpieces should cover the entire canvas with a single design. This Tibetan skull connects with other designs on the arms through the motif of waves.

Contemporary Japanese aesthetics, as practiced by Western European artists, tend to employ full canvases, as is common with traditional Japanese work. They also tend to focus more intensely on perspective and dimension, creating more realistic images and a greater sense of depth, as is seen with the smoke background and receding body of the dragon in this backpiece by Filip Leu.

(Photo by Maren R. Nelson)

Portraits of Jimi Hendrix and John Coltrane by Filip Leu; portrait of
Joni Mitchell by Shotsie Gorman. Photorealism and portraiture are
among the important stylistic developments in custom tattoo art.
Whereas portraits were traditionally reserved for black and grey
designs of approximately 3" square, they are currently done in a
variety of sizes and color schemes. *(Photo by Maren R. Nelson)*

left: Tattoo by Guy Aitchison and Leo Zulueta. Photo by Maren R. Nelson. So-called "tribal" tattoos follow muscle groups with their abstract designs.

(Photo by D. Angus Vail)

below: Tattoo by Guy Aitchison, Kari Barba, Paul Booth, Filip Leu, Marcus Pacheco, and Leo Zulueta. Biomechanical tattoos simulate machinery in bodily contours. Notice how this tattoo incorporates the collector's scar in the design.

(Photo by D. Angus Vail)

Chapter 4

The Tattoo Relationship: Risk and Social Control in the Studio

Although the analysis of socially disvalued commercial activities—prostitution (for example, Bryan, 1966), drug dealing (for example, Adler and Adler, 1983), the distribution of pornography (for example, McKinstry, 1974), and so on—is common in sociological discussions of deviance, the consumer research literature contains little about the consumption of socially marginal, deviant, controversial, or unconventional goods and services. This significant gap in the marketing literature is unfortunate since the study of deviant consumption touches on many issues of interest to consumer researchers. Attention to marginal commercial exchanges provides considerable information on such central concerns as the effect of subcultural groups on consumption decisions (Nicosia and Mayer, 1976), changes in commercial products due to the diffusion of product characteristics from marginal taste publics into mainstream commercial culture (Hirschman, 1981), and the relationship of purchased objects and services to the consumer's identity and definition of self (Hirschman, 1980; Sirgy, 1982; Hirschman and Stampfl, 1980; Solomon, 1983). Further, since these types of commercial activities are potentially discrediting, the marginal consumer normally experiences considerable risk when planning, carrying out, and evaluating the exchange. Attention to this neglected area of consumption, therefore, adds to an understanding of what consumer researchers refer to as "perceived risk" and its impact on commercial interactions and consumer decision-making (Ross, 1975).

The socially disvalued phenomenon of tattooing is a service that involves the direction of a tangible action by a skilled craftsworker at the body of a client/consumer (Lovelock, 1984: 51–52).

As is the case with haircutting, plastic surgery, and similar quasi-tangible services, tattooing requires that the customer be present throughout the service delivery, entails a close personal involvement between the client and service worker, is a relatively non-standardized service, and is produced only upon request. Further, the tattoo service involves technical skills with which the client is commonly unfamiliar and that he or she finds difficult to evaluate. While the service is sold, produced, and purchased simultaneously, the relative permanence of the service outcome means that appreciation or dissatisfaction continue long after the service interaction is terminated (see Kelly and George, 1982).

Tattooing is, therefore, a consumer service which is low in "search qualities" (attributes the buyer can determine prior to purchase). Reliable information on tattooing is almost nonexistent in mainstream social circles. Most members of American society have had little direct experience with tattooed people or the settings in which tattoos are applied. Tattooing is also a service in which "experience qualities" (characteristics the client can determine and evaluate only after purchase) are extremely high. The specialized and somewhat mysterious tattoo service is also high in "credence qualities" (attributes the consumer is unable to ascertain and assess even after having been involved in the purchase experience). Few tattoo consumers, especially first-time recipients, possess the specialized knowledge necessary to judge the technical merits of a tattoo or to evaluate the relative quality of the service delivery (Zeithaml, 1984).

This chapter focuses on the situated experience of the major participants in the "tattoo event" (Govenar, 1977). The first section employs the consumer researcher's concept of "perceived risk" to orient a discussion of tattoo recipients' in-shop encounters with tattooing and the approaches they take to reducing their risk and minimizing post-purchase regret. We then turn to look more closely at a topic introduced in the last chapter—the tattooist's occupationally based categorization of clients and the techniques he or she uses to control the tattoo interaction.

RISK, REGRET, AND THE TATTOO CONSUMER

As we have seen, the person entering the tattoo setting commonly experiences considerable anxiety, especially since he or she typically has little or no prior experience with tattooing. The novice client possesses, at best, minimal knowledge of what the tattooing process entails. Due to the limited number of tattoo studios available in most areas, the potential client generally has little opportunity to compare prices and quality of work. However, the tattooee is usually intensely aware that the tattoo is a permanent addition to the body and that the application process involves some degree of pain. When asked to describe their state of mind when entering the tattoo establishment to receive their first tattoo, interviewees typically spoke of feeling nervous and fearful. Anticipation of "physiological risk" involving significant pain was the major source of their anxiety.

I hadn't really talked with anyone about getting that first tattoo. I just kind of did it on the spur of the moment . . . I was very nervous, didn't know anything about what to expect. The tattooist had to stop after the outline (was put on) to let me catch my breath, so I wouldn't pass out. I was the only person in the place at the time. The tattoo artist was a big biker type with a lot of tattoos. He was very closed mouthed about the process. . . . He really wouldn't talk specifically about anything. Like I said, I had no idea about what to expect. I think that almost passing out was more due to the fear and psychological stuff than it was due to the pain. It didn't hurt as much as I thought it would.

When I walked in I was just looking around; looking at all the different pictures. Just scoping it all out really. (The tattooist) asked if he could help me and I said, "Right now I just want to look at them all and, if I like one, that is probably the one I'll get." I was a little nervous and I didn't want to say, "Oh, that's the one." I was nervous about being in there for the first time and seeing guys with needles going in and out of their arms. It was kind of weird because I never really like needles all that much. . . . (Once I chose the design) I had to lie on my side so

he could get on the side. I had two people working on me. (The
tattooist) did the outline and then started coloring. My other
leg was shaking a little. It wasn't because it was hurting as
much as I was nervous, like I said. . . . It was weird. I expected
needles in and out and it was like a stinging. On the outline he
was pulling it around so that it was going deep enough. At
first, I was like grinding my teeth and holding my arms up and
catching my side. But after a couple of minutes I calmed down
and just let him finish up. . . . I was kind of surprised. You
know, before you go in people tell you—just to scare you a
little—that it's not going to be an easy ride. There were a
couple of kids in there that were going after me and when I
went in they were all saying, "Good luck," like I was going
to the torture chamber. When I came out they said, "Did it
hurt? Did it hurt?" I tried to calm them down and tell them it
wasn't really that bad so they wouldn't be so paranoid about it.

As indicated by this respondent, information provided by one's
everyday associates usually increases the novice tattooee's anxiety
rather than reducing it. The most effective means by which recipients eased their nervousness were talking with the tattooist and
watching while other clients were serviced.

I wouldn't have been as nervous if I had been more familiar
with the situation. It was my first time in a tattoo parlor and I
figured I had better get it done now because I was pretty busy
and I didn't know when I would get back. I wasn't familiar with
what was going on—the noise, the sound of what was going
on. I wasn't nervous because, "Oh, my god, I'm getting a
tattoo." It was just that I wished I knew more about the
procedure. . . . I remember feeling foreign because I was
unfamiliar with the situation . . . not because I was a woman.
(The tattooist) was pretty nice. We had a beer before I decided
to get it. I asked questions as we went along. I asked him how
long it would take. I said, "I'm not going to ask you if it hurts."
I just didn't want to be that much of a fool. I figured it was
going to hurt. I asked him if it hurt could I tell him and would
he stop. He said, "Yes." But it never arose that I needed to say
stop. I asked thing like, "What are you going to do now?" "I'm

going to stencil it on first and then I'm going to color it in." He asked me not to move. He put me really at ease. I was afraid because I was so unfamiliar with the situation that I would say something out of character for people that would normally get tattoos . . . I just was cautious. I didn't want to say anything to offend them or that was offensive to them as artists.

[Quote from fieldnotes] I go back into the waiting area to talk to the guys looking at flash. I ask one what he is going to get and he says he wants a large rose that will cover his left bicep. I go into the back room and get one of the new flash sheets that Ralph has been coloring and show him the rose. He says it is O.K. but that he wants one with scroll work. He eventually finds a design in the sample book and we go with Frank into the back room to have it traced, enlarged, and made into a stencil. While this is being done he confides in me. "I'm a little nervous. I'm scared of needles. That's why I came in with my buddy and was standing there watching him work on that other guy." I say, "I was the same way. I don't like needles, but this really isn't too bad. You can see there isn't all that much blood. It doesn't go in that deep and you get used to it. It stings a little bit at first but it isn't bad after the outline is done." He keeps watching but still looks nervous.

Tattooing also entails the violation of significant norms governing the interaction between strangers. There are few settings in everyday life in which extensive physical contact, the willful infliction of pain, and exposure of intimate parts of the body to virtual strangers are routine aspects of commercial interactions. Since the tattoo studio is largely a male domain and most tattooists are men, body exposure and intimate touch were factors of physiological risk about which women tattooees expressed concern with considerable regularity.

I thought it would be more secretive, not having other people around. . . . I had to take my blouse off and I remember wishing I had something I could put over me because I had to sit there for twenty minutes with my arm over my breasts and my arm got tired. Actually, I never felt that the people there were really just interested in staring at a woman with her blouse off getting a tattoo. I felt that the people there were interested in seeing what I was getting or seeing how someone gets a tattoo.

I had anticipated sitting up and I was surprised when the artist pulled this examining table over. I thought the shape of my breast would change, but I figured he knew what he was doing. I remember changing my clothes right there in the room—just turned my back to the door. It's not that I wasn't aware that the artist was a male person but it just wasn't threatening. I had my shirt off and he applied the outline. He was actually going to touch me. He was so close to me when he was bending over me—you just get a distance there. It's like when a doctor is examining your breasts or something or a gynecological exam. His hands were warm and reassuring. He had to lean against me and, at first, I thought that might be uncomfortable, but while it was actually going on it was reassuring. I didn't have the feeling that he was looking at me in any sexual way. I think he said later that he only sees two inches of flesh at once. He was also rather matter of fact. He said that I should be careful not to place the tattoo too near my nipple. To be explicit and talk about my body—my nipple—was rather matter of fact and reassuring.[1]

The nebulous and largely incorrect information about tattooing that circulates within conventional social networks contains cautions about the longer-term physiological risks tattooees may well encounter. Warnings that one is apt to contract hepatitis, AIDS, herpes, or other diseases from tattooing; that infection is common; and that people often have negative physical reactions to the tattoo pigments are typically presented as significant risk factors. Most tattoo artists are overtly aware of, and take great pains to avoid, these potentially negative consequences. The majority of studios are kept scrupulously clean, equipment is autoclaved or kept in antibacterial solutions, tattoo needles are used on only one client, unused pigments are discarded, and customers are given written instructions on the steps which should be taken in order to insure that the tattoo heals properly. Most tattooees are impressed by the apparent cleanliness of the modern tattoo studio. They are generally careful to follow the aftercare instructions provided (we will see later in this chapter that tattooists negatively define those clients who disregard the basic rules about how to care for a new tattoo). The symbolic hygiene of the tattoo establishment and the tattooist's ritual display of competence are effective in reducing this aspect of the client's risk experience.

Before I got my first tattoo the only other tattoo parlor I had ever been in was near a military base in Texas. I was just a kid and I remember I had shorts on and the guy offered to tattoo my knees for free. The place was real dingy and dark and the guy looked like a bum. Years later when I decided to get a tattoo I went down to the (shop) in N——(city) and looked around. It was like a doctor's office—white walls and plants and a waiting room. The guy even had one of those white coats that doctors wear and he wore rubber gloves. It wasn't like I expected. I thought it was a good experience . . . I went to bed that night, got up the next day and washed it, didn't pick the scab or anything. I did all the things they said—put that vaseline stuff on it. It worked out all right. I'd do it again.

Even when he or she chooses a small design, the tattoo client, armed with minimal pre-purchase information, encounters an unanticipatedly high "financial risk." Confronted by this risk, the tattooee may attempt to bargain for a lower price—a practice that is, as presented in the last chapter, not acceptable in most commercial tattoo studios. Discounts are given only to steady customers with whom the tattooist has a friendly relationship or, less frequently, when business is slow and the tattooist is desperate to have, at least, some income for the day. The following excerpt from my fieldnotes describes a typical encounter with a customer who attempted to reduce his financial risk.

[Quote from fieldnotes] the door to the shop opens and a middle-aged, working-class guy with a sizable beer belly comes in. He says he called before and that he wants to get Yosemite Sam put on his arm. He shows us a standard conventional Marine tattoo on his left forearm—a skull with dagger and "Death Before Dishonor." On the other bicep is a rose with the

name "Rose" in the scrollwork. He finds the design he wants
on a sheet and begins to dicker about the price (I know this is
a prime example of client assholeness in Randy's view).

Randy—That one is fifty bucks—Sam with two smoking guns.
Client—You said it was $45 on the phone. I only brought $50
and have to get some beer for the ride home.
R (annoyed)—I told you it was $45 or $50 on the phone!
C—You think we can work something out? I want to have some
other work done. How much is that? (Points out a large grim
reaper. Randy tells him it is $85.) I really like that. I want to
get my arms covered; none of that other bullshit. I want to be
able to see them. (Pause.) Can I get Sam for $45?
R (very annoyed)—You'll have to wait until the boss gets back
and talk to him.
C—Yeah, I really like that one. I got this (indicates skull with
dagger) twenty years ago for $11.

When confronted with the "sticker shock" generated by the
prices posted on the flash (or, in the case of those requesting custom work, hearing about the estimated length of time the tattoo
will take and the artist's hourly rate), inexperienced tattooees
usually either swallow hard and pay the money up front or they
reduce their risk by revising their expectations and picking a
smaller and less expensive design. It is interesting that tattoo selection on the basis of price—a common approach when a consumer is making an impulse or "low involvement" purchase—is
so common in what should be, by all rights, a "high involvement"
transaction (Assael, 1984: 80–102).

The tattoo process is also more time-consuming than most novice clients anticipate. Typically, tattoo artists are reluctant to
make appointments. Except in the case of complicated custom
work, tattooists usually work on a first-come-first-served basis.
The novice tattooee, therefore, often confronts the problem of
"time loss" (Roselius, 1971) as an aspect of risk. Except for pushy-
client attempts to negotiate cost, dissatisfaction about waiting
and arguments about who-was-here-before-whom were the most
common sources of conflict within the tattoo settings observed.
While commercial tattooists commonly see the rather languid

pace of the shop as a mark of professionalism and artistry (only tattooists who are "only into it for the money" or who are technically unskilled rush the tattooing process), customers are often not as casual about the whole thing. Clients typically enter the tattoo establishment with a single-minded desire to undergo what they anxiously anticipate to be a painful experience. Waiting for long periods of time or being told to "come back tomorrow when we open" have the potential of precipitating significant conflict.

[Quote from fieldnotes] there is a group of four young male customers around the counter when I come in. They turn out to all be on the lacrosse team at (local university). They are all sitting around and drinking beer while Jerry is tattooing a cartoon bear with a lacrosse stick on one guy's hip (jocks always get "hip shots" because coaches hate tattoos and this is an easily hidden body area). I put my case in the back room, come back out and sit on the stool by the mirror in Monty's area. I ask the guy nearest me if they are all getting work done. "Yeah, we were here last night and he (indicates one of the guys) was the only one who could get it done. The rest of us came back today. He (indicates guy who just left to go to the bar across the street) was really psyched. He was going to do it himself but we talked him into doing it today. . . . " (Later) one guy asks me for the time and I tell him it is a little after five. He says they have been there since two. Jerry hears this and says, "It's taking more time because you're getting them on your hips. If you would have them on your arm or someplace like that it wouldn't take as long." I observe that it takes a lot of patience to get a tattoo. One of the other guys says, "This is nothing. I have some friends that got tattoos up in [neighboring state] and after they had been there for five hours the guy said he was closing up. They say you have to go up there and get a motel room because you can never be sure if you are going to get it done that day."

Bob comes into the backroom complaining about the people who are still waiting to get work done. "Man, if some tattoo artist said it was too late for him to work on me I wouldn't complain. These assholes come in here and expect it to be like

S—— R——'s [a popular commercial studio in an adjacent state]. If this was his shop he would have just put some half-assed shit on them and taken their money. All of these people would have been out of here by now but they would have had lousy tattoos."

Proprietors typically provide at least some minimal forms of diversion for waiting customers. Most provide waiting areas in which the client can leaf through dog-eared magazines or look at photo albums containing examples of their finest work. Other establishments have amusement arcades containing electronic games, pinball machines, and pool tables on which clients can wile away the hours. Usually, inexperienced clients use some of this time to increase their knowledge of the tattoo process. They watch as the tattooist readies his or her work space, adjusts the machines, chooses and dispenses the pigments, prepares the skin surface, applies the design, and inscribes the tattoo.[2] For some, this helps to reduce anxiety; others are made even more nervous by their first direct encounter with what tattooing actually entails.[3]

Tattoo clients are also concerned with the "social risk" they run when they decide to have their bodies indelibly marked. While, as we have seen, various subcultures positively value tattooing as a symbol of commitment and belonging, the tattoo is still defined as a stigmatizing mark by most members of mainstream society. The consumer is aware of the potential negative social consequences of being tattooed. Employers, parents, and other representatives of "straight" society are justifiably seen as interpreting the tattoo as a symbol of the general deviance and untrustworthiness of the wearer. The major way in which the novice deals with the potential social risk of tattoo possession is by limiting his or her commitment. The first tattoo is usually small, relatively inexpensive, and placed on a body location which is easily hidden from strangers or casual associates. Choice of a small tattoo placed on a readily concealable body location acts to decrease the potential negative social consequences of tattoo possession. In addition, since the small design is inexpensive, financial risk is minimized and, because a small tattoo is quickly applied, physiological risk is minimized as well.

Positive social responses from friends and other members of the novice tattooee's reference group also help decrease feelings of social risk. As described earlier, getting tattooed is a highly social experience for most first-time tattoo recipients. Most initiates enter the studio in the company of close associates who act as "purchase pals" (Bell, 1967). These companions help generally to reduce the risks involved by consulting with the tattooee about design and location, providing social support for the decision, commiserating during the painful application process, and by helping to fill waiting time. Purchase pals also aid the recipient by acting as surrogate social evaluators. They provide risk-reducing support by positively reacting to and thereby validating the tattoo consumer's decision (cf. Ben-Sira, 1976: 6).

While a certain level of risk is characteristic of all service interactions, it is particularly intense in settings where marginal or deviant services (for example, illegal abortion, prostitution, tattooing) are produced and/or consumed. In addition, because of the potentially negative legal, social, and psychological consequences of acquiring deviant or marginal consumer products (for example, illegal drugs, pornographic materials, tattoos), a high degree of risk is a key feature of all deviant consumption. The typical strategies by which conventional retailers reduce perceived risk are not commonly utilized by suppliers of deviant products and services. Retailers of socially disvalued goods and services rarely offer guarantees of satisfaction; legal recourse is generally not available should the consumer experience dissatisfaction; quality is not standardized; purchase settings are commonly dangerous and unfamiliar; and there is a general understanding that the supplier is not altogether trustworthy.

As a type of marginal service interaction the purchase of a tattoo entails considerable risk. Lack of familiarity with the purchase setting, anticipation of pain, uncertainty about social consequences, unanticipated expense, and other unknown factors lead the client to experience a high degree of risk.

The tattoo consumer uses a variety of strategies to help reduce his or her experience of risk in the tattoo encounter. In particular, the tattooee uses information provided by characteristics of the setting and the interaction within it to ease feelings of anxiety. The cleanliness and order of the studio, the quality and variety of the flash, the appearance and demeanor of fellow customers, and photos of past work are important sources of information. The customer's interaction with the tattooist is of particular importance, since this is the primary source of the information he or she uses to calculate trust.

The literature on patient satisfaction with medical service (for example, Ben-Sira, 1976; Greenley and Schoenherr, 1981) clearly shows that the client's evaluation of the service is, to a major extent, shaped by his or her interactional experience with and relationship to the service deliverer. The tattooee's experience of risk in the tattoo shop and post-purchase satisfaction depend largely upon the psychosocial care provided by the tattooist. Interviewees consistently stated that those tattooists who were friendly, answered their questions patiently, allowed them to play a significant role in planning the tattoo, and behaved in what was often referred to as a "professional" style eased their anxieties and created a tattoo that was a significant source of pride. The key importance of the tattooist's demeanor is especially apparent in these descriptions provided by two women interviewees.

> (The artist) didn't seem to want to get to know me socially. It was very professional. Actually, that was a good attitude that he had. It showed that he was a professional. That was the way our conversation went. He didn't try to persuade me to get anything in particular—like when you go to a hairdresser and they want to cut all your hair off. I expected him to be a little more rugged. He was very nice—answered all my questions and if I would slouch or anything he would just nicely ask me to get back into the position I was in.

> I was standing there in the studio talking to the artist and said, "Well, I want this kind of curly design but can you do a dragon?" Then we sat down and he began to draw—asking me if I wanted whiskers, did I want it to look sleepy, passive, ferocious, or feminine, things like that. I said that I didn't want it too fierce or too passive. It was really lovely what he drew. He drew it backwards on this paper so I could place it where I wanted it. It was good to be sort of able to preview it. He asked me about the color. That I hadn't really decided. . . . After this

experience I would tell someone who was thinking about getting a tattoo, "Don't go by price, go by what you want. Look around. Look at the books of designs. Try to be explicit about what you want with the artist." I would tell them to try to look at the artist's work on other people. I'd tell them to go in and take a look at the shop first—see if it is clean and all. Most important, I'd tell them to talk to the artist. It's like getting your hair cut—you have to have rapport with the person.[4]

It is uncommon for tattooees to express dissatisfaction with being tattooed per se. Those that do tend to focus on the inferior craftsmanship of the service they receive. Concern with inferior quality is most commonly exhibited by more heavily tattooed people who have sufficient experience to evaluate the technical merits of their collection.

I want to get this (tattoo) altered more to my liking. I prefer that to getting it taken off. At first I was totally against it, but now it doesn't really bother me. To tell the truth, if I am going to have one, I want one that I really like and stick with that. I want this one redone because (the tattooist) that did it was absolutely hammered when he did it. I don't think it is centered right. The lines aren't right. You can see that some of it is more pointed where it should be rounded. It's not good enough. It isn't done by someone I would call an artist. His hands probably weren't that steady. I don't like the care and the workmanship that went into it. If I am going to be stuck with something, I want it to be something that I can be relatively proud of. I'm not proud of it now but I'm not resentful anymore.

I don't wish I didn't have any [tattoos]. Well, I do regret this [he indicates a crudely rendered flying money design]. It just seems out of place with everything else. . . . I don't know why I got it. P—— did it when he first got here. You can see how bad his work was then. He scarred me up. I figured I would see what kind of work he did, so I picked something simple with only a few lines. I've been trying to find something for a year to cover it up, something that will go with the rest of my work.

As seen in the quotes above, regretful tattooees tend to feel personally responsible for the unsatisfactory quality of the work they have acquired. They blame themselves for choosing to patronize a particular studio or tattooist prior to searching out information. They also attribute their regret to having chosen the wrong body location or design, not communicating their desires more effectively to the artist, or not conscientiously following the aftercare instructions provided by the tattooist. This attribution of dissatisfaction to errors of consumer choice encountered in tattoo recipients is a feature of the post-purchase regret of service clients generally. This tendency to blame the self is understandable given the central importance of client-serviceworker interaction in service delivery and the relative lack of information carried by consumers of specialized services (see Zeithaml, 1984: 196–197).

Due to the relative permanence of tattooing, there are only a limited number of options available to the dissatisfied tattoo consumer. If he or she is disappointed with the technical quality of the work, the tattooee may return to the artist and request to have the piece relined or recolored. Most reputable commercial tattooists will agree—albeit reluctantly—to redo their own work free of additional charge. The most common option chosen by regretful tattooees—the one chosen by the interviewees quoted above—is to have a "coverup" tattoo placed over the unsatisfactory image. In many tattoo establishments covering up or extensively reworking badly executed tattoos accounts for between 40 and 60 percent of the business.[5]

Individuals who regret having chosen to get a tattoo have three major options. Most simply, they can conceal the offending tattoo with clothing or flesh-colored makeup. A far more extreme response is seen when dissatisfied tattooees attempt to remove the design themselves.[6] More commonly, extremely dissatisfied tattooees seek the services of a dermatologist or plastic surgeon. The major medical approaches to tattoo removal are dermabrasion, salabrasion, surgical excision, and vaporization of the tattoo pigments through the use of a ruby or carbon dioxide laser. Most of these techniques result in unsightly scarring, and even the more sophisticated and experimental laser removal cannot return the dermis to its pretattooed appearance and texture (see Goldstein et al., 1979).

The regretful tattooee, having made a purchase decision that is practically irreversible, experiences a high level of cognitive dissonance. If the more extreme options presented above are not defined as viable, the individual must find ways of readjusting his or her perceptions of the tattoo in order to regain some degree of psychological comfort. Typically, regretful tattooees reestablish consonance either by simply resigning themselves to the unsatisfactory tattoo (like one comes to accept an overlarge nose or a receded hairline), by seeking information that helps to disconfirm the negative evaluation, or by adjusting one's definition of the tattoo so as to see it as having positive attributes (London and Della Bitta, 1984: 694–697; Assael, 1984: 47–49; Cummings and Venkatesan, 1975). The tattooee may seek out other tattooed people who can provide information that will support a definition of the tattoo as being of reasonable, if not outstanding, quality. The tattoo work carried by others provides a basis for direct comparison of technique and design. Since much commercial tattooing is of mediocre quality at best, it is likely that the dissatisfied tattooee will have little difficulty finding work that is inferior to his or her own. Alternatively, the regretful tattoo recipient may readjust his or her perception of the meaning of the disvalued tattoo. While the work may not be entirely satisfactory technically or creatively, it can be seen as having other positive attributes. For example, when asked why she did not get a coverup over a crudely rendered "homemade" tattoo, one interviewee replied:

> I was going to get it covered but I decided not to. I've had it since I was sixteen and I guess it is part of me now. It is the first tattoo I got . . . my boyfriend did it with a needle and india ink. It reminds me of what I was into in that part of my life. It's a way of marking the changes.

THE TATTOOIST'S APPROACHES TO EXERCISING CONTROL OVER INSHOP INTERACTION

As seen in the previous chapter, learning to evaluate clients and developing styles of interaction that will win trust are central elements of the process of becoming a tattooist. The major actors in the tattoo setting have different goals and possess different degrees of knowledge. As a consequence this is one of a number of commercial situations in which the interaction between the buyer and the seller is potentially conflictual (cf. Emerson, 1970; Schroder, 1973: 183–262). The tattooing situation is routine for the tattooist while, as discussed above, it is novel and anxiety-filled for the client. In order to avoid problematic "performance incapacity" (Emerson, 1970) on the part of the recipient, the tattooist structures the tattoo setting and organizes his or her interaction with the client so as to present a clear indication of expected recipient behavior, thereby limiting the chances of conflict. Diplomas, expertly rendered design sheets, technical objects (for example, autoclaves, racks of shiny tattoo machines), signs that overtly present shop regulations (for example, "NO TATTOOING OF DRUNKS," "YOU MUST BE 18 TO GET A TATTOO," "PAY IN CASH—NO CHECKS") represent the ways in which the tattooist structures the setting in order to indicate his or her expertise and the serious nature of the activity. This physical display of professionalism helps to reinforce the tattooist's right to "manage the tattooing event" (Govenar, 1977: 43).

The tattooist's ability to guide the interaction with the client is further supported by his or her display of technical skill and knowledge. Unhesitating responses to the client's questions, routine ease in handling and adjusting the tattooing equipment, and the mater-of-fact, almost ritualized, activities surrounding the preparation of the body area to be tattooed attest to the tattooist's skill and his or her consequent right to control the interaction. This display of expertise is especially important when dealing with novice clients. As one artist stated:

When someone comes in to get their first tattoo they are usually pretty nervous and don't know what to expect. What I do is go through this ritual. I take my time adjusting the machines and I prepare the pigments and stuff like that. I'm getting ready to tattoo them but I'm also showing them how professional I am. They're just sitting there but I know they are watching. I don't need to go through all of that with people who have a lot of work because I know they trust me. I just do it with new people.

Other participants in the setting—fellow tattooists, regular hangers-on, and so forth—help to support the tattooist's controlling definition of the situation. The regulars act as members of the tattooist's "team." By engaging in casual conversations about arcane features of the tattooing subculture and off-hand discussion of technical issues and other matters that are unfamiliar to the client, team members aid the tattooist in creating the "front" that he or she needs in order to exercise interactional control (see Goffman, 1959).

Without this concerted display of expertise, the tattooist would have difficulty managing some of the necessary features of the tattoo process. In most settings in the everyday world extensive physical contact, infliction of pain, and exposure of intimate body parts are severe violations of the norms regulating interaction among strangers. Tattooing interaction—which routinely involves these elements—would be highly conflictual if clients did not define the tattooist as skilled, knowledgeable, in control, and, consequently, cede to him or her the right to treat them as technical objects.

But the objectification of the client can increase the potential for conflict and threaten the tattooist's interactional control. Therefore, the tattooist must also develop certain "expressive skills" (Govenar, 1977: 48–50), which indicate to the client that he or she is being dealt with as a person. Skilled tattooists employ humor, indicate concern, ask clients about aspects of their lives, and provide reassurance in order to put them at ease. Through the use of these acquired interpersonal skills the tattooist affirms the client's individuality and further decreases the likelihood of conflict.

Tattooists' Typifications of Clients

The general discussions of service work (for example, Mennerick, 1974; Spiggle and Sanders, 1983) and sociological analyses of specific service delivery interactions (for example, Sudnow, 1965; Browne, 1976; Roebuck and Frese, 1976; Faulkner, 1983) clearly demonstrate two key features of commercial settings in which there is direct contact between buyer and seller of an intangible and relatively nonstandardized product. Service workers, from tattoo artists to psychiatrists, are determined to control the service interaction. They show a related tendency to typologize their clients in order to better predict interactional problems and devise utilitarian approaches to cope with conflict. In general, the typologies employed by service deliverers are based on five definitional dimensions.

1. Facilitation of work: does the client assist or hinder the service worker in his or her service delivery activities?
2. Control: does the client allow the service worker to exercise maximum control over service delivery or does he or she attempt to wrest control from the service provider?
3. Gain: does the client allow the worker to profit or does the interaction require extensive expenditures of time and effort while providing little payoff?
4. Danger: does the client pose a physical and/or psychological threat to the service worker?
5. Moral acceptability: is the client morally acceptable or does he or she violate the service worker's values and normative expectations (Mennerick, 1974: 400–406)?

Although tattooists routinely employ all of these dimensions to catergorize customers, their typological schemes are relatively simple—clients are typically defined as either "good" or "bad." The simplicity of the tattooist's client typology is due to three important characteristics of the tattoo service and the corresponding interactional settings. First, commercial tattooing, while it requires, at least, a minimum of technical skill and experience, is not particularly complex relative to other service activities (for example, that of airline ticket agents or plastic surgeons). Secondly, even with the recent diffusion of tattooing into an increasingly wide variety of economic groups and subcultures, the clientele encountered in most commercial studios is relatively homogenous. Finally, the tattooist's customer typology is not particularly complex because the tattoo service is provided in a setting over which the service deliverer exercises significant control. Tattooists work in their familiar "home territory" with clients who are commonly inexperienced, unknowledgeable, fearful, and interactionally tentative. (See Mennerick, 1974: 407–411 for a general discussion of these issues.)

Factors that are both behavioral and physiological affect the tattoo clients' facilitation of the work and their consequent categorization by tattooists. Certain characteristics of the organic "canvas," which the client presents to the tattooists, aid or impede the tattoo process. "Good" clients have finely textured, clear, light skin ("like fine vellum paper"). Dark, coarse skin presents artistic and technical problems.

> Clear, white, unwrinkled, and unblemished skin is the best. That's one reason I like to work on women. The worst kind of skin is on those guys who have laboring jobs or who are out in the sun all the time. The sun breaks down the elasticity of the skin. That's why when you see sailors or old cowboys they have loose, wrinkled skin that just seems to hang there. You see a lot of that in shops around seaports. Some guys come into the shop and you can't really tattoo them. You just mark up their skin.

> I had one gentleman come in. He worked for twenty-five years in a heat treating plant. His skin is like gritty sandpaper. It is a terrible thing to think that this happened to this human being because of the place he worked. You can't even shave his skin. Red headed people have like albino white skin. All red headed skin is like rubber. The elasticity is unreal. I have small hands and you have a big man come in and it is almost impossible to stretch the skin and get a nice tattoo. Blond headed people with light skin . . . say someone of your size. . . . Tight skin is excellent to work on. The color flows in well; you don't have to repeat yourself. You can do a tattoo in a third of the time it would take you to do a normal person. There are some men that I can't tattoo. I won't because I can't guarantee that the tattoo will come out right. Their arms are so big and the skin is like buffalo hide. You can't seem to puncture the skin under the epidermis. It just stays on the top. I was taught that if the color doesn't go in the first time don't overwork it. By overworking it, it is going to bleed out anyway.

Clients who bleed profusely, whose skin swells in reaction to the needle, or who faint during the process also tend to be negatively defined by tattooists. All tattooists possess a wealth of "horror stories" about the 4 or 5 percent of clients who do not facilitate the tattoo process due to their tendency to faint or get sick.

A very small proportion pass out but, generally, they are younger men who come in and try to impress upon me their bravado. Those are always the ones that go out. It's not the ones that come in and say, "I'm scared to shit." They never go. It's the one who says, "Fuck man, just give it to me." Bam! They're gone like that. I really don't like that. That scares me. I had some guy go into some sort of bizarre fit in front of me at one point early in my career when I first started tattooing. I got about five minutes into the tattoo and he started to pale a little bit. So I said, "Ok. Look, just relax. Loosen your pants. . . ." I went through the routine as I know it to be done. Head between the knees. And before he got his hands to his pants he went out. I pushed him back into the chair and I took a popper which I have here all the time—I have ammonia caps. I snapped the popper under his nose and at that point his entire body went rigid. He sprung back out of the chair, arched up, his arms and legs went out. It was the summer time and he had shorts on and he had these flip flop shoes on—his toes spread and his fingers spread and he began to tremble all over his entire body. I sat there with this guy in front of me doing this, not having any idea what the fuck was happening. I stood up and I punched him in the chest as hard as I could. He folded up into a little ball, pissed all over the floor and came back to consciousness. I died a thousand deaths at that point. That's it. That's what I don't like about tattooing. There's the potential for that kind of trauma; it does occur every now and then. That's the most distasteful aspect of tattooing.

Although the tattooing process is not especially painful, as we have seen, pain is a major concern in the minds of most novice clients. How troublesome the pain of the tattooing process is to the recipient depends on the location of the tattoo, the skill of the tattooist, the quality of the equipment (especially the condition of the needles), and the pain threshold of the client. Because of the consistent concern about pain expressed by recipients, most tattooists have standard lines they use to ease, make light of, or deflect the client's fear. One tattooist with whom I worked, when asked the routine question, "Does it hurt?" usually replied, "No, I don't feel a thing." When not employing some form of humorous response most tattooists usually attempt to get the client to relax by offering a more straightforward description of the tattoo process. "It's not too bad. Sort of a stinging or burning feeling. You kind of get used to it. The outline will hurt a little more than the coloring I'll do later. I'll stop for a while if it gets too uncomfortable" (see also Govenar, 1977: 49; Morse, 1977: 70; St. Clair and Govenar, 1981: 112, 117, 119).

Interestingly, most tattooists maintain that women seem to be less bothered by the pain of tattooing than are men. I quote from an interaction between the proprietor of a shop and a visiting tattooist.

[Quote from fieldnotes]
TJ—The worst part of getting a tattoo is waiting. (Clients) get real nervous. I had this chick come in yesterday to get a rose put on her breast and she didn't move at all. She did look kinda pale.
Mitch—Yeah, women are usually better than guys. I see these big tough guys come in here and you start working on them and you have to stop before they pass out. It's not the pain; it's the idea of the thing. It's like getting a needle; it's all in the mind.

Other tattooists account for the difference of the responses of men and women to the pain of the process by saying that child-bearing makes women more accustomed to pain, women are more used to having their bodies altered and worked on, or that women who get tattooed have thought more about and are more committed to the process than are men (Tucker, 1976: 31).

How one responds to the pain and negative psychological features of tattooing significantly effects how one is evaluated by the tattooist. Tattooees who stoically accept the pain facilitate the tattoo process. Those who flinch or pull away from the needle present a problem. Tattooists respond to the clients who display little tolerance for the pain in various ways. Some speed up the tattoo application so as to dispense with the problematic client as quickly as possible. Others are more patient, stopping at frequent intervals to ask how the customer is doing and providing instructions on how to manage the pain.

> I've always tried to be open, friendly, reassuring . . . especially with a first-time tatty. You can usually sense when a person is extremely nervous or apprehensive. This is natural. In this business you get them day in and day out. I think you have to have a rather soothing approach. Sometimes it is necessary to go into a detailed explanation of what it is you are doing . . . which comforts them. (You tell them) that you are simply putting a little pigment barely under the skin. They know you do it with a needle and they think of that long sharp thing the doctor jams into your backside. You have to show them what it is about . . . show them how it works.

> [Quote from fieldnotes] a young man who brought in a stag's head insignia from a rifle manufacturer is getting the piece put on the left side of his back at the shoulder. I know from previous conversations that back work is somewhat more painful—reportedly because it is a boney area and the recipient is unable to watch the process—but this guy is making quite a show of the pain. As he continues to squirm about and complain (the tattooist) gets increasingly annoyed. (The tattooist) takes a deep breath and gives instruction. "Just let the pain pass through you—think of it that way. When you tense up you just make it worse. Feel the pain when you breath in and let it out of you when you breath out." A bit later the guy complains that it is taking a long time. With considerable show of exasperation (the tattooist) responds, "You would have been out of here a long time ago if we didn't have to keep dancing around like this."[7]

The client's choice of body location not only affects how much pain is experienced. The location's physical characteristics either aid or impede the tattooist's activities. Problematic clients choose body sites that present special technical problems, while "good" tattooees receive work on conventional locations that present minimal technical problems and are more easily manipulated by the tattooist. As described in the previous discussion of the tattooee's choice of location, body areas that are especially boney or fatty or that make it difficult for the tattooist to stretch the skin are particularly problematic.

Tattooists also experience problems when client's choose a site at or near their genital area. The male tattooists consistently expressed distaste for jobs that were not only technically difficult but which also required them to have contact with a male client's genitals.

[Quote from fieldnotes] Bob is doing a cartoon bird on the inside of a young man's leg. He is doing the coloring as I enter and I notice he is not being very careful and is not very concerned with keeping the pigment and blood from staining the client's underwear. After being bandaged and ritually given hygiene instructions, the kid pays $45 and leaves. When he is gone Bob heatedly states, "I hate to do shit like that!" I assume he is referring to the lame design the kid chose but I ask what he means. "All the time I was doing it I had to hold onto the guy's cock. It really creeps me out. The next time I have to do that I'm going to charge $100 minimum. I don't care what design they choose."

Someone called and wanted their wife's vulva tattooed like a butterfly. I didn't do that. I'm really not too tickled with the idea of someone I know nothing about coming in and I'll have to handle their genitals . . . man or woman. I'm really not into handling the genitals of strangers. I don't know where the hell they've been or what they got. They just want dumb things. These bikers will come in and they just want to make a joke out of their body. Like one guy wanted eyes tattooed on his buttocks. I don't need the money bad enough to get involved in stuff like that. Then you give them the price. They think that because it is a practical joke it shouldn't cost that much. But it's not a joke to me because I have to do it. Who wants to stare at somebody's ass.[8]

Following the application and bandaging of the tattoo the recipient is routinely instructed on how to care for the new acquisition during the healing process. Commonly, the client is given a set of written instructions (often printed on the back of the tattooist's business card) in addition to verbal advice on hygiene. While there is some variation in aftercare instructions, the extent of the client's adherence has significant impact on the quality of the final product. Recipients who disregard or haphazardly follow hygiene instructions are routinely defined as problematic by tattooists. Tattoos that become infected or heal improperly will typically loose color or have spotty outlines. Consequently, the "bad" client who fails to comply with aftercare instructions impedes the tattooist's work.

> [Quotes from fieldnotes] as I come in Ray is finishing up doing some work on a young latino guy who has a classic spread eagle design on his right forearm. Apparently this is the second time the guy has come in for a recoloring. As he finished the bandaging Ray gives the kid the standard card with aftercare instructions and says with some heat, "Now keep it clean. Leave the bandage on for 24 hours—that's this time tomorrow. Don't get it wet; don't put anything on it." "Not even Bacitracin?" the guy asks. "NOTHING! Don't fuck with it! When the scab comes off you can do anything you want with it, but I don't want to have to do this again."

Much of the legal and medical concern with tattooing centers on problems of infection or the communication of certain diseases due to improper or sloppy sterilization procedures (see Goldstein, 1979). Even if they themselves rigidly exercise hygienic caution, tattooists whose clients develop infections run the risk of encountering legal problems or coming into conflict with local health authorities. Further, clients who are dissatisfied with the quality of their tattoo—even if they, rather than the tattooist, are at fault— may not return for additional work or recommend the studio to associates who desire tattoos. Because satisfied clients are repeat customers and the major source of new business, most tattooists will recolor or reline a piece that is flawed due to improper healing. This service is typically provided free of charge and can affect the busy tattooist's profits. Touchup work is time-consuming but does not generate additional income for the tattooist.

The appropriate receiving demeanor, which greatly facilitates the tattooist's work and is expected and rigorously enforced by tattooists, requires the tattooee to remain essentially motionless and silent and to retain the posture determined by the tattooist. Because stillness is such a virtue, tattooists typically discourage the client from smoking, talking, or watching the tattoo process ("You don't need to see it. I need to see it. You'll have the rest of your life to look at it!"). The best recipients are quiet, relaxed, malleable, and commonly stare into the middle-distance during the process. Troublesome clients, on the other hand, jerk away, attempt to engage the tattooist in conversation, or try to observe the work. Without exception tattooists demand fairly rigid adherence to this key behavioral expectation. The quality of clients' tattoos is directly related to their maintaining this demeanor.

Intoxicated or drugged clients are most apt to display disrespect, overtly violate the norms of the tattoo setting, and fail to adhere to the appropriate receiving demeanor. As seen in the previous chapter, tattooists consistently see drunks as being their most problematic customers. Most tattooists typically refuse to work on people who are obviously intoxicated. Sometimes this general rule is applied flexibly, however, when the customer appears to be sufficiently straight that the tattooist believes that the customer is making a conscious decision, there is a chance to make a significant profit, and a reasonable degree of control can be maintained over the tattoo interaction. One interviewee, an apprentice in an established shop, described an encounter in which he effectively managed interaction with a drunken customer.

One time these two drunk guys come in. [Shop proprietor] don't like to tattoo drunks, but he figured one wanted a big tattoo and the other wanted a smaller tattoo. (He) could do the big one and I could do the small one. This guy wasn't really, like, fallin' down drunk—like "fuck-you-asshole" drunk. He wanted something and if he wasn't going to get it he would beg and plead until he got it. So, I was givin' him this tattoo and he was movin' around so I was just pullin' on his arm. I expected him to hit me for holdin' onto his arm too tight. But, fuck it, I can handle myself that way. After a while he mellowed out because he was gettin' his tattoo and he started to explain that he only had a few beers and he might be a little drunk but he really wanted this. He says, like, it doesn't really matter does it? I told him, like, the way I thought about it. "Would you like it if I were drunk doin' your tattoo? There are, like, two sides to it. Why can't I get drunk if you are going to get drunk to get it, you know?" He thought about it and I figured I got through to him. Like, I don't mind it if the person is a little high while you are doin' it. People come in on coke and they shake. I don't bother with them.

Service work is a commercial activity characterized by a certain degree of client control. Typically, the service customer partici-pates in the definition and production of the service rendered (Zeithaml, 1984). In most service delivery settings, however, the extent of the client's control and the interactive style he or she employs affect the way he or she is defined and dealt with by the worker. Good tattoo customers facilitate the tattooist's work and participate in a satisfying service negotiation when they are thoughtful and knowledgeable about design and location. They have a general sense of what they want but, at the same time, they are amenable to accepting the tattooist's suggestions, display respect for his or her expertise, and cede a certain amount of ar-tistic control. Here, for example, is one artist's description of a good client.

If someone comes in and they have thought about (what tattoo they want) and they have some artistic ideas and class, then I take care in working on them. A chick came in to get a tattoo yesterday. She was really serious about it. She brought in all of these books and we spent over an hour deciding on the design and where it should go. She was really artistic herself. She finally decided on a stylized Indian bird design on the side of her breast. That kind of person is really satisfying for me. It gives me a lot more freedom.

While tattooists—as demonstrated in the preceding quote—cling to some degree of artistic self-definition, most also acknowledge that they are involved in a profit-oriented business. Consequently, tattooees are evaluated on the basis of the potential (largely economic) gain they offer measured against the amount of time and energy they require. Recipients who shop for a tattoo on the basis of price or who enter the setting with no clear concept of what they want and are unable to find a suitable tattoo on the standard flash sheets are commonly defined by tattooists as interfering with their opportunity to make a profit and, thereby, being more trouble than they are worth. Here is a description of an interaction with a problematic client whose uncertainty interferes with the tattooist's interest in maximizing gain while limiting time and energy expended.

> [Quote from fieldnotes] the shop is unusually busy for a weekday afternoon. A husky biker type has been waiting for some custom work. He has a large skeleton with a gun on his left bicep and wants Fred to do some work around the existing piece. "I don't care what you do. Just make it look good. You know, maybe a cemetery or something like that." Fred grimaces as he takes out his hectograph pen and begins to draw tombstones on the guy's arm. He works slowly—drawing, making a face, spraying the arm with green soap and rubbing off the sketch, trying again. Finally, he puts down the pen and says, "Why don't you just look around at the flash and see if there is something you want. We're busy here and I can't take the time with this shit. If you want a tattoo I'll do it, but you come in here and don't know what you want and expect me to do it all for you. You don't want a piece, you just want to get tattooed."

There is a certain amount of danger associated with all businesses that operate on a cash basis. Tattooists, who commonly work at night, frequently have sizable quantities of cash on hand, and tend to encounter a rather rough clientele, are well aware of the risks they run. They typologize clients with regard to their apparent dangerousness. Like police officers (Wilson, 1970), prostitutes (Hirschi, 1962), cab drivers (Henslin, 1968), and other service workers who routinely find themselves in high-risk situations, tattooists are attentive to clientele who make furtive movements, ask unusual questions, or exhibit other forms of behavior that are out of the ordinary.

In recent years tattooists have also become more aware of the physical risks inherent in working in such close proximity to the blood of strangers. The possibility of contracting hepatitis, herpes, AIDS, and other diseases transmitted through contact with blood is of increasing concern to tattooists (cf. Becker et al., 1961: 317–318). Most will refuse to work on customers with rashes or obvious skin lesions. It has also becoming conventional for tattooists to wear surgical gloves while working on clients.[9]

Finally, tattooists typologize recipients on the basis of their moral acceptability. Objectionable personal hygiene, choice of overtly socially deviant symbols, and requests for tattoo placement on genital areas or highly visible and stigmatizing body sites are the major cues used by tattooists to make negative judgments about the values, lifestyles, and attitudes of certain clients. It is common for tattooists to refuse to service those individuals who overtly appear to violate standards of good taste and propriety.

Given the close physical contact involved in the delivery of the tattoo service, it is understandable that cleanliness is one of the most common characteristics tattooists mention when asked about the differential acceptability of clients. One of the more misanthropic interviewees put it this way:

> On the negative side of tattooing you have the scum element of the public; the ones that don't think it is necessary to bathe, or change their clothes, or whatever after work before coming to the tattoo shop. They think dirt is fine. There's the asshole biker types who thrive on dirt and want to talk about their motorcycle life constantly while you are tattooing them. These are the ones I dislike the most because I could care less about their motorcycles or their biker life-style. But when you work with the public you have to expect a certain percentage of geeks, filthy people, and scum in general because a large percentage of tattooing is done on this type of person.

As discussed in a preceding chapter, the tattoo recipient's choice of design and body location reveal much about his or her interests, values, and attitudes. Tattooee choice is, therefore, an important indicator tattooists use to evaluate the taste and moral acceptability of their clients. Under most circumstances, most reputable tattooists frown on and will refuse to tattoo those who request work on their faces or hands. The desire to make such a public display of the tattoo/stigma is seen as thoughtlessly deviant. Requests for tattoos on public skin are also routinely denied because facial or hand tattoos could potentially have negative impact on the tattooist's reputation and business while perpetuating the general public's antipathy for tattooing, tattoo workers, and tattoo art.

> This guy came in and wanted me to tattoo something on his forehead. I refused to do that. Large designs on people's faces. . . . I don't think the world is ready to accept that yet . . . unless you are a Maori chief. The society doesn't accept it and I don't want my name associated with something like that. Tattooing should not be flaunted in the face of the public. If someone wants "fuck you" written across his forehead I don't want it known that I was the one that did it. I wouldn't do it because I think it is a stupid thing to do. You have to draw the line somewhere.

The tattooist also uses the design a client requests as an indication of his or her taste and acceptability. As we have seen, most commercial tattooists do not feel that their economic circumstances allow them to refuse to apply the joking, cartoonish designs or the name/vow tattoos which continue to be conventional in street tattooing. Yet, they will often attempt to redirect the interests of those people whose hearts are set on getting Yosemite Sam making an obscene gesture, the pink panther smoking a joint, or the name of their current girlfriend or boyfriend permanently affixed to their bodies. Those clients who persist in desiring images of this kind are deemed to be tasteless, if not morally deficient, and are commonly objects of some derision. On the other hand, recipients who request extreme right wing symbols (for example, swastikas) or overtly anti-social phrases (for example, "fuck niggers") typically are deemed unacceptable and are routinely denied service. Like the tattooist's choice not to mark public skin, the decision to refuse morally repugnant and image-threatening requests of this kind is often based on his or her desire to avoid negative public reaction. The typical approach tattooists use in response to these customers is to point out the consequences of their choice and try to persuade them to reconsider.

> A young chick came in the other day and had "born to be wild" put on her wrist. She's going to have a hell of a time getting a job when they see that. (Are there any tattoos you won't do?) I don't refuse to do many things. I try to talk people out of some of the things they want. I don't do political stuff—swastikas and things like that. I don't want people thinking this is a place for a bunch of Nazis.

Another tattooist interpreted the customer's design choice as an indication of his or her intelligence.

> If someone comes in here with an arm full of garbage from swap meets and they think that it is really nice stuff and they can't see the difference between that and something that is really nice, then what's the sense. I'm not saying do something as shitty as what they got. I just do the outline, shade it, color it solid. Whereas maybe with someone else I would get into putting in highlights, feather in the colors. But this guy, fuck it, just color it in solid. They're happy. It's bright, solid. It's not shitty if it is done technically right. Now someone who really appreciates tattooing and has got a lot of nice work . . . I'll do water shading and white highlights, put white instead of just leaving skin. On the leaf I'll make the outer edges dark green to light green to yellow green and white highlights. I won't do that on some bozo. But they won't get shitty work in the sense that I got bad needles and won't stop to change them. No one gets the bum's rush. You can usually assess someone's intelligence. If at age thirty they want a pink panther smoking a joint with a can of beer in the other hand then the guy's kind of a bozo.

Tattooists' definitions of their clients and the resultant relationships are, to a major degree, based on their design and location choices, their physical condition and demeanor, their apparent dangerousness, and their willingness to accede to the tattooist's attempts to control the tattoo event. The tattoo client also has a vested interest in fostering a positive and conflict-free relationship with the tattooist. Within the immediate tattoo setting the recipient's experience will be more intrinsically rewarding and less anxiety-producing if he or she attends to the cues by which the service provider communicates the normative expectations that constrain the service interaction. In turn, the care exercised by the tattooist in the service delivery process and the final outcome of the transaction are, to a large measure, dependent on the quality of the relationship which develops.

> I can assess people when they come in the door and I know what it is going to take to please that person and who not to waste the effort on. I don't mean not do a good job on them, cheat them. It's always going to be done properly in here— they're going to get what they see on the picture. Someone who comes with Yosemite Sam over here and down here they got the Tasmanian Devil throwing the finger or something and they want a Donald Duck over here and they think these crudely done things are great . . . I realize that I don't have to bend over backwards for this guy. I used to try to go overboard for everybody and they didn't really appreciate it. There's a difference between doing it and putting your heart into it. It's going to always be technically right. I'm not going to put any extra effort into something or get into custom free-hand like stuff on someone who I don't have the rapport with and I can't spend that time with.

CONCLUSION

Conflict is an everpresent possibility in the service delivery setting of the tattoo studio. Clients typically are unfamiliar with the situation, unknowledgeable about the normative constraints to which they are expected to conform, and fearful of the pain of the tattoo process. Within this context of risk—physiological, financial, temporal, and social—tattooees make choices of design and location based on intrapersonal, aesthetic, and socially symbolic criteria that they have often only vaguely examined and defined. In order to increase their store of information and reduce purchase risk, they limit the size and price of the tattoo, spend time watching and interacting with the tattooist, and commonly enter the tattoo establishment in the company of supportive associates. Should they come to regret the consequences of their tattoo purchase, tattooees can simply chalk it up to experience or they may deal more directly with the negative outcome by having the offending product removed, covered, or redone.

Concerned with minimizing conflict while maximizing economic and interpersonal rewards, the tattooist has a clear interest in understanding the client and channeling his or her intentions and behavior. The tattooist/service worker's understanding of and consequent interaction with the client are facilitated by the use of a basic typological system, which allows the differentiation between good and bad recipients. Customers are categorized, and interactional strategies are employed based on the tattooist's evaluation of whether or not the client will facilitate the tattooist's work, cede appropriate control, provide sufficient gain for the time and energy expended, present danger, and/or demonstrate an acceptable level of taste and morality. By means of overt instruction and symbolic representation of competence, the tattooist communicates behavioral expectations and exercises control over the service delivery interaction. The quality of this emergent relationship has considerable impact on the experience of both the tattooist and his or her customer. The smoother and more coordinated the commercial "dance" of the tattoo event, the greater the likelihood that the tattooee will receive a service/product that will meet his or her defined needs and not be a significant source of remorse. In turn, easy and predictable interaction with tattooees improves tattooists' ongoing occupational experience, maximizes their ability to reap financial gain, and reinforces their positive self-evaluations as creative workers providing a valued and technically proficient aesthetic product.

Chapter 5

Conclusion: Tattooing and the Social Definition of Art

 In addition to their overt functions—keeping us warm, holding liquids, brightening our living spaces, firing projectiles, and so forth—all of the products conceived, created, distributed, obtained, consumed, and displayed carry symbolic meaning. Most importantly, they hold information about how we define ourselves (Solomon, 1983), how we want those with whom we interact to identify us (Csikszentmihalyi and Rochberg-Halton, 1981), and the scope and intensity of our associations with others (Douglas and Isherwood, 1979).

The social world of tattooing centers around the production of a unique cultural artifact. As highly symbolic objects produced within the context of commercial interactions, tattoos are of special interest. The historical path by which tattooing entered western society and came to be incorporated as a cultural practice imbued it with intense and widely held deviant associations. As we have seen, the deviant character of tattooing has shaped, and continues to constrain, the occupational enterprise of tattooing, the collective activity of the purchase process, the identity and self-definition of tattoo consumers, the style of the product, and the organization of the social world surrounding the phenomenon.

In addition to its association with deviance, tattooing is sociologically significant because it exhibits many of the features that characterize various other cultural practices conventionally regarded as "artistic" and that result in the creation of products customarily awarded the honorific title of "art" (Dickie, 1971). The differentiation between art and non-art is socially constructed and, therefore, subject to significant change over time. This change, like social change more generally, is typically brought about through the conscious, cooperative, and goal-directed efforts of social actors who have a vested interest in having their activities defined as artistic and their product legitimated as art. To the extent that they are successful, they gain status, their occupational lives may be more satisfying, their chances of achieving significant financial reward are enhanced, and the pressures exerted by agents of social control are reduced or deflected (DiMaggio, 1987; Wolff, 1983).

The boundaries of the contemporary tattoo production world rub against those of the larger, conventionally legitimated art world. Key actors in the former are increasingly engaged in concerted efforts to broach these boundaries, thereby achieving the valued redefinition of tattooing as art and the related advantages, which will follow. This endeavor is proceeding in spite of internal resistance from tattooists who are satisfied with the current commercial status quo and external opposition by agents of the conventional art world who refuse to acknowledge the legitimacy claims of tattooing. Consequently, an examination of the tattoo world can help to identify those factors that impede the incorporation of a cultural production activity into the accepted repertoire of artistry or, on the other hand, increase the likelihood that the practice and product will be socially sanctioned as "real" art. This is the issue I will explore in these concluding paragraphs.

FACTORS AFFECTING ARTISTIC DEFINITION

Art exists in much more than "the eye of the beholder." Like deviance (Becker, 1963; Schur, 1971), objects that are identified as art and activities that are deemed artistic are labeled as such through the conflictual, cooperative, and negotiative process of social interaction. Having one's activities socially certified as "artistic," the outcomes of those activities defined as "art," and the consumption of the products regarded as "art collection," hold significant advantages for all those involved. Direct participation in the institutional networks of the art world confers status, affords significant control over occupational activities, promotes an enhanced definition of self, and offers the potential of increased economic gain. Since "anything whatever may become art" (Dickie, 1971: 107; 1974: 49–50), the key question around which an institutional theory of art revolves is: What factors increase the likelihood that an activity or object will be consensually labeled as art and, conversely, what characteristics impede this process of artistic definition?

Art works exist within an historical and cross-cultural context (Dickie, 1971: 101). Creative practices that have identifiable *historical and cultural roots*—which can be connected to a tradition that notes stylistic precedents, charts the development of defined value and identifies exemplary practitioners and artifacts—are excellent candidates for artistic legitimation. As Janson (1964: 15) observes:

> Every work of art occupies its own specific place . . . which we call *tradition*. Without tradition—the word means "that which has been handed down to us"—no originality would be possible; it provides, as it were, the firm platform from which the artist makes his leap of the imagination. The place where he lands will then become part of the web and serve as a point of departure for further leaps. . . . Tradition is the framework within which we inevitably form our opinions of works of art and assess their degree of originality (cf., Mukerji, 1978: 351; Manfredi, 1982: 120–148).

On the other hand, production activities that cannot be connected to historical or cultural precedent or that have little or no demonstrable foundation in accepted theoretical or technical development are unlikely to achieve institutional certification.

Within the conventional boundaries imposed by historical and cultural tradition, objects that are unique, original, and, consequently, scarce and expensive are prime candidates for artistic legitimation. *Originality* is the conventional hallmark of artistry (Janson, 1964: 12; Dickie, 1974: 47–48). Cultural items that are mechanically reproduced, widely available, inexpensive, and overtly designed as commodities for mass consumption are, by definition, excluded from the category of "real" art. While there is often an interesting cross-fertilizing connection between popular cultural materials and so-called "high" art (see Crane, 1987; Nye, 1972; Gans, 1974; Browne, 1983; Hirschman, 1981), the overt consumer focus and highly formulaic character of popular culture makes these materials unlikely candidates for artistic certification. Popular cultural themes and objects intrude upon the art world only when they are removed from their intended commercial context and used as icons by "acknowledged" artists.

The chances that products of certain activities will be labeled as art are further enhanced if the materials display attributes that have come to be conventionally defined as indicating *aesthetic worth*. In general, this means that the candidate object has no overt utilitarian purpose and is presented as a focus of attention simply for the sake of the pleasurable experience derived from that attention (see Holbrook and Moore, 1981; Dickie, 1971; Wallendorf et al., 1981; Becker, 1982: 131–145).

The apparent amount of labor and *technical skill* that went into the creation of the object is related to the defined aesthetic value of that object (Mukerji, 1978: 352). If anyone, no matter what their level of ability and experience, can make something in a relatively brief period of time, it is less likely that it will be labeled with the honorific title of art than if the object overtly exhibits skill, knowledge, and a degree of toil. Articles that do not represent any particular amount of skilled labor; are overtly sloppy, ill-conceived, or ugly; and are mechanically reproduced as commodities for mass consumption rather than as a source of aesthetic enjoyment suffer a severe definitional handicap.

A product's chances of being defined as art are also related to the kinds of *materials employed and the procedures creators pursue* in the course of the production process. Objects made from conventional materials such as paint, canvas, marble, or clay through the conventional use of conventional equipment—brushes, pens, pottery wheels, and so forth—enjoy legitimational advantages. When, however, products are made through the use of unconventional resources and procedures, chances of institutional acceptance are greatly reduced (see Becker, 1982: 57–59; cf. Lyon, 1974).

The amount of *serious, typically academic, attention* devoted to an object or activity also affects its chances of artistic certification. Products and production enterprises derive importance from being the focus of abstracted, critical, theoretically oriented discussion. Universities are major sources of institutional legitimation. When students in programs specifically devoted to art learn about the historical context in which a productive activity has arisen and learn from acknowledged practitioners how to engage in that activity themselves, the practice must be artistic and the product must be art (see Manfredi, 1982: 76–85; Crane, 1987: 9–11). On the other hand, when academicians and certified art critics ridicule or, worse yet, totally ignore a body of objects, it is unlikely that those objects will achieve artistic legitimacy. Practices that are easily mastered by the common person or that result in products that are not regarded as being worthy of serious theoretical analysis—that is, which can be "understood" without "explanation" by expert critics—are, at best, weak candidates for recognition by the conventional art world.

Within the organizational structure surrounding any mode of cultural production, primary control of production and the product is derived from control over the distribution apparatus (Hirsch, 1972; Monaco, 1978). Consequently, *the physical setting in which objects are presented for (aesthetic) appreciation or sale* is an important factor in their institutional authentication. Gallery owners and museum directors act as key gatekeepers in the art world and *art* museums or *art* galleries contain objects which are, by definition, art (Becker, 1982: 93–130; Mukerji, 1978: 360; Pellegrini, 1966: 301–303; Dickie, 1971: 102–103; Crane, 1987: 110–136). If the results of a specific activity are ignored or disdained by the controllers of legitimating settings—either because they are regarded as being unworthy or because they are so unconventional in scale (for example, earthworks) or organization (for example, conceptual art) that they present logistic problems within the setting—the products are handicapped in their definitional career.

Presentation in museums or galleries does more for classes of objects than simply certifying them as art; it also imbues objects and activities with commercial worth. Art is a commodity acquired for its *investment value* as well as it aesthetic characteristics and its status symbolizing functions (Mukerji, 1978: 351; Pellegrini, 1966: 299, 308–309). As Crane (1987: 112) observes in her discussion of avant-garde art:

> While in a sense all the objects are alike (for example, paintings are pieces of canvas with paint or other substances spread over them), enormous differences in price exist. Value is not

attributed to these objects on the basis of production costs, as in other markets, and, only to a small extent, on the basis of the costs of merchandising them. Instead, value is attributed entirely on the basis of evaluations of quality by experts, including critics, museum curators, and, to some extent, eminent collectors.

Therefore, if something is sold at a high cost to collectors who purchase the item with the anticipation that it will appreciate in value over time, that object has passed through the initial stages of artistic definition and has a good chance of continuing to be regarded as art. If, on the other hand, the article is not consensually defined as carrying significant investment value and/or due to its physical characteristics is difficult or impossible to collect and *pass on* to another owner, it is not a good candidate for artistic legitimation.

The *status characteristics of producers* are also important factors that contribute to or impede the movement of an object or activity into the category of art. "Fine" (elite, conventional, studio) art is *creator oriented* (Lewis, 1972: 20)—art is what (certified) artists create and their productive endeavors are the dominant focus of critical attention. Cultural artifacts purposefully produced by "professional" artists—in the sense that artistic production is their major source of income (Manfredi, 1982: 63–65) and self-identification (Becker, 1982: 95–99)—who have gained some degree of reputation in the art world are likely to be defined as "authentic" art (Mukerji, 1978: 356). However, the more anonymous the creator and the lower his or her social status, the lesser the likelihood that the result of his or her creative undertakings will be certified as art by representatives of the conventional art world and presented as a viable candidate for appreciation.[1]

Similarly, the *social status and class position of those who collect, consume, criticize, or otherwise attend to the cultural artifact* promotes or impedes the process of artistic definition.[2] If those who enjoy a high degree of social repute and hold positions of power (academics, the wealthy, acknowledged art critics, "cultured" members of society, and so forth) discuss an object, collect it, present it in settings they control, offer learned critiques of it, and give money to its creators, then it is likely to be consensually regarded as art (see Peterson, 1983; Bronner, 1986: 146–148). The appreciation of members of upper-class "taste publics" (Gans, 1974; Lewis, 1981) is, in short, a source of "cultural capital" (DiMaggio, 1987). Value and esteem are afforded on the assumption that those in positions of power are especially qualified to separate the artistic wheat from the base cultural chaff and to determine a product's artistic merit. In contrast, objects and activities (for example, bowling balls, country music, break-dancing, professional wrestling, tattoos) that are valued and consumed by members of the "inferior" classes or by those in stigmatized social networks have little chance of acquiring the honorific artistic designation.[3]

Finally, since whether or not something comes to be regarded as art is, to a major degree, dependent on whether it is *promoted* as art and how those promotional activities proceed (see Lewis, 1986), concerted social action plays a considerable part in increasing or reducing an object's chances of artistic legitimation. When production personnel, their enterprises, and the resultant product are *sponsored by an organized social group* that possesses significant promotional resources, the chances that the product will be defined as art and the producers defined as artists are significantly enhanced. Lack of an organized base of support and formalized promotional structure impedes the process of artistic legitimation. An even greater impediment to a creative practice's artistic candidacy is generated when organized forces come to be marshalled *against* that activity. Artistic definition is especially difficult to achieve if governmental agencies regard the product or the production process as presenting a moral or physical danger and take legal steps to regulate it or prohibit it entirely (Becker, 1982: 176–191) (see Figure 4 for a summary presentation of these points).[4]

THE ARTISTIC REDEFINITION OF TATTOOING

Given these factors that increase or reduce the likelihood a product will be defined as art, the production process defined as artistic, and the producer ascribed the honorific title of artist,

Figure 4. Factors Affecting a Product's Definition as Art

Promoting Characteristics	Impeding Characteristics
A. Product Features	
1. Historical or cross-cultural connection to creative practices	Lack of historical or cultural antecedents
2. Uniqueness	Mass production
3. Overt display of aesthetic characteristics, evidence of technical skill	Lack of aesthetic content, little evidence of creator talent
4. Collectibility	Lack of "artifactuality," no defined investment value
5. Use of conventional materials	Use of unconventional resources
B. Production Features	
1. Producer has artistic reputation and elite class characteristics	Producer is anonymous, lacks social status
2. Organizational promotion	No organizational support, organized constraint on production or organized presentation as "non-art"
3. Employing conventional production process	Engaging in unconventional production activities
C. Art World Response	
1. Focus of academic discussion and critical attention	Product deemed unworthy of legitimating attention
2. Display in museum and gallery settings	Lack of museum display or gallery marketing
3. Purchase/collection by elite, affluent consumers	Consumers primarily drawn from low status, socially disvalued groups

what are the chances that tattooing will be incorporated as an artistic genre within the institutional context of the conventional art world? Tattooing is a particularly interesting phenomenon in this regard because, unlike the process whereby craft activities (cf. Kealy, 1979; Neapolitan, 1986; Christopherson, 1974) or folk products (cf. Vlach and Bronner, 1986; Fried and Fried, 1978) have gained artistic legitimacy, tattooing must first be separated from its deviant associations before it can hope to be included in the repertoire of art forms.[5] As is seen in those situations in which deviant activities and marginal actors have attempted to gain public recognition and acceptance, the promotional efforts of organized groups are of key importance.

In general, deviant organizations work to reeducate the public by recasting the behavior as socially nonthreatening—or even beneficial—and emphasizing the normative conformity commonly displayed by most of those who have previously been stigmatized and subjected to social reaction (see, Sagarin, 1979; Trice and Roman, 1979). Like groups representing homosexuals, the mentally disordered, alcoholics, and other disvalued social actors, formal organizations such as the National Tattoo Association and similar alliances are actively involved in redefining tattooing. Information directed at the general public by tattooing organizations and tattooists who have a vested interest in expanding the artistic reputation of tattooing emphasizes conventionally accepted values. Promotional materials refer to tattoo *studios* and tattoo *art*, display exemplary work exhibiting aesthetic content and technical skill, stress the historical and cultural roots of contemporary tattooing (especially classical Japanese work), and emphasize the academic training and conventional artistic experience of key practitioners (see, for example, Ward, 1986; Tucker, 1976, 1981; Green, 1982; *The New Yorker*, February 9, 1987, pp. 29–31). In addition, tattoo organizations take steps to enforce and promote public knowledge of normative conformity within the tattoo community. Practitioners are actively encouraged to "work clean," present and maintain a neat and professional work setting, avoid tattooing minors or those who are intoxicated, decline client requests for marking public skin or inscribing overtly obscene or racist images, and to otherwise avoid practices that would perpetuate the negative reputation of tattooing and tattooists. To the extent that these organizational and individual actors are successful in freeing tattooing from its disreputable background and public image, the process of artistic definition can progress more smoothly and result in at least some degree of institutional acceptance.

In addition to its symbolic connection to deviant social groups, the definition of tattooing as a legitimate art form is impeded by its limited "artifactuality" (Dickie, 1974: 22–27). Separating the tattoo from the body of the original purchaser in order to resell it to another owner is not, for all practical purposes, a reasonable or particularly appealing alternative. Consequently, although tattooing is a fairly expensive creative service, with collectors of large, custom designed pieces spending thousands of dollars for their work, tattoo art is lacking in direct investment value.[6]

Tattooing also employs a unique production process and unconventional material resources—a needle or group of needles is used to inject pigment under the recipient's skin. A creative practice that requires collectors to experience considerable pain and lose blood and that results in the permanent alteration of their bodies presents a significant violation of artistic convention. These "distasteful" attributes reduce the chances of tattooing's certification as an accepted mode of artistic production.

The inability to separate the tattoo object from its owner in order to display or resell it and the physical trauma involved in the production activity violate important conventions in the institutional art world. However, other creative practices that result in the production of objects with similar limitations *have* achieved artistic acceptance. Ballet and other forms of strenuous performance typically entail considerable pain and result in the loss of body fluids. The short, but controversial, history of the institutional acceptance of Conceptual Art provides another instructive example. Like tattooing, Conceptual Art violated conventions of artifactuality and, as a consequence, resulted in works which were impossible to collect directly or market as artistic commodities. As a commercial alternative, documents representing the artist's ideas and the operationalization of those ideas were produced and sold to collectors.

Works of Idea Art frequently did not actually exist as objects. Rather, they remained ideas; frequently, what did exist was only some kind of documentation referring to the concept. . . . Initially, it appeared that this new art movement rejected the usual commercial, marketplace aspects of artmaking. Indeed, it was difficult to understand how such Conceptual works could be bought or sold; nor could they be "collected" in the usual sense (Battcock, 1973: 1).

Despite its overt symbolic rejection of the consumer aspects of contemporary art, Conceptual Art did eventually gain (limited) acceptance as a fine art genre. To a large degree the institutionalization of Idea Art was promoted by the pre-existing artistic reputations of its major creators. Even when they created unconventional, uncollectible, nonobjectifiable products, the things that legitimated artists did in the name of art were labeled as art and accepted as such by the established art world—though not without considerable conflict (see Battcock, 1973; Meyer, 1972; Rosenberg, 1972: 28–38).

Despite the inherent problems in separating the tattoo artifact from its collector, tattooing does display the other characteristics that increase the chances of artistic legitimation. As noted earlier, presentation in the conventional settings in which art is appreciated and purchased is a key factor leading to institutional redefinition. Since the mid-1970s, tattoo art has come to enjoy this type of legitimating exposure with increased frequency. While gallery and museum shows of tattooing sometimes contain the art "in the flesh," it is more common for exhibits to emphasize photographic representations of exemplary work and other documents and objects associated with the creative practice, such as design sheets and ornately carved hand implements.[7]

In addition to its exposure in museums and galleries, tattooing is coming increasingly to be the focus of academic discussion. A major legitimating event took place in 1983 when the art history department and the Museum of Cultural History at UCLA sponsored an "Art of the Body" symposium at which anthropologists, art historians, dermatologists, sociologists, and various other participants with conventional academic credentials met to present papers on tattooing and other modes of decorative body alteration (see the papers in Rubin, 1988). Analyses of tattooing also have been published in established art journals (see Tucker, 1981; Sanders, 1986). These articles typically focus on exemplary practitioners and emphasize their technical skill, innovative styles, and experience with other, more conventionally accepted, artistic media.

The recent spate of expensive "coffee-table" books presenting photographs of some of the most striking examples of contemporary western and Japanese tattooing provides another outlet for serious critical discussions. The written material in these works is, for the most part, produced by authors with academic credentials and tends to focus on the historical, anthropological, and aesthetic context of the displayed work (see Wroblewski, 1987; Rondinella, 1985; Fellman, 1986; Richter, 1985). Finally, a few specialized tattoo journals have appeared in recent years that employ the writing style favored by academics and contain articles by social scientists, physicians, folklorists, and influential tattoo artists. *Tattootime, The Tattoo Historian*, and *The Tattoo Advocate* are examples of this type of serious tattoo publication.

A primary thrust of much of the legitimating discussion found in general interest magazines, academic publications, catalogues accompanying tattoo exhibitions, and published materials directed at members of the tattoo community is on the changing characteristics of the new tattooee. The new tattoo client is consistently presented as being drawn from the middle and upper-middle class—generally affluent, well educated, and involved in professional and managerial occupations (see, for example, Green, 1982; Tucker, 1976). While this focus on the changing social background of the contemporary tattoo consumer is somewhat overblown and often part of a more-or-less consciously constructed promotional strategy, it does reflect a general trend that has been accelerating for almost two decades. A significant amount of diffusion of interest in and purchasing of tattooing is occurring across class lines. The cooptive assimilation by elites of cultural phenomena such as jazz (Bjorn, 1981) and film (Mukerji, 1978) that were originally enjoyed by low status groups resulted in the artistic redefinition of those cultural materials. To the extent that a similar process of diffusion continues, gains momentum, and draws further attention, the likelihood that tattooing will achieve some measure of legitimacy as an artistic phenomenon appears rather good (see DiMaggio, 1987: 447–448). Further, as major tattooists continue to explore new forms of stylistic innovation—especially as they incorporate styles that have flourished in the conventional art world (for example, primitivism, photo-realism, abstraction, minimalism)—influential representatives of the art establishment can be expected to pay more sympathetic attention, thereby increasing the prospect of redefinition and artistic legitimation (DiMaggio, 1987: 449, 452).

The recent history of graffiti-as-art offers a particularly relevant example. In the 1970s graffiti made a minor incursion into the established fine art world. Like tattooing, graffiti is a mode of cultural production connected to marginal and disvalued social groups—principally poor, minority, urban males. Further, it functions, like tattooing, as a "disenfranchised gesture" symbolizing territorial boundaries, group membership, personal identity, and protest against the control exercised by the social establishment (Klofas and Cutshall, 1985; Castleman, 1982: 26–31; Pearlstein, 1978). Largely through the efforts of sympathetic academics, graffiti "writers" in New York were brought together to form organizations such as the United Graffiti Artists (UGA) and the Nation of Graffiti Artists (NOGA) (Castleman, 1982: 117–133). In turn, these academically connected sponsors used their establishment associations to move the work of organization members off the streets and into legitimating academic, marketing, and display settings.[8]

Drawn by the nascent artistic legitimation of graffiti, the media, which previously had strongly condemned the practice as criminal vandalism, began to praise graffiti for its vitality and exuberance.[9] Although intense social control activities by governmental organizations effectively truncated the creative work done by the original artists in the original public environments (see Castleman, 1982: 134–175), established artists enthusiastically coopted the themes and stylistic features of graffiti. In the late 1970s curator Rolando Castellon mounted an exhibit entitled

"The Aesthetics of Graffiti" at the San Francisco Museum of Modern Art. The show contained both graffiti-influenced work by established artists and art-photographic documents of "real" graffiti. In his introduction to the exhibit's catalogue, Castellon called attention to the process of cultural imperialism whereby disvalued forms of cultural production are coopted, sanitized, and transformed into art.

> In general, this exhibition defines two main categories of graffiti. First, there are traditional examples which are found on streets, buildings, doorways, hallways and sidewalks. By taking these graffiti out of their normal environment, it is hoped that a new appreciation for their visual and aesthetic qualities can be achieved. Secondly, there is graffiti art, an increasingly thriving and richly varied mode which draws emotionally, intellectually and/or visually from the street graffiti of the everyday world. *Through the process of conscious integration by studio artists, graffiti thus become officially sanctioned "fine art"* (emphasis added, San Francisco Museum of Modern Art, 1978: 1).[10]

It is imminently reasonable to anticipate that contemporary tattooing, with its demonstration of technical skill, consistent aesthetic appeal, organizational promotion, changing audience, gallery and museum exposure, and increasing academic and critical attention, will be at least as successful as was graffiti in achieving the status of a minor art form and acting as a source of stylistic innovation in established artistic genres. However, as we have seen, not all tattooists are in favor of disrupting the commercial status quo nor are all tattoo enthusiasts interested in seeing tattooing accepted within conventional social circles. What is lost when a deviant cultural activity is coopted by agents of the institutional art world and gains—at least to some degree—artistic legitimacy?

The *power* of tattoo, like that of street graffiti, is primarily derived from its ability to outrage members of conventional society. For tattoo devotees much of the appeal of tattooing comes from its symbolic demonstration of co-membership in a unique and somewhat alienated cultural group (see DiMaggio, 1987: 443; Laba, 1986). The central issue to be confronted by key members of the tattoo community is whether the advantages that originate from producing and consuming yet another mode of establishment cultural capital outweigh the intense pleasures of exclusionary identification with the deviant social group symbolized by the tattoo mark. In the final accounting, an enlarged market, increased income, decreased stigmatization, and artistic status can be very costly when purchased from those who control the social resources. Imperialism rarely works out well for those who are subjected to it.

Epilogue 2008:
Body Modification
Then and Now

CLINTON R. SANDERS with D. ANGUS VAIL

The only thing about social relationships, social structures, and other elements of social life that doesn't change is that they are constantly changing. The perpetual emergence of social worlds is the rule rather than the exception and the worlds that *Customizing the Body* addressed in the late 1980s—the academic world of ethnographers, the intellectual world of those concerned with a sociology of the body and its modification, and the tattoo world—have been especially active sites of social change, development, and evolution.

Good ethnography tends to transcend many of the changes in the worlds it describes because it explains the processes through which people produce those worlds, not the outcome of those processes. From this perspective, *Customizing the Body* is not specifically a book about tattooing. It is a book about how people experience, respond to, and enact definitions of the kinds of activities that are socially acceptable or unacceptable. It is a book about how people produce and define art. It is a book about how peoples' relationships are characterized by both conflict and cooperation and how their identities, both purposively chosen and involuntarily assigned, are shaped by their physical appearance. These processes do not change, even if their manifestations might.

Tattoos may look different today than they did in the late 1980s, but people still have to decide whether they think tattoos are tacky, sleazy, dangerous, or fun, and, more importantly, they still have to decide whether being tacky, sleazy, dangerous, or fun are characteristics they want to embody and display. Although sociologists and other social scientists disagree about many matters, all would likely agree that one's appearance has significant impact on how he or she gets along with others. Ethnographers also may disagree about techniques and writing styles, but all responsible ethnographers would agree that the goal should be to come as close as possible to creating a rich description of specific social worlds and faithfully representing the experiences of people who live within them.

While the description of the world of tattooing and the experiences of the people inhabiting it offered in the first edition of *Customizing the Body* continues to be of considerable value, significant changes have occurred. Some of these changes have happened independently of the book, some of them have happened because of it, and some have built on its foundation. In this new Epilogue, we discuss recent developments in the tattoo world and how changes in technology and the people and institutions that make up this world have shaped these developments. We also examine other forms of body alteration that have emerged as tattooing has moved from being a disvalued practice to being part of the popular cultural world of fads and fashions. As predicted in the first edition, this transition has caused tattooing to lose its power as a "mark of disaffiliation." Consequently, those who want to demonstrate their marginality or uniqueness must find different ways of generating "conspicuous outrage" among members of conventional society. New modes of body modification have arisen out the desire of some to symbolize this disaffection and mark their membership in a distinctive social group.

We also discuss the established scholarship on tattooing that has emerged in the past fifteen years or so. These works are central to the burgeoning literature in the sociology of the body, and it can be argued that the first edition of *Customizing the Body* provided an important part of the foundation upon which this literature is grounded.

TATTOOING TODAY

The late 1980s was an exciting time in the tattoo world. The full-body aesthetic typified by Japanese tattooing was established in the United States, and the number of skilled artists capable of working in that scale was increasing rapidly. Magazines devoted to tattooing were becoming easily available, and they were produced by people who wanted to show more than chopped motor-cycles and the bodily decorations of the people who rode them. Tattoo conventions were becoming more common, and they were sponsored by organizations other than National Tattoo Association. There were more art school-trained tattooists and they were taking tattooing in directions not considered possible even ten years earlier.

It is unclear whether we are still in the tattoo renaissance that emerged in the 1960s, but there is no question that tattooing is still a vibrant art form, and its technical merits and thematic repertoire continue to expand exponentially. When *Customizing the Body* was first published, many would have maintained that there were only a handful of tattoo artists worthy of that title east of California. But now it is hard to find a city or town that does not have at least one tattoo artist who is technically skilled and capable of working in a variety of styles. Tattoo clients across the country expect artists to have at least rudimentary ability to create tribal, traditional Americana, Celtic, biomechanical, fine line, and Japanese style works, and many seek rather extensive coverage, from "sleeves" and "backpieces" to full body suits.

Many of the stylistic changes in tattoo art that have come about in the last fifteen years are the result of changes in the tools of the tattoo trade, especially the pigments available and needle configurations used to inscribe the designs. Until the mid-1970s, tattooers had an available pallet of only five colored inks (red, blue, black, brown, and yellow). The invention of a purple pigment in the mid-1970s was revolutionary, and some maintain that this was partly responsible for the solidification and expansion of the tattoo renaissance that had emerged some ten years earlier. However, it was not until the mid-1990s that the available pallet genuinely opened up—today, there are literally hundreds of colors available from established pigment manufacturers. The expanded availability of tattoo inks allowed artists to work in styles and create images that were not previously possible.

As an illustration, one dramatic stylistic movement began as a revolutionary departure from the abstract psychedelia practiced by San Francisco's Bill Salmon and his imitators. This style, known colloquially as "the French School," is attributed to the early pioneering work done in the 1990s by the European artists Tin Tin and Stephane Chaudesaigues. The absence of outlines and the emphasis on intense colors that characterize this style allow for soft transitions in the designs so that the artist can create tattoos that display photo-realistic precision and simulate watercolor painting. Other styles have emerged from this style, such as the largely black and grey "Dark Art" associated with New York artist Paul Booth and the colorful biomechanical work pioneered by Guy Aitchison. (For more about these and other artists and to view examples of their work, see the list of Selected Tattoo Artist Websites at the back of this book.)

Less obviously influenced by the French School, but still owing a substantial debt to the increased pallet, is the so-called "New Skool" of tattooing, pioneered by Grime and other members of the New Skool Tattoo Collective in California. New Skool tattooing reflects the traditional Americana aesthetic of heavy, bold outlines and flat, dense colors but is composed of images that are typically bizarre, ironic, and uniquely individual (see Irwin, 2001, 2003).

The other major stylistic movements in tattooing follow fairly loosely in the footsteps of Japanese tattoo masters like Horiyoshi I, II, and III, Horitoshi, Horihide, and others. Often called "Neo-Japanese" or "Contemporary Japanese" (or even "American Japanese"), this style focuses on large-scale work that is more subtle and precise than traditional Japanese tattooing.

Changes in needle configurations are an important technological component in Neo-Japanese tattooing and other contemporary styles. Swiss artist Filip Leu is known for a variety of artistic innovations, but perhaps his most enduring contribution to tattooing is his pioneering work with large "magnum" needles. Leu began experimenting with 25-, 35-, and 45-point magnums in the early 2000s because he was dissatisfied with the amount of space he could cover with more traditional 7-, 9-, or 11-point configurations. Moving to the larger format required fashioning new needle tubes that could accommodate the substantially larger needle groups (a 45 magnum is about an inch wide), as well as adjusting the voltage at which his machines ran. The end result, however, was revolutionary for tattoo artists working in large scale since it allowed the artist to complete a full backpiece in as little as 12 hours, with less damage to the skin and substantially less pain for the client.

While learning to tattoo with the large magnum needles required a bit of practice, these configurations have made large-scale work easier to accomplish, easier to endure, and even less expensive, as artists who are in high demand often charge by the hour. The major pioneers in this style of tattooing are Filip Leu in Lausanne, Switzerland; Mick Tattoo in Zurich, Switzerland; Luke Atkinson in Stuttgart, Germany; and Tin Tin in Paris.

As these movements have developed along parallel lines, their eventual merger was almost inevitable. This merger is currently happening in American custom tattooing where a variety of artists are now using the magnums to create works in the large scale associated with Japanese work that incorporate decidedly American imagery such as scenes from American horror movies and the fantasy paintings of Frank Frazetta. As often happens with new movements in tattoo art, some are wondering how well the boldness of the colors and subtlety of the designs will hold up over time.

The tattoo world is constituted by more than practitioners, equipment, and styles. Tattoo clients are an essential component. The tattooists presented in the first edition of *Customizing the Body* spoke enthusiastically about the diffusion of tattooing and the increasing diversity of their clientele. Recent discussions (for example, Kang and Jones, 2007) continue to stress that doctors, lawyers, priests, housewives, and university professors are acquiring tattoos. While the increased popularity of tattooing is clear, the decreased stigma associated with wearing a tattoo has meant that people are more willing to display their tattoos in public. This era, then, is marked as much by the increased visibility of tattoos, as by their increased prevalence.

Tattoo Collectors

The most striking change in how people acquire and wear tattoos comes from the confluence of increased artistic standards and abilities among tattooers and tattoo artists, increased prevalence of tattoo shops and studios, and the decreased intensity of the stigma associated with visible tattoos. These changes are seen in the growing number of "collectors" in the tattoo world. While it is difficult to say with any precision how much more prevalent collectors now are among the ranks of the tattooed, one thing is almost certain: the time, energy, skin, and money people invest in getting tattooed have increased markedly over the last ten to fifteen years.

The term "collector" is an honorific title that refers to a number of characteristics—both social and physical—of the tattooee. The most important feature is the amount of his or her body the tattooee has devoted, or is in the process of devoting, to tattoo work. While there certainly are exceptions, collectors tend to invest significantly more time, energy, skin, and money into getting tattooed than do other tattooees. These investments often take form in a variety of relatively standardized "suit" aesthetics, based fairly directly on the Japanese full-body style. While each suit is comprised of unique designs or combinations of designs, there are conventional constraints regulating the length of the "sleeves" and coverage of legs and torso.

In a body suit, the central and defining component is the "backpiece," which is typically a single design covering the entire back and often the buttocks. Backpieces usually center on a single figure, often a fantasy creature such as a dragon or a heroic mythological character. This figure is set off by background motifs most commonly symbolizing wind, water, and/or earth. The back is the largest uninterrupted canvas on the human body, so a backpiece clearly demonstrates the collector's artistic, financial, and temporal commitment to the process of becoming tattooed.

Not only are they prized by their owners, backpieces also are marks of status for the artist who designs and executes them. Because the backpiece is such an important piece in the collection, collectors invest considerable time and research in finding, commissioning, and "sitting for" the "right" artist. One of the most important attributes collectors consider is an artist's experience with large-scale work. Skin is pliable and the body surface is irregular. This means that designs that work on paper do not necessarily translate well to skin, and, while an artist's study of anatomy and the human form are necessary at some level, nothing can replace experience in designing and executing backpieces. Artists who work successfully in such a large scale also need to learn how to "pull a line" with sufficient speed, accuracy, and agility that they can complete the outline of at least the central figure in one sitting. Since outlines are the most difficult part of a tattoo for the tattooee to endure, experience outlining large-scale tattoos will affect artists' designs for those tattoos.

"Sleeves" are somewhat less important large-scale tattoos among serious tattoo collectors, but they are common components of a full-body suit. All sleeves begin at a "shoulder cap" and extend with varying degrees of relatively solid coverage down the arm. "Short sleeves" go to the mid bicep, "half sleeves" go to the elbow, "three-quarter sleeves" go to mid forearm, and "full sleeves" go to the wrist. While a well-executed sleeve will appear to be a single design concept, sleeves are often constructed fairly piecemeal with discrete designs building around one another, all of which are subsequently "tied in" with a background motif of some sort (most commonly "wind bars" and/or waves patterned after traditional Japanese designs).

The other major canvases of the body are "rib panels," "chest caps," and legs. A matched set of legs is called "pants." Rib panels often feature complimentary single designs covering the tattooee's right and left sides from the hips to the base of the pectoral muscles. Chest caps typically are symmetrical, built around a central design, and ultimately connected to the backpiece. Legs tend either to reflect and support the design of the backpiece or function as slightly larger-scale sleeves. Legs also tend to go from the hips either to the knee, mid calf, or ankle. Each of these pieces of tattoo "canvas" generates a different level of status within the community of serious collectors, depending on how solid the coverage is and/or how painful the area is to get tattooed.

This description of a tattoo collection and how it is conventionally acquired reflects some of the most common methods by which people get tattooed in America. As earlier chapters of this book make clear, men often start with tattoos on the upper arm, and women often start with small tattoos in intimate places like the buttocks, hips, or breasts. Placement of early tattoos can affect how a person chooses to build his or her collection should she or he decide to make the requisite financial, physical, and temporal commitment. The one assured means of not having early tattoos interfere with the design of a suit is fairly common among Japanese collectors and is starting to become more common among American and European collectors. This approach involves commissioning an entire suit as the first (and often only) tattoo the collector acquires.

The aesthetic advantage of beginning with an entire suit is readily apparent. The collector can be relatively assured that each section of the body will work with the others and the continuity of the complete tattoo will benefit from having the same person design and execute it. Stylistically, the collection will have a continuity that is hard to achieve when individual tattoos or segments of a body suit are acquired piecemeal over time. Full-suit commissions are still rare in the West, however, and the skills and experience necessary for an artist to design a full suit are even less common. Understandably, collectors who commission full suits typically must engage in a considerable amount of logistical planning and consultation with an artist. Collectors also frequently travel great distances at substantial expense to see the project through to its completion.

Tattoo Media and Tattoo Conventions

In the late 1980s there were a few films about tattooing, but none were readily available. Peter Fonda hosted a documentary-style film called *Signatures of the Soul: A Look at Modern Tattooing* (1987, directed by Geoff Steven), and there was a B-movie suspense thriller called *Tattoo* (1981, directed by Bob Brooks and starring Maude Adams and Bruce Dern). But if you wanted genuinely informative documentary material about tattooing, you had to read *Tattootime* or *The Tattoo Advocate*, the only available "serious" tattoo publications, or you had to have access to ethnographer Alan Govenar's film on the old-time tattooer, Stoney St. Clair (*Stoney Knows How*, 1981), or the documentary focused on artist Don Ed Hardy and the San Francisco tattoo scene produced by *Tattootime* (*Tattooing Reality: Hardy and Associates Make their Marks*, 1988). In contrast, at this writing, there are almost too many documentaries to count, many of them airing on PBS, Discovery Channel, A&E, and other standard cable channels. There are also two reality programs (A&E's "Inked" and The Learning Channel's "Miami Ink") centered on tattoo shops. While the tattooists working in those shops are not always as informed as they might seem to the everyday casual viewer, they do encounter a wide variety of requests for different tattooing styles from their clientele. As moderately competent tattoo artists, they need to know what "kanji" are (currently fashionable Japanese ideography often used to represent spiritual principles in tattooing), what a "koi" is (a Japanese carp used to symbolize perseverance in Japanese tattoo iconography), and how symmetry works in tribal tattooing in order to make a living at their trade. Even in Las Vegas and Miami where the shows are set (neither city is known as a center of tattooing culture), clients want full sets of sleeves in the traditional Japanese style. Before "Miami Ink," many of these tattooees were getting their educations from tattoo magazines.

Fifteen years ago tattoo magazines were still a subcultural phenomenon. Those who knew about artistic tattooing read *Tattootime* when it came out, provided they could find it. The only readily available sources of information were the biker magazines that periodically covered tattooing. Shortly after the first edition of *Customizing the Body* was published, however, several magazines appeared that changed things dramatically. *Outlaw Biker Tattoo Review*, *Skin Art*, and *International Tattoo Art* each had a profound impact on the tattoo world by placing knowledgeable tattoo artists on their editorial staffs and focusing on showing cutting-edge tattoo art. Now there were magazines that presented strikingly original tattoos and gave credit to and featured interviews with the artists who did them. These same magazines sent correspondents to cover tattoo conventions and made it a point to emphasize the importance of custom tattooing over conventional pieces chosen from the flash sheets on the walls of commercial street shops. Their readers saw that artistically trained, talented, and experienced tattoo artists were producing artistic products whose beauty and complexity rivaled works in other, more accepted, media.

Success often yields cheap imitation, and it was not long before the number of tattoo magazines had expanded beyond what the market could reasonably bear, with *Easyrider* (publishing three tattoo periodicals plus special issues), *Outlaw Biker* (publishing two magazines plus special issues), *International Tattoo Art*, and *Skin & Ink* all competing for the same market. This glut of tattoo magazines led to a marked decline in standards. While many of these magazines are still published, established and reputable artists are now less likely to submit photos of their work with any frequency. The result is that the publications tend to present the work of lesser practitioners and increasingly to emphasize coverage of the parties held at tattoo conventions.

When *Customizing the Body* was first published there was one annual convention in the United States run by the National Tattoo Association, and it operated much the same way as any professional trade convention. It met in a different city each year for three or four days during which industry insiders could talk shop, attend seminars on health codes or specialized tattooing techniques, and enjoy a concluding awards banquet. Unlike at other trade conventions, however, there were competitions for the "best" tattoos, designs, and artists, and members of the public were welcome. Here, both visitors and participants were able to get tattooed by some of the major figures in the tattoo world, who often came from as far away as Japan or Austria.

In the early 1990s, however, the National Tattoo Association lost its monopoly on conventions when Dennis Dwyer and J. D. Crowe launched Tattoo Tour. Tattoo Tour became a populist alternative to what many saw as National's elitism. While National charged separate admission prices for members and non-members, Tattoo Tour had one rate, and it was lower than National's. Tattoo Tour had no membership requirements for operators of the booths in which tattooists worked. As a consequence, this new gathering offered a significantly larger selection of tattoo artists to the public than did the National convention. There were still competitions, but Tattoo Tour did not hold a banquet. Tattoo Tour provided a way for people living in places other than the East or West coasts to get tattooed by some of the best known figures in the industry. It also provided an opportunity for those artists to have their work displayed and to develop their reputations outside of their home locales.

With the ascendance in influence of each, the magazines and conventions developed what cultural sociologist Pierre Bourdieu (1984) calls a "homologous relationship"—they appeared to be independent but actually influenced each other. Magazines provided a means for artists to become more widely known, and conventions provided a way for them to spread their work into increasingly diversified geographical markets. The conventions became big events in the tattoo world and the magazines would cover them, thereby building interest for conventions being held in more places and with greater frequency. Eventually, it became apparent to people outside the tattoo world that there was considerable profit to be made in sponsoring tattoo conventions. This is, according to many in the tattoo community, the point at which the tattoo world lost control of the tattoo world.

Conventions now are almost too frequent to count, and that of the National Tattoo Association is one of the few remaining that is sponsored by people in the tattoo world. Production companies and media conglomerates currently organize most conventions. For example, Clear Channel Communications, Inc., provided the funding for *Tattoo the Earth*, a convention tour that visited twenty-two cities over the course of two years (2002–2003), featured forty-two artists, and was covered in twenty-seven local and national media outlets. These conventions draw audiences by providing free booths to a handful of well-known tattoo artists and fill the rest of the booths with second-tier artists willing to pay for their booths so they can gain exposure. They are most frequently held in major-arena venues such as San Francisco's Cow Palace and the Oakland Coliseum that offer what the artists often see as less than ideal working conditions.

Thus, as with magazines, over the past decade conventions have become less and less popular among those at the artistic vanguard of the tattoo world. Nonetheless, the nexus of power that connects the magazines and conventions makes them difficult to ignore or reject for those artists seeking to develop or maintain a client base. As seen in Chapters 2 and 3, word of mouth has always been the best way to generate satisfying business for artists and clients alike. But serious collectors and their friends only have a finite amount of skin. Even well-known artists must promote themselves with advertising and by actively participating in even the less desirable outlets in the tattoo world.

Tattoo Artists' Training

If one thing about the tattoo world has changed—sociologically speaking—since *Customizing the Body* first came out, it would be the system of apprenticeship. In the late 1980s the only viable means of entering the tattoo trade was through apprenticeship with an established artist. During the apprenticeship, the novice learned how to build and tune machines, make needles, mix pigments, draw and color flash, and where to find the supplies necessary for all these elements of the occupation. The apprenticeship also provided training in the ethics of the trade. Initiates learned about the importance of respecting other people's custom work, not to "poach" other artists' clients, not to open shops in the same neighborhood as established artists, and so on. To the disappointment of many of the more established and long-term members of the tattoo world, apprenticeships have, since the

1990s, become an increasingly less common point of entry into the tattoo profession.

One reason tattooing has thrived over the last two decades or so is that formally trained artists have come to be increasingly influential. While tattooing used to be a "craft" practiced by men who worked in seaports and other centers of the Americana tradition, the tattoo renaissance made tattooing available to new audiences and new practitioners who saw new potential in the medium. Beginning in the late 1980s, art-school students began trying their hands at tattooing. Their movement into tattooing intersected with rise of tattoo magazines and the influence of tattoo conventions described above.

Magazines support themselves with advertising revenue, and tattoo equipment suppliers pay well for advertising space in tattoo magazines. For a number of years *International Tattoo Art* and *Skin & Ink* refused to accept advertising from equipment suppliers since, they reasonably assumed, the ready availability of tattoo equipment would lead to the influx of inexperienced and untrained people into the trade (that is, those who had not been apprentices). Eventually, however, economic necessity forced even these relatively upscale publications to give in. Armed with equipment purchased through the mail, novice artists typically began by practicing on themselves and their friends, and some eventually developed large enough followings to begin professional careers as tattoo artists. These self-taught practitioners (who, not infrequently, have formal art-school training) are often called New Skool tattooists.

To be fair, apprenticeships are still the primary route through which people enter the tattoo trade. What has changed is the point at which novice tattooists enter the apprenticeship. While people wanting to become tattoo artists most commonly began their apprenticeships without any experience applying tattoos, now they often begin with experience and a portfolio of work. Thus, rather than learning the trade from scratch, they enter apprenticeships seeking to refine, rather than acquire, tattooing skills.

Few would question the quality of the portfolios put together by many of these New Skool artists, but they have changed, undeniably and profoundly (for better or worse), the ethical and cultural landscape of the tattoo world. Due to the changed nature of the apprenticeship system, New Skool artists fail to acquire the institutional memory that had been passed from teacher to apprentice for decades. Having not received instruction in the ethics of tattooing, they engage in activities that sow discord in the tattoo community. Many of them, for example, have no compunction about copying other artists' custom designs. This has led artistic visionaries to stop sending photographs of their work to magazines in order to protect their, and their clients', investment of time and creative energy in designing unique tattoos. They break agreements with established artists not to open shops in the same neighborhood, and they derogate the people who provided them the opportunity to establish themselves. While blatantly unethical and disrespectful behavior of this type is more the exception than the rule, its prevalence is increasing and its source in the decline of the traditional apprenticeship system is clear.

OTHER FORMS OF BODY MODIFICATION

When *Customizing the Body* was first published, tattoos were still an effective means of symbolically thumbing one's nose at conventional society. Visible tattoos served (however unjustly) as markers of a person's willingness or desire to reject accepted behaviors and expected appearance. However, tattooing's ability to shock, inflame, or upset more conventional members of society decreased as more people received tattoos, the artistic quality of the work available improved, and heavily tattooed people became increasingly visible. Piercing, scarification, and other dramatic and less popular forms of permanent body modification have provided an outlet for those who wish to arouse "conspicuous outrage."

So-called "radical" piercing is a shifting category, largely because "radical" is a relative term. However, there are a few forms that will likely continue to shock most people for the foreseeable future. These escalated symbols of outrage include hole stretching, facial piercing, and genital piercing.

Hole stretching is practiced widely among "modern primitives" (see Vale and Juno, 2005 [1989]) who use body modification practices to demonstrate their alienation from contemporary consumer culture. Modern primitives emulate "primitive" cultures with "tribal" tattoos, stretched earlobes (and now even stretched holes in nose piercings), facial piercings (most commonly in the eyebrows and "labrets" located about half-way between the lower lip and chin), and a variety of other body modifications. Modern primitives have also embraced rituals such as "suspensions," in which people hang by wires or ropes looped through their piercings. Two common forms of this practice are the "sun worship ritual," in which the person is suspended by metal hooks run through the pectoral region, or back suspensions, where one is lifted off the ground with chains attached to rings or hooks perforating the shoulders, back, and sometimes the lower legs.

Genital and nipple piercing are also fairly common among modern primitives, but these modifications are most directly connected to segments of society that celebrate "body play." Body play is common among practitioners of BD/SM (Bondage-Discipline/Sado-Masochism [or Slave-Master]) who derive pleasure from unconventional forms of stimulation. Wearing jewelry through the nipples or genitals provides numerous opportunities for playing with, enjoying, imposing, and receiving a wide range of physical sensations. From the perspective of those who wear genital piercings, pleasurable sensation, not pain, is the goal.

The most common piercings are, for both sexes, through the nipples. However, genital piercings are common enough to have specific names. Women tend to favor wearing jewelry through the clitoral hood or labia, but more radical piercings like the fourchette (which runs from the base of the vagina to the perineum), the triangle (which runs horizontally through the clitoral hood, behind the nerve bundle of the clitoris), and the Princess Diana (which runs parallel to the clitoris through the clitoral hood) are also possible. Male genital piercings include the Prince Albert (which enters through the urethra and exits below the crown of the glans, or head, on the underside of the penis), the dolphin (which enters the lower hole of a Prince Albert and runs further down the urethra on the underside of the penis), the ampallang (horizontally through the glans), the apadravya (vertically through the glans), the frenum (through the pinchable tissue on the underside of the penis below the glans and usually worn with hoop jewelry that wraps around the glans below the corona, or ridge), the lorum (similar to the frenum but worn where the shaft of the penis reaches the scrotum), the hafada (hoops, usually worn in pairs, piercing the outside of the scrotum), the Dydoe (a piercing through the corona of the glans; Dydoes are usually worn in pairs), and the guiche (a horizontal piercing of the perineum). Men often combine piercings in "ladders," usually a series of frenum piercings that run down the shaft of the penis, often continuing to run the length of the scrotum and ending in a guiche.

The term "scarification" refers to a wide range of permanent body modifications that result in a scar. The most common scarification practices are cutting, burning (or branding), and "flesh peeling." Cutting is the most precise of these techniques and it allows for the creation of scars that display the most obvious artistic features. Designs are usually incised with a scalpel on an outline placed on the skin with a stencil. The fresh wound is then coated in flammable liquid such as alcohol or lighter fluid and then set alight to cauterize the wound channel. The process is often repeated several times to create a sufficiently deep wound channel and, thus, a more visible scar.

Branding has a rich history in sub-Saharan Africa, where members of tribal groups were often branded in honor of, or to simulate the appearance of, religious totems (for example, raising keloids to simulate the bumps on the backs of crocodiles [Roberts, 1988]). The most common contemporary form of branding is found within traditionally African American fraternities. Those who wear brands often describe their marks as co-opting a symbol of oppression from slavery and embracing it as a statement of pride in their black heritage. Branding also addresses purely pragmatic issues. Tattoo pigment is often masked by melanin and thus hard to see in dark skin. Further, the skin of those with African heritage tends to raise larger, and therefore more dramatic, keloid scars. Brands can be applied in a variety of ways, the most common of which features heating strips of metal held in pliers with a torch until they become red hot. The hot metal is then applied to the recipient's skin. The metal strips can be shaped to create a variety of designs or to achieve various effects. Practitioners and recipients of brands often call this process "the kiss of fire."

Flesh peeling is the most recent innovation in scarification practices. It involves cutting designs composed of two parallel lines into the skin and removing the ribbons of flesh between the double outline. This practice allows for broader lines in the scar, an effect that is difficult to achieve with standard cutting practice and difficult to control with branding.

The most recent modes of body modification involve a variety of applications of plastic surgery. The most common of these is the sub-dermal implant. Implants are usually made of surgical steel or surgical grade plastics, and they are placed under the skin to augment, enhance, or change the shape of the face (most commonly) or other regions of the body. Thus, a person might implant ridges over the eyes to simulate a lizard's brow, install in his forehead a bladder that can be filled with air to change the size and shape of the head, or implant ridges over her collar bones for decorative effect. These practices are most common among modern primitives who wish to create a "cyborg appearance" as part of a critique of modern consumer culture (see Hewitt, 1997; Pitts, 2003; and Polhemus and Randall, 1996; for extensive discussions of these practices).

As the means by which people modify their bodies become more varied, people seek out newer, more radical, sometimes permanent methods of playing with their appearance and bodily structure. The most radical among these to date involve dramatic and irreversible surgical techniques. Members of the body-modification world have been known to split their penises down the center; sever, bisect, and pierce their testes; remove sections of their ears and stitch them back together so they will simulate the ears of a zebra; file their teeth into points and split their tongues so as to simulate the appearance of a lizard; and even remove finger joints or entire fingers. While these forms of body modification are available for those who are strongly inclined to physically demonstrate their alienation from conventional society, they are rare practices that are unlikely to become especially popular, at least in the near future.

TATTOO SCHOLARSHIP TODAY

When the first edition of *Customizing the Body* was published, the scholarly literature on tattooing and other forms of permanent body alterations was relatively limited. It consisted largely of a few psychological treatments of tattooing as an indicator of social pathology. As is still the case with many of the more contemporary psychological discussions of tattooing, these studies were based on studies of residents of institutions such as prisons or in-patient mental health facilities. Since data are drawn from groups who are psychologically and socially atypical, the insights and conclusions contained in these studies tend to have little relevance for understanding the phenomenon of body alteration outside of those settings. In the past few years, as general attention to and awareness of tattooing have increased, social scientists and humanists have done more research and writing directly focused on providing a general understanding and explanation of tattooing.

Psychological treatments of tattooing remain concerned with explaining the connection between tattooing and psychopathology. In their study of high-school-age adolescents in Australia, Houghton and associates (1996), for example, seek to explain the "reasons, experiences, methods, *and perceived health consequences of obtaining tattoos*" (p. 420, emphasis added). Their results suggest a correlation between tattoos and self-reports of "school problem behavior," although this concept is not explicitly defined in the article. The study does not discuss whether becoming tattooed precedes or comes after one is involved in problem behavior nor does it explore the teens' motivations for acquiring tattoos.

In another recent discussion of body modification, Jeffreys (2000) makes the questionable claim that cutting, tattooing, and piercing need "to be understood . . . as being the result of, rather than resistance to, the occupation of a despised social status under male dominance" (p. 410). Given this orientation toward the function of tattooing and other modes of body modification, Jeffreys would probably have a difficult time explaining the fact that the majority of those who choose to be involved in these practices are male.

Other studies that have appeared after the initial publication of *Customizing the Body* have described tattooing (and other forms of body modification) as "adolescent risk behaviors" (Armstrong and Pace, 1997), a form of "Russian roulette" (Ceniceros, 1998), and related to illegal drug use (Loimer and Werner, 1992). The common thread in these articles is an assumption that body modification is somehow harmful or pathological. These conclusions are, however, highly problematic since, in addition to often focusing on institutionalized populations, the authors lump together a variety of very different phenomena. For example, they fail to separate those who wear amateur or self-applied tattoos from those who wear the work of professional tattooists. These researchers also tend not to distinguish among tattooing, piercing, self-cutting, and other forms of body alteration.

Typically, academic discussions of body modification are premised on the conventional, but often unstated, assumption that body modification is pathological. Guided by this initial assumption, researchers often fail to collect data that would provide the basis for a discussion of the phenomenon as the consequence of choices "normal" people make for a variety of understandable, eminently social, and usually quite ordinary reasons.

This tendency to pathologize body alteration is not limited to any particular academic discipline. Quantitative studies conducted by sociologists also try to demonstrate what is wrong with people who choose to modify or adorn their bodies in fairly permanent ways. Carol and Anderson's (2002) study of girls in a residential program for at-risk youth correlates tattoos and body piercings with "trait anger." Koch and his associates (2005) applied the "Health Belief Model" to the decision-making process of young adults in order to discover the social and psychological influences that could prevent a person from engaging in such "risky" behavior as getting a tattoo. Hawkes, Senn, and Thorn's (2004) experimental study was designed to test whether the size and visibility of women's tattoos have negative impact on how other people see them. Though somewhat less judgmental, Jacobson and Luzzatto (2004) use data drawn from participant observation to support their claims that tattoos and other body adornments are faddish affectations and help provide adolescents with a sense of individuality.

The anthropological treatment of tattooing has followed several distinct paths. The most traditionally "anthropological" of these approaches focuses on tattooing as it is practiced in tribal societies. A notable example of this approach is Alfred Gell's (1993) *Wrapping in Images*. This book offers a rich analysis of Polynesian tattooing that connects the decorative activity to the mythology, cosmology, and identity practices in six Polynesian cultures and traditions. Gell's work is especially notable in that it offers careful and complete documentation of cultural practices in cultures that, for all intents and purposes, no longer exist.

A second form of anthropological analysis extends traditional attention to relatively simple cultures by focusing on the co-optation of cultural meanings of "tribal" and "primitive" tattooing and body modification practices by contemporary social groups. Pritchard (1999, 2000, 2001), for example, focuses on the appropriation of Maori tattoo practices (*ta moko*) by "modern primitives." The author focuses particularly on the issue of whether cultural meanings and identities can be appropriated by one culture without severely distorting their significance within the cultural group in which they originated.

Along similar lines, the selections in the volumes edited by Caplan (2000) and Thomas, Cole, and Douglas (2005) combine historical and anthropological approaches to examine the complex movement of tattooing from Polynesia to Europe and America. While Captain Cook's role in this process is well documented and widely known, the works in these two collections show that the typical accounts of his influence are overly simplistic and fail to acknowledge the influences of a variety of other indigenous cultures.

The final path of anthropological analysis follows most directly in the tradition of *Customizing the Body* in that it employs information collected through direct interaction with people involved with body modification and tends to avoid pathologizing the phenomenon. DeMello's (2000) *Bodies of Inscription*, for example, moves from a historical discussion of tattooing to focus on the central role played by tattoo conventions and publications in forming styles and orientations within the tattoo world. DeMello's discussion is grounded in extensive interview data and emphasizes the importance of body alteration in shaping the identities and social connections of the largely middle class members of the tattoo world on which she focused. Like sociologist Katherine Irwin (2001, 2003), DeMello emphasizes inequalities that she sees in the tattoo subculture, especially those based on gender and class.

In the 1990s serious discussions of body modification often reflected the postmodern analytic and presentational conventions that had become popular in certain social scientific circles. These works tended to be obscurely worded, based on rather speculative "readings" of limited data, and employ an analytic frame premised on the central role played by social inequality. For example, Rosenblatt's (1997) secondary analysis of *Modern Primitives* (Vale and Juno, 2005 [1989]) presents modern primitivism as a form of resistance to social and cultural structures that have supposedly made identity construction problematic in contemporary society. For example, in typically convoluted postmodernist prose, Rosenblatt contends that

> [a] comparison of modern primitivism with "invented traditions" and "revivals of traditional culture" could be more than an ironic or decentering device. . . . A study of the discourse surrounding primitivism taking place in the shadows of anthropological discussions of culture movements can illuminate the ways in which, in each case, creative political practice and structures of meaning render each other intelligible (p. 288; see also DeMello, 1993).

Two edited collections also reflect this postmodernist orientation. Mascia-Lees and Sharpe in the flamboyantly titled *Tattoo, Torture, Mutilation, and Adornment* (1992) and Featherstone (2000) in *Body Modification* offer a variety of pieces that treat the body as a "cultural text." As is, or was, typical of postmodern discussions, the selections in both of these volumes are not based on direct empirical data (save for occasional use of the author's personal experience) and tend toward abstracted analyses of films and written materials. The authors do not appear to be overly concerned with the failure to ground their discussions on empirical data. In their introduction, for example, Mascia-Lees and Sharpe offer a postmodernist explanation for the fact that the authors of the chapters in their collection have avoided dealing with the complications involved with the direct investigation of body modification and the culture that surrounds it. As they state:

> Contemporary theorizing, whether feminist, postmodernist, or anthropological, has contributed recently to exposing "the natural" as a Western cultural construct, calling into question the often taken for granted dichotomy between nature and culture and the ways in which this distinction has acted to reinforce relations of power and domination. Indeed, the body has become an important site for rethinking such binary oppositions as masculinity and femininity, gender and sex, the public and the private, and the cultural and the natural. Contemporary attempts to expose these categories as ideological constructions buttressing Western and/or male supremacy

and to disrupt them have focused on the body. Understanding the body not as simple materiality, but rather as constituted within language as in much contemporary thought, is intended to question traditional notions of the body as prior to, or outside of, culture. This move is, of course, just one of the latest attempts in the West to grapple with the relationship between the natural and the cultural and to put the body, and representations of it, in service to this struggle (p. 3).

While some of the basic ideas offered by authors influenced by the postmodern "turn" are of potential value, in placing the body and representations of it on equal analytic footing, postmodern analysis does away with the need to investigate people's actual embodied experiences. From a postmodern perspective empirical research such as that upon which *Customizing the Body* is based holds limited value because, in focusing on collective experiences and empirically verified phenomena, it fails to account sufficiently for "narratives," "discourses," and other personalistic constructs and stories. We take issue with such claims. However, some discussions directly influenced by postmodernism are of considerable value.

Victoria Pitts's (2003) *In the Flesh* is an example of what can happen when a skilled analyst combines postmodern theory with systematic data derived through the use of more or less conventional methods. Pitts examines the politics of body modification in discussions of the piercing, tattooing, scarification, and subdermal implantation practices of a number of segments of the body-modification world—primarily modern primitive culture, queer culture, and cyberpunk culture. She demonstrates how people use body modification as an ongoing activity through which they construct their social selves. According to Pitts, people use body-modification practices as methods of reclaiming their bodies from a contemporary culture they find alienating, hostile, and repressive.

Michael Atkinson's (2003) *Tattooed: The Sociogenesis of a Body Art* is a discussion of tattooing practices in Canada based on systematic ethnographic research. Atkinson grounds his understanding of tattooing largely on ideas developed by Norbert Elias (1991, 1994) that emphasize how social experience shapes individual and collective personality structures and how people's use and perceptions of the body arise out of social interaction. Atkinson develops a "figurational" sociology that offers a picture of tattooing as shaped both by social structure and the creative personal decisions of those who choose to acquire tattoos. Imbedded within a matrix of complex relationships and interdependencies, people, Atkinson maintains, use tattooing as a life-long body project that allows them to define, negotiate, and maintain definitions of self, identity, and social position.

Finally, Angus Vail's (1999a, 1999b, 2000, 2001) research on fine-art tattoo collectors and artists builds on and moves beyond some of the themes introduced in *Customizing the Body*. Based on interviews, fieldwork, and his experiences participating in the fine art-tattoo world, Vail emphasizes the process through which people convince one another that their own consumption or production of art is legitimate, valuable, and important.

Taken as a body of research, Vail's work is an explicit extension of the themes laid out in the original edition of *Customizing the Body*. For instance, in his treatment of the process through which people become tattoo collectors, Vail (1999b) extends the discussion in Chapter 2 of *Customizing the Body* to show how collectors undergo processes of self definition as they learn how to treat their bodies as explicit sites of artistic activity ("canvases"). In charting the process through which collectors come to enlarge their collections and thereby come to incorporate their tattoos as a central feature of their identities, Vail makes the key distinction between those who *have tattoos* and those who *are tattooed*. As he puts it:

[The] tattoos [of the person who merely has tattoos] are no different than the car she or he drives or the hair style she or he sports on any given day. Like these adornments, tattoos represent possessions that can be considered with or without the individual who wears them. . . . To the collector [in contrast], tattoos are not something one owns. Rather, they are part of him or her, no less important than the color of his or her hair or skin and no more easily removed from his or her identity than his or her deepest beliefs, most profound concerns, or idiosyncratic sense of humor (p. 270).

In a similar vein, Vail's (2000) article on the socialization of tattoo artists builds on the discussions of apprenticeship and

street-shop social control covered in Chapters 3 and 4 of *Customizing the Body*. He focuses on the moral and ethical instruction that tattoo artists undergo as they come to see themselves as
artists and as they seek validation for those claims among their
peers in the broader world of professional tattooing. Part of this
process involves a form of retroactive apprenticeship that many
artists seek after they have bypassed the formal apprenticeship
system. Realizing that their autodidactic instruction in tattooing
has left out the history and ethics of the trade, they seek instruction from those who are more established and who have access to
the institutional memory that is such an important part of the
social networks that comprise the broader professional world of
tattooing.

In his most explicit departure from *Customizing the Body*, Vail's
(1999a) comparison of tattoo collectors and opera fans shows how
members of art worlds use the time they have spent developing
and refining their taste in art as a resource in convincing others
of the legitimacy of their claims to membership in elite art worlds.
In focusing on the time it takes to learn about and consume art,
and the often strenuous physical demands of consuming art, Vail
shows how art-world participants justify their claims to sophisticated, and sometimes explicitly superior, taste.

CONCLUSION

Predicting the future of any social phenomenon is always a haz-
ardous endeavor. However, it is not unreasonable to expect that,
for a time, tattooing will continue to expand since more people are
now wearing or choosing to acquire tattoos and, as emphasized in
Chapter 2, the choice to get tattooed typically is prompted by the
fact that a person one knows is tattooed. In short, the more
people who are tattooed, the more "unmarked" people have contact with friends and acquaintances who are tattooed and the
more likely they themselves are to move along the path to being
tattooed. There are also more tattoo shops available to both serious and novice tattooees. The increased opportunity to acquire a
tattoo is also likely help to prolong tattooing's popularity.

But, like all fads, tattooing will probably decline as a widespread decorative practice. Because a certain, relatively small,
proportion of those who get tattooed move on to eventually

become more committed collectors and the tattoo will continue to have the identity-display functions discussed in Chapter 2, tattooing certainly will not die out altogether. It seems reasonable to predict that most likely to survive will be those street shops that put out the cheapest and most conventional tattoos for casual recipients and custom shops where the most talented artists provide work for the most committed collectors.

However, the spread of tattooing has sapped, and will continue to diminish, the power of the tattoo to frighten or annoy members of mainstream society (see DeMello, 2000; Irwin, 2001). This means that tattooing no longer is effective as a mechanism of conspicuous outrage and, in order to symbolically divide "us" from "them," marginal, alienated, or unconventional members of the society must continue to find innovative ways to induce outrage. This process of the escalation of outrage is ongoing and is seen in the spread of the alternative forms of body alteration discussed above and in the continuing search for new and different ways of modifying the body. As is frequently emphasized by sociologists interested in social change, one of the factors most responsible for this process is technological innovation. As advances in medical, artistic, computer, and other technologies change and diffuse, the available means of modifying the body—and outraging ordinary folks—will expand in turn. Bladders that are surgically implanted and can be expanded or deflated at will to alter one's physiognomy, tattoo inks that glow in the dark, computer-directed instruments that inscribe burned or cut designs, tattoo images that move on the wearer's body because of some form of animation process, decorative piercings of the torso or large muscles in the arms and legs, and automated vending machines in public settings that dispense permanent or semi-permanent body markings and piercings are but a few of the conceivable possibilities. Since deviant activities and styles typically act as the sources of innovation in popular culture (see Sanders, 1990), it is reasonable to anticipate that the process of spread, commercialization, and eventual decline of these new forms of outrage will unfold in much the way it did in tattooing.

It is far easier to predict that social, medical, and behavioral analysts will continue to focus attention on body modification than it is to predict the direction of or changes in purposive body alteration itself. As seen above, these discussions tend to be limited by the blinders provided by disciplinary perspectives. Psychologists and psychiatrists see body modification as indicative of some form of psychopathology, members of the medical community see it as a threat to individual and public health, criminologists see it as being related to involvement with dangerous deviant social groups, and so forth. It would seem far more reasonable to see body-modification activities and other features of social life as involving people who are relatively aware of their circumstances working together to make purposive decisions to live their lives in particular kinds of ways. These people typically negotiate the complexities of social worlds with relative skill, choose paths of behavior based on what they see as reasonable alternatives, and assemble a collection of selves and present them to others based on how they understand the situation they are in and what they want to accomplish within it. Consequently, those who seek to explain social worlds like that surrounding tattooing and other forms of body modification need to respect the perspectives of those who live within those social worlds. They should avoid imposing judgments about the relative legitimacy of these practices and should remain open to understanding the world as the people they are studying understand it. Sociologically "appreciating" certain groups and their collective activities is not the same as condoning, agreeing with, or even partaking in those activities. Understanding is not the same as, nor does it necessarily require, appreciation. While the body-modification phenomenon upon which *Customizing the Body* focuses is touching, uplifting, creative, and expressive on the one hand, it is also bizarre, unfortunate, and stigmatizing. What is central, however, is to recognize that these social practices are the consequences of people's normal desires to have close relationships with others, see themselves as special, and mark the passage of their lives on earth.

Methodological Appendix

I'd been teaching at the university level in Chicago for 20 years. I was an associate Professor of English Literature and had received my Ph.D. from Ohio State in 1936. I spent my summers in Europe and became very friendly with Gertrude Stein and Alice B. Toklas. Somehow I became awfully tired of teaching and I decided I would get out of it if I could. I had always been fascinated with tattooing and thought it would be as far away from academia as I could get.

Tattooist Phil Sparrow,
Morse, 1977: 50

In the course of the last twenty years or so, fieldwork methodology has undergone significant development. Some field researchers, seduced by the legitimacy and supposed rigor of positivism, have focused on devising highly structured procedures for collecting field data designed to counter the accusations of bias and unreliability leveled by scientistic critics (see, for example, Sykes, 1977; Miles and Huberman, 1984; Werner and Schoepfle, 1987). Others, heartened by the post-positivist skepticism about applying the methods and assumptions of the natural sciences to the unique phenomenon of human behavior (see Sass, 1986), have reaffirmed their commitment to the flexible, creative, and interpretive search for meaning that has long been the cornerstone of disciplined ethnographic research. One theme consistently stressed in recent methodological discussions by writers dedicated to traditional modes of fieldwork practice has been the importance of an explicit and reflexive account of the complex interactional experience through which the researcher collected the data and grew to understand their meaning (Adler and Adler, 1987; Emerson, 1987). What follows is my attempt to be responsive to this prescription.

Fairly early in my academic career I realized that sociology had something special to offer me. It provided what I saw to be a useful and sensible analytic perspective and offered a legitimate context in which I could focus on social activities and objects that were of personal interest and sources of private pleasure. Attracted by people and phenomena that are generally outside the boundaries imposed by conventional society, I have tended to focus on what I have come to think of as the "soft, white underbelly of American culture." Among other things, I have researched and written about narcotics police, underground comix, horror films, drug use by GIs in Vietnam, various domestic drug-using subcultures, club performers and other cultural producers, and now tattooing.

Since my graduate school experience in the 1960s I have also been drawn to participant observation. It is a research approach that allows me to work independently (I have usually found interaction with anyone in the role of "boss" to be, at best, annoying), and I find I possess a certain ability to interact comfortably with a fairly wide range of people. Doing this sort of "lone-ranger" fieldwork (Adler and Adler, 1987: 14) in the kinds of social settings I tend to choose has always provided me with a certain measure of adventure and allowed me to escape legitimately from the narrow confines of academia. In general, I am more at ease interacting with junkies, freaks, night-people, bikers, musicians, and other unsavory sorts than I am in rubbing shoulders with academics. *Doing* sociology provides me with the opportunity to interact within settings and social networks that I have come to feel comfortable in, and that are commonly closed to, and therefore unexplored by, my more conventional colleagues. I do not intend this to sound overly cavalier or derogatory. Instead, I am taking to heart the advice of Mills, Hughes, Park, and others who have emphasized the importance of deriving an understanding of the complex richness of human behavior from information collected within a variety of social settings. My own inclinations and experiences have drawn me to employ what skills and knowledge I possess to participate in the illumination of some of the darker corners of American culture.

My initial first-hand contact with tattooing came about when I was visiting San Francisco during the summer of 1979. Since the

American Sociological Association (ASA) meetings were in session, I had a bit of time on my hands. The "Museums" section of the Yellow Pages offered some promising diversions, and I walked over to the Museum of Conceptual Art. At the address listed I encountered a somewhat seedy building that was locked. On the door was a series of brass plaques commemorating each time someone had broken into the premises. I found this exhibit to be appropriate and amusing, but it did not take much time.

Climbing the dingy stairway leading to Lyle Tuttle's Tattoo Art Museum a short time later, I found myself in a new and fascinating world of cultural production. After looking at the sizable collection of tattoo memorabilia, I entered the tattoo studio adjacent to the museum and, like many first-time visitors to tattoo establishments, impulsively decided to join the ranks of the tattooed. After choosing a small scarab design from the wall flash, I submitted to the unexpectedly painful tattoo experience. Although the resident tattooist was not especially forthcoming in response to the questions I forced out between clenched teeth, I did come to realize that this was a phenomenon that combined my research interests in social deviance, artistic production, and body alteration. At the same time, it offered a research experience that would provide a much needed escape from the thankless task of writing a textbook in which I had been involved for the last couple of years.

Returning to the East coast, I visited a small street shop in a "transitional neighborhood" located a few minutes from my office. The owner appeared flattered that a "professor" would want to hang out and listen to him talk about himself; and I soon became a regular participant in the shop, observing the work, talking to the participants, and—despite my original vow never again to undergo the pain of indelible body alteration—eventually receiving considerable tattoo work from a variety of well-known tattoo artists with whom I came into contact during the subsequent seven years.

This book is based primarily on data collected during participant observation in four tattoo studios located in or near major urban centers in the East. Three were traditional shops specializing in the formulaic images favored by military personnel, bikers, laborers, and occasional groups of college students and secretaries. One establishment was a custom studio in which a tattooist with extensive professional experience in a variety of artistic media created original and unique works of art for a generally more select, monied, and aesthetically sophisticated clientele.

For the most part, my role was that of one of a number of regular hangers-on who either lived in the neighborhood or were friends of the local artist. My participation in the establishment to which I originally gained access was considerably more extensive. In addition to (apparently) just standing around and chatting, I routinely helped with the business of the shop. I made change for the amusement games, provided information about cost and availability of designs, stretched the skin of customers who were receiving tattoos on body areas other than arms or legs, calmed the anxiety of first-time recipients, and, in a variety of ways, made myself useful.

As my involvement with and knowledge of the world of tattooing progressed, my role in the national tattoo community also expanded. In a variety of circumstances, my status as university based sociologist proved useful in helping to legitimize tattooing as a commercial and cultural activity. I participated in television talk shows, offered testimony to zoning boards considering the advisability of allowing tattoo studios to open in downtown business areas, wrote letters to lawyers handling cases for tattooists being persecuted by the local authorities, and, in other ways, selectively used my knowledge and more or less respected social position to help redefine tattooing in the face of widespread public distaste and misunderstanding. I emphasize the selectivity of the assistance I provided. While most tattooists are principled, reasonably skilled, and acceptably hygienic, a minority continue to fit into and reinforce the common stereotype. I was careful to qualify my support for tattooing when talking with media representatives— emphasizing the artistic qualities of the work done by certain tattooists—and decline to assist those practitioners about whom I had no first-hand knowledge. The nonacademic writing I did on tattooing was directed primarily at those who were already members of the subculture. For example, I wrote an article for a motorcycle magazine advising readers on how to evaluate the quality of a tattooist's work, published a piece on the stigmatized presentation of tattooing by "scientific" analysts in a major tattoo journal, and had a piece included in the catalogue accompanying a major exhibit of tattoo art and photography mounted in Rome.

To supplement the data drawn from my direct and intimate participation with the tattoo subculture, I conducted a series of lengthy, semi-structured, tape-recorded interviews with tattoo recipients contacted during the course of the research. I collected interviews with 16 people (10 men and 6 women) who were representative of the sex, age, tattoo experience, and social status categories I encountered in the field settings. Their average age was 24 years (from 17 to 39) and, as a group, they carried 35 tattoos (9 had one, 3 had two, and 4 had three or more).

A somewhat more structured body of data was drawn from the four-page questionnaires completed by 163 tattooees contacted in three separate settings. Fifty-six were filled out by tattoo enthusiasts attending the 1984 convention of the National Tattoo Association in Philadelphia, 44 were returned by clients in the "artistic" studio, and 63 respondents completed the questionnaire following their tattoo experience in the street shop in which I initially began to collect field data. Sixty-eight percent of the respondents were men and 32 percent were women. They ranged in ages from 17 to 71 with an average age of 30 years. Sixty-two percent had received some education past high school and 5 percent had graduate degrees. Skilled craftwork, machine operation, and general labor were the most common occupations pursued by the men; service and clerical workers were most heavily represented among the women. Twelve percent of the men and 6 percent of the women were involved in professional or technical occupations (see Figure 5).

Although I have a healthy skepticism with regard to the data provided by self-administered questionnaires, I still chose to supplement the qualitative information I had collected by using this mechanism for the following reasons. It provided me with a broader general picture of the people who are tattooed, and there was no systematic body of data numerically representing tattooees in the United States (cf. Dube, 1985). I had little trouble in getting the people in the tattoo shops to fill out the questionnaire, since

Figure 5: Selected Characteristics of Tattooees
(Questionnaire Respondents, N = 163)

	Male (N = 111)	Female (N = 52)
Mean age (years)	27.4	27.7
Occupation (percent)		
professional/technical	12	6
business manager/owner official/proprietor	14	4
sales/clerical	1	27
skilled craft	38	19
operative (machine/vehicle)	14	4
service	3	10
laborer/unskilled/domestic	12	6
student	4	12
unemployed (incl. housewife)	1	12
no response	3	0
Total	102*	100
Income (percent)		
under $6000	7	23
$6000 to $9999	6	19
$10,000 to $14,999	16	21
$15,000 to $19,999	26	15
$20,000 to $24,999	14	4
$25,000 or more	27	10
no response	4	8
Total	100	100
Education (percent)		
some high school	14	19
high school graduate	27	17
some school after h.s.	37	42
college degree	11	13
some school after college	5	4
graduate degree	7	4
Total	101*	99*

*percentages do not total 100 due to rounding

it was offered as simply another piece of the paperwork involved in purchasing a tattoo. (Recipients are routinely required to fill out a form on which they give their age, name, and address, and to sign a pledge of dubious legality that, should the tattoo result in some type of untoward consequence, they will not bring legal action against the tattooists.) The data collection experience at the National Tattoo Convention went somewhat less smoothly.

I had been asked by one of the convention organizers to offer a lecture based on my current findings that would be interesting and useful for attending tattooists. I agreed to do this if, in return, I would be provided with a table and allowed to commandeer tattooee respondents. For the most part, things went pretty well. I socialized with old friends, gawked at the colorful participants, provided some decent copy for a flock of newspaper reporters who wanted to know why anybody in their right mind would want to get a tattoo, and, sandwiched between a lawyer and a dermatologist, delivered a well-received talk on how tattooists could structure a relatively unproblematic relationship with clients. Prior to the lecture there had been a lot of action at my table in the exhibition hall as I successfully cajoled tattooees into completing questionnaires. I returned to my table and resumed mining the data motherlode until, for some reason, one of the few conventioncers who had refused to have anything to do with the survey decided to stand in the way of scientific progress. Looking like a biker's "ol' lady" from central casting, this recalcitrant young woman was not to be convinced by my smiling assurances about the anonymity of the respondents and the general value of the information for the societal legitimation of tattooing and tattooed people. She heatedly offered the opinion to all those within earshot that I was probably "a narc" and, at best, was just "ripping people off" for information, so that I could "make a lot of money" off of a book about them. Not only did this unexpected tirade significantly slow the traffic around my post, but the woman continued to hang around and whisper discouraging words to the few people I subsequently able to convince to look at the questionnaire. My suggestion that she go find someone else to annoy seemed to aggravate her even more. She disappeared only to return shortly with a couple of male colleagues who looked like the guys who are usually called "Animal" in the movies. It is hard to fool a trained observer, and this situation definitely looked as if it held the potential for significant blood loss. Deciding that coward-ice was the better part of valor, I packed up my stuff and beat a hasty, albeit dignified, retreat.

Fortunately, I rarely encountered this kind of unpleasantness in the course of the research. As it turned out those who did fill out the questionnaire were fairly conscientious about it, and only about 10 percent had to be discarded because they were incom-plete or otherwise unusable. However, the possibility of danger apparent in the convention altercation was an occasional consid-eration throughout the course of the research. Tattooing is a cash business and tattooists typically work late into the night. It was not uncommon for the street tattooist—who regularly worked with a somewhat rougher clientele than did the fine art tattoo-ists—to carry a handgun or have one readily at hand in the shop. On one occasion I stopped off at one of the studios on my way home following the evening class I was teaching. There were no customers so I just sat around socializing with the owner and his assistant. I noticed two young men walk by the shop a couple of times. They eventually came inside and started to look at the flash close to the door. They did not appear to be particularly in-terested in the designs and after a brief whispered conversation one of them disappeared into the adjoining room that contained amusement machines while the other one stayed by the door. I began to feel decidedly uneasy. The shop had been burglarized a few weeks before and the proprietor—who had a rather misan-thropic and suspicious perspective in the best of situations—was even more attuned to possible victimization than was usually the case. He quietly instructed his assistant to retrieve the 38 caliber revolver from the desk in the back room and removed his own weapon from the holster resting in the small of his back under his short blue lab coat. The assistant reentered the main room with the brown and grey butt of the pistol protruding from the waist-band of his pants and, walking slowly into the adjoining room in-quired if the man could "use any help." Both of the suspicious characters replied that they were "just looking" and soon left. Per-haps it was all very innocent but, as I said, fieldwork can sometimes be an adventure. During the course of the research a well-known tattooist was murdered by an intruder with a shotgun. On another occasion two men entered the studio of a renowned East Coast tattoo artist a couple of weeks after I had spent much of the day with him and robbed the shop while waving a pair of Uzi machine guns in a decidedly threatening manner. This experience convinced the understandably unnerved tattooist to relocate his operation to a hopefully more tranquil setting on the West Coast.

This book describes a social world in which I have lived and worked, learned and played for about seven years. In so doing I have participated in ways which have gone somewhat beyond the formal necessities of building what would generally be regarded as an adequate academic analysis of the tattoo phenomenon and the webs of social interaction that surround it. The experience has changed me significantly, both psychologically and physically. Through literally "becoming the phenomenon" I have been able to attain a level of "intimate familiarity" possessed by few other social observers.

Upon initially entering the field I was struck by the apparent trust-enhancing value of the tattoo I already wore—especially since the small piece had been done by a "name" tattooist. The tattoo overtly demonstrated my symbolic membership in, and commitment to, the tattoo community. I was more than simply a journalist or other outsider who wanted to produce yet another amusing article or otherwise exploit the phenomenon because of its exotic features. As the fieldwork proceeded I also realized that enlarging my tattoo collection, especially through receiving work from the tattooists with whom I regularly interacted, was an important step. Once again, I put my body on the line and acquired a medium-sized image on my forearm and a small design on my right earlobe. This latter marking of public skin—an area where only tattooists or committed enthusiasts carry pieces—clearly demonstrated symbolically the level of my own involvement.

Although not held entirely seriously, the idea that tattooing is addictive—that the tattoo pigment enters the bloodstream and impels one to "get more ink"—is a commonplace within the tattoo subculture. As my time in the field and my knowledge of the quality of the work being produced by the most skilled tattoo artists increased, I came to experience personally an almost irresistible desire to enlarge my own collection. I fantasized about possible designs and body placement, found myself feeling embarrassed that I did not have more "coverage" when I encountered heavily tattooed enthusiasts, and even began to have dreams in which my body was festooned with large colorful examples of the best work contemporary fine art tattooing had to offer.

As is often the case with addictions, this one began to affect my personal relationships. Friends and lovers were initially supportive, or at least tactfully tolerant, largely because they could understand the methodological importance of my direct involvement in the tattoo experience. At one point, however, I had to promise the woman with whom I have a long-term relationship that, if I could acquire one more tattoo from a nationally recognized artist without her throwing up her hands and calling it quits, I would kick the tattoo habit (we later had to renegotiate this agreement).

It was through a variety of experiences such as this that I developed a *feeling* (that key source of qualitative data) for the impact of the tattoo mark on the tattooee's relationships with intimates, associates, strangers, and his or her self. I came to truly *understand* how the tattoo collector's social life is shaped significantly by considerations of practical secrecy and delighted revelation.

The focus on the tattoo as a symbol of both affiliation and disassociation, which is central to my discussion of the tattooee's career, was enhanced greatly by my own experience as a tattooed person. Soon after I left the San Francisco studio with that first tattoo, I began to realize that I was now confronted with a new category of routine social decisions—to whom and under what circumstances should I reveal my potentially discrediting decoration? Those with whom I came into contact were now classified on the basis of their anticipated response, ranging from those who would be appreciative and supportive (primarily, close friends and other tattooees) to those who would react negatively (for example, my parents and most of my colleagues). Even such routine decisions as what clothes to wear—particularly during the summer months—were now shaped by new considerations.

My transitory encounters with total strangers in public settings were similarly affected by my personal and professional involvement with tattooing. I regularly began to approach people I saw with tattoos and ask them about where they had gotten their "work" done and what had led them to choose that particular image. Tattooees accosted in this way initially tended to respond with considerable suspicion and hostility. Their affect changed dramatically, however, when I displayed my own tattoos and could demonstrate some familiarity with the tattooist they had patronized. I was no longer a curious (and, probably, unsympathetic) stranger; we were both members of a select and often stigmatized group. The fact that we would often touch each other—stretching the tattooed skin and feeling the texture of each other's design—was a special indication of the affiliative significance of the tattoo symbol. It was through social encounters such as this that I came to build an understanding of the *meaning* of the tattoo experience beyond that which could have been derived from structured information collected solely through more conventionally distanced techniques.

My experience with putting together my own tattoo collection over the course of some eight years was also a major source of insight into the perspective of committed members of the tattoo subculture. As I said before, my first piece was chosen more or less impulsively at the time of my initial visit to the museum-studio in San Francisco. Prompted by a casual interest in the development of the Art Deco style, I had done a bit of reading about Egyptian designs and symbolism (the artifacts discovered when Tutankhamen's tomb was opened in 1922 had been an important influence on Art Deco [see Hillier, 1971]). As I looked at the flash showing available tattoo designs a small winged scarab caught my eye. The design was relatively small and inexpensive, interestingly detailed and I was drawn by the fact the scarab had symbolized immortality to the Egyptians. I chose to have it applied to my right forearm because I wanted to watch the application process and I could easily hide or display a tattoo placed there depending upon the circumstances and the potential audience.

My second experience with the tattooist's needle came after I became involved in the fieldwork. I again chose an Egyptian symbol, an eye of Horus, and had it inscribed on my right earlobe. I had it placed there because of the unconventionality of the location and because I had been very much taken by the small rose tattooed on Eiko Matsuda's ear in Oshima's film *In the Realm of the Senses* (1976).

Like the Horus eye, my third tattoo was also done by the tattooist with whom I became friendly early in the fieldwork. I chose a flaming eye design that the tattooist had adopted from a book on Tibetan art largely because it was unusual, brightly colored, and of moderate size. I had it placed with the scarab on my forearm because I had no desire to expand to other body locations and wasn't very much taken by the here-and-there badge motif which is fairly conventional in western folk art tattooing.

My next piece was a six inch dragon grouped with the rest of the tattoos on my arm. By the time I decided to get this work I was a reasonably knowledgeable member of the tattoo subculture. I had heard many glowing reports of the abilities of an artist who had a studio in New York City and had seen examples of his highly detailed work in various tattoo publications. I decided that I wanted a dragon design both because of my involvement with fantasy art and because I was becoming more and more interested in the powerful Japanese style, which is a key influence in contemporary western fine art tattooing. Symbolizing strength and wisdom, the dragon is a common design in Japanese work. In the company of another tattooist and carrying a half dozen books containing drawings of dragons, I traveled to New York. After an hour or so of discussion and work on sample designs the artist and I settled on an image which combined features of both western and oriental dragons and I received the largest and most ornate piece in my growing collection.

Some months later I again traveled to New York, this time to participate in a television talk show segment on tattooing. I felt an immediate sense of connection to the tattooist who was also on the program—an artist about whom I had heard but whose work was unfamiliar to me. Seeing for the first time the examples of his art, I realized that this young man was creating tattoos that displayed a level of technical skill and striking beauty unlike anything I had yet seen. Though I had planned to close my career as a tattoo collector with the dragon, I began to reconsider as my personal relationship with the tattoo artist developed and I came to realize that carrying custom work done by him was, within the tattoo community, equivalent to owning a Picasso in the larger fine art world. Over the next few years we planned and worked on completely filling the available space on my right arm. I was interested in continuing the theme of mythological creatures while combining major elements of both the Japanese style and contemporary western tattooing. A large griffen modeled after a German block print was inscribed on my shoulder with its tail snaking down my upper arm. The image was integrated with my other pieces by using "fill work" consisting of flames and dark spiraling whirlwind designs which are conventional in Japanese tattooing (see Hardy, 1987a). The artist also covered the flaming eye piece on my forearm with a spider chrysanthemum and placed a small cherry blossom over the Horus eye on my ear. I had become dissatisfied with the technical quality of the original tattoos and both of these floral designs were important elements in classical Japanese tattooing—the chrysanthemum symbolizes determination and the cherry blossom represents the briefness of life (Richie and Buruma, 1980: 40–41). Later, as the artist began to focus on creating photo-realistic images of plants, animals, insects, and other objects found in nature, I had a dragon fly and lotus placed in the inner surface of my forearm. Water designs were used to fill in and integrate these elements with the rest of the work.

Given the duration, intensity, and permanence of this research voyage, I would be a very odd person indeed if I did not feel an emotional attachment to tattooing and many members of the tattoo community. Although I have taken some pains to polish my presentation and pull back from what could be seen as overt displays of bias, this book contains an account grounded on passionate—albeit consistently disciplined—personal experience (cf., Manning, 1982). I also admit to a certain degree of discomfort with the inevitable distortion that results when the complex flow of real-people-doing-real-things is subjected to the simplifying constraints of sociological analysis. Even the fairly flexible conventions of ethnography tend to wash much of the emotion, play, ambiguity, and all of the other characteristics which make everyday life so wonderfully confusing and engaging out of the phenomenon being presented (see Young, 1981; Irwin, 1987). The language of the presentation may seem occasionally intemperate but it is based on a rich and extensive body of empirical material. I have made an honest effort to avoid the conceptual blinders created by "sentimentality" (Becker, 1967). At times I believe this account captures much of the life of the tattoo experience and provides an empathic taste of the "juice" which flows through this world. It is a beginning step, an initial picture that, I hope, others will use, enlarge, elaborate, and correct. The work I have done and the account I offer are successful if the reader comes away feeling that he or she has looked into a previously unfamiliar world that now makes some sense and if this presentation acts as a small step in building a larger understanding of how cultural objects—even those as seemingly marginal as tattoos—are conceived, created, evaluated, marketed, consumed, and joyfully or regretfully incorporated into the self.

Selected Tattoo Artist Websites

Biomechanical

Guy Aitchison: http://www.hyperspacestudios.com/
Aaron Cain: http://www.aaroncain.com/

Contemporary and Traditional Japanese

Dutchman: http://www.dutchman-tattoos.com/
Sabine Gaffron: http://www.sabinegaffrontattoo.de/
Don Ed Hardy & Associates: http://www.tattoocitysf.com/
Hori Tsuki Kage (a.k.a. Shad): http://www.tattoobyshad.com/
Horiyoshi III: http://www.ne.jp/asahi/tattoo/horiyoshi3/
Junii and Bill Salmon: http://myspace.com/10117559
Shige: http://www.yellowblaze.net/
Tin Tin: http://www.tin-tin-tattoos.com/

Dark Art

Paul Booth: http://darkimages.com/enter.asp
Tim Kern: http://www.myspace.com/ymonster
Liorcifer: http://www.myspace.com/liorcifer666
Dan Marshall: http://www.myspace.com/lastritesdanmarshall
Ethan Morgan: http://www.myspace.com/ethanmorgan

French School and Color Specialists

Brandon Bond & Associates: http://www.allornothingtattoo.com/
Stephane Chaudesaigues:
    http://www.stephanechaudesaigues.com/tatouage/tattoo,paris.htm
Tin Tin: http://www.tin-tin-tattoos.com/
Michele Wortman: http://www.hyperspacestudios.com/

New Skool

Joe Capobianco: http://www.joecapobianco.com/tattoos/
Grime, Marcus Pacheco & Associates:
   http://www.primalurgesf.com/phil.html
Adrian Lee & Associates: http://www.newskooltattoo.com/

Photo-realism and Portraiture

Nikko: http://www.myspace.com/nikkotattsu
Tom Renshaw: http://www.tomrenshaw.com/
Tin Tin: http://www.tin-tin-tattoos.com/
Bob Tyrrell: http://www.myspace.com/bobtyrrell

Tibetan Tattooing

Jondix: http://www.holytrauma.com/
Rinzing Thaptsangky: http://www.rinzing-tattoo.ch/

Tribal

Alex Binnie: http://www.alexbinnie.com/tattoo_97_00.htm
Trevor Marshall: http://www.oceanictatau.com/

Notes

Preface to the Revised and Expanded Edition

1. A recent survey of teenagers found that 62 percent agreed that when celebrities get a piercing it prompts teens to do the same and 58 percent said that celebrities getting tattooed causes teens to make the same choice (Majewski, Lori, "Teens and Celebrities," *USA Weekend*, May 19–21, pp. 6–7).

2. In mid 2007, a search on Amazon.com using "tattoo" as the search term yielded over 26,000 hits.

3. For extended lists of labels applied to this collection of graphic materials, see *Juxtapoz* 3 #1 (Winter 1996): 4 and *Juxtapoz* 7 #2 (March/April 2000): 4.

4. For evidence of the major part played by tattooing in lowbrow art, see the Spring 2004 Special Tattoo issue of *Juxtapoz*. For a discussion of the work of Greg Irons, the artist who moved most effectively between the worlds of commercial, serious, underground, and tattoo art, see Rosenkranz (2006).

5. For manifestos of lowbrow art, see *Juxtapoz* #1 (Winter 1994): 1 and *Juxtapoz* #48 (January/February 2004): 4. For extended discussions of this artistic genre, see Jordon (2005) and the essays in Anderson (2004).

6. The derogation of tattooing also occurs in more authoritarian or traditionalist cultures. Recruits who wish to become officers in the Chinese People's Liberation Army are banned from admission to military academies if they are deemed to be too short, too fat, too skinny, or have tattoos (*The Week*, May 5, 2006, p. 7).

7. A minority of those who are tattooed—around 15 percent (Read, 2006)—wear them on their faces, hands, or necks.

8. On the other hand, some employers—Bank of America and Borders Books for example—do not have "dress codes" that prohibit tattoos (Kang and Jones, 2007: 42; Read, 2006). Presumably, these more "accepting" firms are more interested in their employees' skill than in their body decorations or wish to appeal to a younger clientele. There is even a listing of "mod-friendly" employers who hire people with visible tattoos and piercings on the modifiedmind.com website (Wessel, 2007).

9. In 2006 a medical researcher from the University of California

warned women that they could experience problems during childbirth if they wore "tramp stamp" tattoos on their lower backs since this was the site at which epidural anesthetic was injected and these injections could cause a negative reaction if pigment is transmitted into deep tissue (*The Week*, May 19, 2006, p. 6).

10. Perhaps the most unexpected mention of the book was in *Chemical and Engineering News* (August 28, 1989, p. 60).

11. Atkinson (2003) is fairly direct about the significance of *Customizing the Body* for his work: "My first academic encounter with tattooing occurred about ten years ago. Enrolled in a course in the sociology of deviance, I read a piece from Clinton Sanders's well-known work, *Customizing the Body: The Art and Culture of Tattooing* (1989). Contextualizing tattooing as an example of stigma management and secondary deviance, Sanders skillfully presented it as an exotic, disrespected, and marginal social activity" (p. viii).

12. Since the first edition of *Customizing the Body* appeared, my own tattoo collection (as pictured on the original cover) has expanded. I continued my association with Shotsie Gorman as both a friend and a client and received a Celtic dragon wrist-piece based on the graphic on the title page of the first edition, a classic water lily, a photo-realistic dragonfly, and a large dragon with its tail on my inner forearm and its head on my chest. This—when filled in with classic Japanese water, air and, fire designs—completed a full right "sleeve." Having made a promise to my partner not to cover my body with tattoos, I stopped there. Angus's collection is more extensive and of recent vintage. He is working toward a "body suit" featuring five-sevenths-length sleeves and half legs, and with full coverage of his ribs, back, and "chest plates." His collection features the work of noted tattoo innovators such as Jen Billig, Dave Bobrick, Fred Corbin, Suzanne Fauser, Claus Fuhrmann, Henry Goldfield, Shotsie Gorman, Marty Holcomb, Horiwaka, Filip Leu, Joe Levin, Jack Rudy, Shad, and Bill Salmon. The collection has been featured in a variety of tattoo magazines and books, and his right leg (a series of full-color, life-sized portraits of musicians John Coltrane, Jimi Hendrix, and Carlos Santana, done by Filip Leu) has won awards for realism and portraiture. These portraits changed the practice of portraiture in tattooing, which had previously remained restricted to black and grey images, usually of three-inch by four-inch size. His collection also features a variety of styles of tattooing from traditional Japanese to hotrod flames, from photo-realism to psychedelia, from traditional Americana to biomechanical. As of this writing, his back and right ribs remain open, although he has plans for their completion.

Chapter 2

1. It is interesting to note that tattoos appear to be less prevalent among hospitalized mental patients than among the general population.

Tattooists and other knowledgeable observers estimate that approximately 10 percent of Americans wear tattoos (see Post, 1968: 519; Webb, 1979: 38), whereas between 3 and 5 percent of institutionalized mental patients are tattooed (see Pollack and McKenna, 1945; Edgerton and Dingman, 1963)

2. See Scutt and Gotch (1974: 15–88) for an extensive discussion of the sexual symbolism of tattoos.

3. On the other hand, Mosher et al. (1967) found that tattooed prisoners had a more positive body image than their unmarked fellows. Tattooed prisoners also scored high on measures designed to indicate "integrated, adaptive, and socially acceptable patterns of behavior."

4. In some cases tattoos are used as a badge commemorating prison experience. Hispanic males in Los Angeles, for example, have developed a convention in which a small tear is tattooed at the corner of the eye for each year spent in prison (cf. Agris, 1977: 28). Tattooing has also been used by those in power to symbolize negative social status. For example, by the early seventeenth century Japanese authorities had developed an elaborate tattoo system that indicated the nature and geographic location of the criminal's violation (Richie and Buruma, 1980: 12–13; see also Brain, 1979: 160–162).

5. The central importance of personal recommendation as the source of tattoo clients is well known to tattooists. All tattooists have business cards that they hand out quite freely (one maintained that he had dispensed over 50,000 cards in the past two years). Listing one's services in the Yellow Pages is the other major means employed to draw customers since it provides location information to those who, for a variety of reasons, do not have interpersonal sources. A tattooist whose shop was located near a large naval base stated:

> I'm dropping most of my Yellow Page ads. It's just a waste of money.
> I'd rather have that thousand bucks a year and do something else
> with it. I'm in every phone book in the state, I'm dropping it in all
> but [naval base]. That's the only one I've found that is worthwhile
> because it is a transient population that does use the Yellow Pages
> for a reference. Most people come here by word of mouth. They see
> the work and they come. Or they hear about it. A lot of people come
> because it is close and there aren't a lot of studios around. Cards
> are your best investment.

6. Questionnaire respondents were given an open-ended question that asked them to speculate as to why people get tattooed. Of the 163 respondents, 135 provided some sort of reply to this item. Forty-four percent of those responding emphasized that becoming tattooed was motivated by a desire for self-expression (for example, "vanity," "it's a personal preference," "a statement of who you are"), 21 percent emphasized tattooing as a mechanism for asserting uniqueness and individuality (for

example, "people like to be different," "personal originality," "it makes you special"), and 28 percent made some form of aesthetic statement (for example, "because it is beautiful," "a form of art that lasts forever," "body jewelry"). On their part, tattooists tend to recognize the aesthetic importance of their work as seen by their clients. One tattooist, for example, observed:

> If you ask most people why they got (a particular tattoo) they aren't going to have any deep Freudian answer for you. The most obvious reason that someone gets a tattoo is because they like it for some reason and just want it. I mean, why do people wear rings on their fingers or any sort of nonfunctional decorative stuff—put on make-up or dye their hair? People have the motivation to decorate themselves and be different and unique. . . . Tattooing is really the most intimate art form. You carry it on your body. The people that come in here are really mostly just "working bumpkins." They just want to have some art they can understand. This stuff in museums is bullshit. Nobody ever really sees it. It doesn't get to the people like tattoo art.

7. Of the thirty-five tattoos worn by the sixteen interviewees, 14 percent (five) represented a bird, 6 percent (two) represented a mammal, 14 percent (five) represented a mythical animal, 9 percent (three) represented an insect, 3 percent (one) represented a human female, 17 percent (six) represented a human male, 14 percent (five) were noncommercial symbols (hearts, crosses, military insignia, and so on), 14 percent (five) were floral, 3 percent (one) were names or vow tattoos, and 6 percent (two) were some other image.

Questionnaire respondents were asked to indicate the design of their first tattoo. They were: 14 percent (twenty-three) bird, 11 percent (eighteen) mammal, 12 percent (nineteen) mythical animal, 10 percent (seventeen) insect, 1 percent (two) human female, 6 percent (ten) human male, 4 percent (six) commercial symbols, 8 percent (thirteen) noncommercial symbols, 21 percent (thirty-four) floral/arboreal, 4 percent (seven) name/vow, and 9 percent (fourteen) other.

8. The painfulness of the tattoo process is the most unpleasant element of the tattoo event. Only 33 percent (fifty-four) of the questionnaire respondents maintained that there was something about the tattoo experience that they disliked. One third of these (eighteen) said that the pain was what they found most unpleasant. Fourteen of the sixteen interviewees mentioned pain as a troublesome factor. Numerous observations of groups of young men discussing pain or expressing stoic disregard for the pain as they received tattoos demonstrated the importance of the tattoo event as a form of initiation ritual. In some cases the tattoo process provides a situation in which the male tattooed can demonstrate his manliness to his peers. Here, for example, is a description of an incident in

which five members of a local college football team acquired identical tattoos on their hips:

> [Quote from fieldnotes] I ask the guy nearest to me if they are all getting work done. "Yeah. He (indicates friend) was so hot for it he would have done it himself if we couldn't get it done today." (You all getting hip shots?) "Yeah, that's where all jocks get them. The coach would shit if he found out." The conversation among the jocks turns to the issue of pain. They laugh as the guy being worked on grimaces as W (artist) finishes the outline and wipes the piece down with alcohol. The client observes that this experience isn't bad compared to the time "I fucked up my hand in a game and had to have steel pins put in the knuckles. One of them got bent and the doctor had to cut it out. That was bad. I got the cold sweats." Some of the others join in by telling their "worst pain I ever experienced" stories. The guy being worked on is something of a bleeder and the others kid him about this. As W begins shading one of them shouts, "Come on, really grind it in there."

The cross-cultural literature on body alteration indicates that the pain of the process is an important factor. Ebin (1979: 88–89), for example, in discussing tattooing in the Marquesas Islands, states:

> The tattoo was not only an artistic achievement: it also demonstrated that its recipient could bear pain. On one island, the word to describe a person who was completely covered with tattoos is ne'one'o, based on a word meaning either "to cry for a long time" or "horrific." One observer in the Marquesas noted that whenever people discussed the tattoo design, they emphasized the pain with which it was acquired.

See also Brain, 1979: 183–184; Ross and McKay, 1979: 44–49, 67–69; Becker and Clark, 1979: 10, 19; St. Clair and Govenar, 1981: 100–135.

9. Other than simply accepting the regretted mark, there are few avenues of resolution open to dissatisfied tattooers. In the most extreme cases, the tattooed may try to obliterate the offending mark with acid or attempt to cut it off. A somewhat more reasoned (and considerably less painful) approach entails seeking the aid of a dermatologist or plastic surgeon who will medically remove the tattoo. The most common alternative, however, is to have the technically inferior piece redone or covered with another tattoo created by a more skilled practitioner. Tattooists estimate that 40 to 50 percent of their work entails reworking or applying cover-ups to poor quality tattoos. See Goldstein et al., 1979, and Hardy, 1983.

10. One traditional use of tattooing has been to mark indelibly social outcasts and defined deviants so that they can be easily identified and/or avoided by officials and "normals." In sixth-century Japan, for example, criminals and social outcasts were tattooed on the face or arms as a form

of negative public identification and punishment (Richie and Buruma, 1980: 12–13). Similarly, in the nineteenth century, inmates of the Massachusetts prison system had "Mass S. P." and the date of their release tattooed on their left arms (Ebensten, 1953: 20). More recently, the Nazis tattooed identification numbers on the arms of concentration camp inmates. In April of 1986 conservative columnist William Buckley suggested that victims of AIDS (Acquired Immune Deficiency Syndrome) be tattooed on the buttocks in order to limit the spread of the disease among homosexuals (*The Hartford Courant*, April 19,1986, p. C6).

11. The literature directed at the fan world surrounding tattooing consistently makes reference to the "tattoo community." For example:

> The choice of the artist and the image are of paramount importance. The collector is not only making a statement about himself, but is also visually displaying the art of tattooing. The collector has an obligation that goes far beyond commitment to oneself. The tattoo community as a whole is dependent on the critical abilities of those who look upon tattooing as a serious art form. . . . Like any other area of the arts that has a large following, tattooing creates for both the artist and the patron a culture that is familiar and appreciated. The tattooing community has a close bond between the artist and the collector, a bond much closer than in most artistic communities because of the intimate nature of a tattoo. Everyone who is part of the community shares in the responsibilities involved in keeping the art form alive and responsive (Brachfeld, 1982: 24–25).

Chapter 3

1. Prior to entering tattooing interviewees had been truck drivers, car salesmen, automobile or motorcycle mechanics, construction workers, hospital attendants.

2. All but three of the interviewees reported that the idea of pursuing the occupation of tattooing was initiated while being personally tattooed.

3. Eleven (79 percent) of the fourteen interviewed tattooists reported that they had acquired their first tattoo machine from another artist. Five of the eleven purchased equipment from the tattooist who was doing their own work.

4. See Zeis, 1984 [1952]; Lemes, 1978.

5. Dr. Andrew Lemes (1978) reports that his life was threatened when word got out that he intended to publish "tattoo trade secrets." This market-limiting secrecy within the tattoo world also has obvious implications for the researcher. In the early stages of my fieldwork tattooists were rather overt about expressing their suspicions that I might be interested in acquiring "secret information."

6. Of the nine tattooist/interviewees who had received some form of training, one had been involved in formal, remunerated training; five were hired as apprentice-gofers and three learned by hanging out and observing in tattoo studios.

7. Japanese tattooist/initiates typically practice on radishes (Richie and Buruma, 1980: 97), hams or sausages (Fellman, 1986: 13).

8. When asked who was the recipient of their first tattoo, six respondents (43 percent) said they had done their initial work on customers in the shop where they were working or hanging out, two (14 percent) said they had tattooed themselves first, and six (43 percent) said they had done their first work as coverups or reworking of the crude work carried by trusting or naive personal friends or acquaintances (cf. Schroder, 1973: 108–111).

9. Five of the fourteen interviewees were basically self-taught.

10. Interviewees estimated that between 40 and 80 percent of the customers who come to them for a first tattoo eventually return for more work.

11. Of the fourteen tattooist interviewees, six worked in shops owned by another tattooist (two were apprentices), three were proprietors of shops in which there were two or more artists, four were situated in shops in which they were the sole tattooist, and one was a "bootlegger" tattooing out of his apartment in a state in which tattooing was legally prohibited.

12. Of the fourteen tattooists interviewed, nine cited pleasurable interaction with clients and customer satisfaction with the tattoo/service as the primary reward of their occupation.

13. It is interesting to think of this issue of the tattoo "artist" covering or reworking the product of another "artist" in light of Becker's (1982: 217–225) discussion of the editing, destruction, and "death" of art products.

14. Eleven of fourteen interviewees cited the negative social status of being a tattooist as a major occupational problem.

15. The legal problems encountered by the tattooist are an excellent example of a specific instance in which the state attempts to structure an art world and shape the artistic activity to its own liking. See Becker, 1982: 165–191 for a general discussion of this issue.

16. One tattooist prided himself on the quantity and diversity of the tattoo designs he had on display. He estimated, however, that of the some 2,000 tattoos he offered he only applied 100 with any regularity.

Chapter 4

1. Given the male dominance within tattooing, I was surprised at the relative infrequency with which overtly sexual talk and sexual come-ons occurred in the studios. Male tattooists consistently maintained that they were not sexually excited by the exposure of or contact with intimate parts

of female clients' bodies. When I observed tattooists working on or near women's "private" areas they routinely maintained a serious facial expression and did not engage in the usual joking interaction. Like some gynecologists (see Emerson, 1970) they adopted a rigid business-like demeanor so as to avoid the potentially conflictual sexual implications of the intimate physical contact. On their part, women clients commonly exercised some care when planning for and receiving tattoos on their breasts, buttocks, hips, thighs, or other private locations. They usually were accompanied by a female friend and wore leotards or bathing suits under their clothes. In the shops I frequented curtains commonly were used to conceal the process from the casual observer (cf. Becker and Clark, 1979: 14–15).

2. Those shops in which commercial values are dominant—especially those which cater primarily to military personnel—deal with the time problem by speeding up the process. Some shops employ an assembly line mode of organization. The least experienced employee applies the chosen design using a plastic stencil and fine carbon powder, the senior tattooist does the most exacting work of outlining the design with black pigment and, finally, the client is passed on to assistants who shade and color the design. While this procedure was generally denigrated by the tattooists I interviewed, it was, at the same time, seen as a reasonable approach for high volume shops located near military bases.

3. At times, watching customers react negatively to their experientially enlarged understanding of the tattoo process. For example:

> Did I tell you about the guy who fainted in here the other day? Well,
> actually he didn't do it in here, he did it outside. He had come in
> with his friend, not even getting a tattoo, just watching. I noticed
> him leave. He was out sitting on the front step and he just went
> over. We thought he was dead. He was foaming at the mouth and
> didn't move a muscle. He had wet himself and there was all this
> blood on the sidewalk—he had cut himself when he went down. We
> did the thing with the poppers and the wet towels. His buddy—the
> guy who was getting the tattoo—said he "had a weak stomach."
> Needless to say he didn't get a tattoo.

4. It is understandable, therefore, that experienced tattoo collectors who purchase custom work and who have developed a personal relationship with an artist consistently express the highest level of satisfaction. On the other hand, tattoo initiates with little or no experience and who impulsively decide to be tattooed in the first studio they enter are far more likely to regret their decision. As would be predicted on the basis of the literature on high risk purchases (for example, Cunningham, 1967), tattoo consumers who have been satisfied with past work and who choose to get additional tattoos display considerable "brand loyalty." Returning to a tattooist who has provided satisfactory service in the past significantly

increases the certainty that the performance of the service deliverer will be acceptable. The artist's technical and creative skills, while perhaps not of the highest caliber available, are a known quantity. Another reason for the loyalty to a particular tattooist typically shown by returnees is found in the personal relationship which is a core feature of all service interactions, especially those which involve significant perceived risk and are correspondingly high in experience and credence qualities (Zeithaml, 1984). Tattoo collectors cultivate and value the relationship with "their" artist. They routinely visit the studio, even when not desiring work, to socialize and discuss tattoo lore. They act as part of the tattooist's "performance team" by testifying to his or her skill, displacing completed work to potential clients, and generally helping the tattooist to maintain interactional control over the tattoo setting. By fostering a personal relationship with the tattooist the collector is increasing the chances that his or her work will be of the best technical quality possible and thereby maximizing the likelihood that he or she will be satisfied with the service provided.

5. As discussed in Chapter 3, cover-up work on dissatisfied tattooees is the bread-and-butter of even the most moderately competent tattooist. To some extent, the tattooist will purposefully "educate" a customer about the inferior quality of his or her other work in order to prompt dissatisfaction and generate more business.

There are what—seven or eight tattoo artists in (the state) and probably about forty bootleggers. There are a lot of butchers out there. This guy came in the other day and he had gotten some work by a scratcher out in R——. It was a disgrace. He came in with a friend who was going to get some work. He wasn't going to get anything done but he showed it to me and he could see from the work I was doing and from how I responded how shitty it was. Most people don't know bad work from good work. I convinced him to let me fix it up because I just wanted to see if I could do it. I usually give people like that a break. People like that are usually so tickled with the cover-up or some reworking that they tell all of their friends and they come in and get more tattoos and so on. It pays dividends.

In addition to covering or reworking a technically inferior piece, tattooists ease client dissatisfaction by obliterating names or initials which tattooees commonly have indelibly inscribed on their bodies. Usually, these cover-up clients come to the establishment propelled by the intense prompting of the people with whom they currently have relationships or because they want to symbolically obliterate the last vestiges of relationships which ended unhappily. One tattooist recounted a unique name cover-up story:

I hold the record for name cover-ups. (This comes after he has concluded a rather snippy conversation with a guy who wants to get his girl's name put on him. S—— [artist] had said, "You really shouldn't do this. Didn't I just cover up another name on you? Is this

your mother or daughter? You know the way things are. Tattoos last
a lot longer than relationships.") I talk to other artists and I know I
hold the record. This guy came in and he wanted some girl's name
put on him. I tried to talk him out of it like I always do, but he was
not to be dissuaded. So, I put his girlfriend's name on him and he
leaves. A half hour later the phone rings and this guy says, "Can you
cover up the tattoo?" and I say, "Who is this?" *It's the guy who just
left!* It turns out that he left here and went home and walked into a
totally empty apartment. The woman had taken everything they
owned and moved out while he was in here getting her name put on
him. That *has* to be a record.

At times this form of relational tattooing may become rather extreme.
One mid-western tattooist recounted the following story.

I have this chick that comes in every once in a while—a black chick.
Her boyfriend is some hot soul musician who has had a couple of
hits on the soul charts. Everytime she comes in she gets the same
thing. She gets his name put on her thigh. I don't know, she's a real
nice looking chick but she has G—— T—— about fifteen times on
her thigh. I try to get her to let me put a heart or a butterfly or
something on but she just wants the name. Last time she was in she
got something different. She got "property of" put before the name.

6. While this extreme form of desperate self-mutilation is rarely pursued, I have, in the course of the research, encountered people who
attempted to remove tattoos by abrading them with sandpaper, painting
them with acid and other caustic substances, or by cutting them off with
knives. For example:

[Quote from fieldnotes] I saw the crudest attempt at self-removal I
have ever seen down at R——'s (studio) today. A young, fairly well-
dressed oriental guy came in to get some cover-up work. I'm not
often shocked by this time but this one really took me aback. When
he took off his shirt I could see that much of his back was covered
with massive keloid scars which only partially obliterated the outline of a crude demon's head and four playing cards. It turns out
that he had the back piece put on when he was in prison in Hong
Kong for some sort of petty crime. When he got out he was intensely
ashamed of the tattoo. He proceeded to purchase a bottle of acid
and, after fortifying himself with booze, poured the acid down his
back. The pain must have been unbelievable. I was impressed by
how gently R—— treated him. He told him that he had consulted
with a doctor after the young man had initially come to him and,
because the skin had been so seriously traumatized and the blood
vessels were so close to the surface, he could not tattoo directly
over the scars themselves. Instead, what he proceeded to do was to

cover up the unscarred tattoo which remained with an ornate oriental dragon. The scar tissue was outlined in the traditional Japanese cloud style. The ugly and uneven scars were used to create part of a unique and beautiful back piece.

7. Tattooists see the ability to apply a piece with minimal pain to the recipient as a mark of expertise. One interviewee spoke of a fellow tattooist with some disdain:

> [He's] a funny guy. He thinks that anything he doesn't do is just adequate. A guy I know went in there with one of my pieces and was saying how good it was. He asked the guy who did it and when he found out that it was mine he said something like, "Well, it's not TOO BAD." He doesn't give you very much. He's really rough, too. Really likes to hurt'em. He's still using those paper towels from the Sunoco restrooms—with all the wood chips in them—to wipe with. I went in to have him do this piece and he worked it and worked it. I said, "Hey V——, leave it alone." And he says, "No, just a little more. I still see white spots." He just gets off on hurting people. (cf. Richie and Buruma, 1980: 98.)

8. Some psychoanalytic analysts would interpret this kind of distaste as being related to the tattooist's latent homosexual fears. In the 1934 volume of *Psychoanalytic Quarterly* Susanna Haigh presented the sexual analysis of tattooing in no uncertain terms:

> The symbolism of the act of tattooing is pointed out as observing the needle as the penis introducing the tattooing fluid into a cavity. The tattooist is the more or less sadistic aggressor; the person tattooed, the passive recipient. . . . As might be expected the tattoo is used often as an unconscious representation of a penis both by men and women. . . . (There is an) anal element in the tattoo. There is surely a definite relationship between the impulse of the child to smear itself with feces and that of the adult to have himself smeared with indelible paint (quoted in Morse, 1977: 122).

9. Rubber glove manufacturers are enjoying a booming business due to the rising fear of contracting serum communicated diseases, especially AIDS. One manufacturer, Global-Crown Bio-Med Lab in Manchester, Connecticut, for example, reports an 80 percent increase in rubber glove sales (*The Hartford Courant*, July 17, 1987, p. B3). Dermatologist Gary Brauner emphasized the potential health hazards associated with the tattooist's contact with clients in a lecture delivered at the 1984 convention of the National Tattoo Association in Philadelphia. He strongly advised attendees to wear surgical gloves during the tattoo process.

Chapter 5

1. The importance of the social status of the creator in determining whether a product is defined as art or as something else (and consequently inferior) is well illustrated by the ongoing resistance of the art world to certifying material objects typically produced by women as being "real" art. Most commonly, women's creations are either ignored by the male dominated art world (see Heller, 1987) or relegated to the second-class category of "craft" (see Banks, 1987; Needleman, 1979; Crane, 1987: 60; Becker, 1982: 247–258; Maines, 1985).

2. The class structure of the social system in which the art world exists has been the dominant structural feature of interest in most sociological discussions of art forms and artistic style. See, for example, Hauser, 1982: 94–307; Fischer, 1970; Lomax, 1970; Pellegrini, 1966.

3. The major way in which cultural items created, enjoyed, and consumed by disvalued social groups come to affect the materials and activities of upper-class taste publics is through "bottom-up" cultural diffusion or, to use a less neutral term, cultural imperialism. Much of the innovation that takes place in high fashion and modern dance, for example, comes from the sanitizing appropriation of stylistic elements initiated in "street culture" (see Hirschman, 1981b) and by members of impoverished social groups (see Gans, 1971).

4. Due largely to its physical intrusiveness and historical connections to marginal groups, tattooing is prohibited or the focus of extensive regulation by local governmental agencies in most states. Despite official disapproval and restraint, the tattoo service is readily available throughout the United States. Best's (1981) discussion of the effectiveness of social control directed at the media points to the reasons why regulation is relatively ineffective in decreasing the availability of tattooing. He maintains that legal restraint is most effective when the cost of production and distribution is high, the number of artifacts and available distribution channels is low, the production industry displays a heavy reliance on advertising, and the audience/consumer group is heterogeneous and includes children. These conditions do not characterize contemporary commercial tattooing.

5. The mass media are the major source of public information about the physical and normative reality of American society. When tattooing is presented in the media it is associated almost exclusively with unconventional, dishonorable, dangerous, and otherwise deviant social types. (See, for example, the mentally disordered character played by Bruce Dern in Bob Brooks' *Tattoo* [1981], the heavily tattooed "hero" in Clive Barker's *Hellraiser* [1987] and the extensive publicity given to Richard Speck's "born to raise hell" tattoo.) The disreputable symbolic baggage carried by tattooing is well illustrated in the copy used in a current mailorder catalogue which is intended to entice people to purchase a set of "stick-on" tattoos.

Painless Tattoos are so realistic, they'll even *fool* mom. Use to *shock* friends and co-workers; to *scare* away muscle-bound beasts. Water-applied tattoo lasts several days, but can be instantly removed with rubbing alcohol (emphasis added).

6. A few heavily tattooed collectors, such as "Krystyne the Kolorful" (Krystyne Chipchar) and Neil Grant, who are well known in the tattooing subculture, do make a limited amount of money from their extensive collections by marketing photographs of themselves. A significantly more macabre approach is seen at the Medical Pathology Museum of Tokyo University which houses a collection of over 105 preserved tattooed skins. The collection was originally begun in the mid-1920s by Dr. Masaichi Fukushi. Athough the collection is largely a medical curiosity, this is one of only a few situations in which extensive, fine art tattooing has been separated from its original owner and maintained as a cultural artifact (Hardy, 1987b; see also Richie and Buruma, 1980: 69).

7. For example, Jeff Crisman, a photography professor at the University of Illinois Chicago campus exhibited his photos of tattooing and tattooists at the Chicago Public Library Cultural Center in 1983 (Fondiller, 1984) and at the Arc Gallery in 1986 (*St. Louis Post-Dispatch*, June 12, 1986, p. 21). Sandi Fellman, a photography professor at Rutgers University, exhibited her photos of full-body Japanese tattooing at the Clarence Kennedy Gallery in Cambridge, Massachusetts in 1987 and Masato Sudo's exhibition of Japanese work was on display in San Diego's Museum of Photographic Art (Jamiol, 1987: 37). Sudo and Fellman also had photographs in a major exhibit entitled "The Art of the Japanese Tattoo" presented by the respected Peabody Museum in Salem, Massachusetts. This show was a particularly significant event in the course of tattooing's legitimation as an art form. The Peabody exhibit included a large collection of ukiyo-e prints by Utagawa Kuniyoshi representing tattooed heros from the *Suikoden*. Japanese tattoo master Aki Ohwada—the owner of the Kuniyoshi prints—and his wife attended the show and proudly displayed their own extensive tattoos. Most importantly, the Peabody exhibit was significant because it was supported by a grant from the National Endowment for the Arts and, as DiMaggio (1987: 452) emphasizes, grants from public agencies "set out *explicit* classifications of artistic work" (see *The Hartford Courant*, November 9, 1986, p. H25; Jamiol, 1987). Other exhibitions of tattoo art have been presented at the Oakland Art Museum (1978), Mercati Traianei in Rome (1985), the Paradiso in Amsterdam (1986), and the Sixth Sense Gallery in New York (1987). Museums specifically devoted to displaying historical memorabilia and examples of a wide range of classic and contemporary tattooing have been established by Lyle Tuttle in San Francisco (the Tattoo Art Museum) and "Philadelphia Eddie" Funk in Philadelphia (the National Tattoo Museum).

8. For example, in December of 1972 the UGA had an exhibition of work in City College's Eisner Hall which was reviewed by the *New York Times*

and resulted in the hiring of UGA artists by choreographer Twyla Tharp to create the backgrounds for her new ballet "Deuce Coupe" (Castleman, 1982: 119). Subsequently the work of graffiti writers was shown, among other places, in the Razor Gallery, the Bank Street College of Education, and Chicago's Museum of Science and Industry and the NOGA received funding from the New York State Council on the Arts (Castleman, 1982: 121–122, 128, 131, 133).

9. In his review of the UGA'S Razor Gallery show Peter Schjeldahl of the *New York Times* wrote:

It is a pleasure to report that respectable standing and the *"art" context* have not cowed most of the UGA *artists*. The show-off ebullience of their work has, if anything been heightened by the comforts of a studio situation. . . . For all their untutored crudities, none of these (canvases) would do discredit to a *collection of contemporary art* (emphasis added, quoted in Castleman, 1982: 122; see also Gardner, 1985; Rosenberg, 1972: 49–54).

10. The connections between graffiti and tattooing as disvalued modes of cultural production are apparent in plates 138 and 173 of the San Francisco Museum of Modern Art's *Aesthetics of Graffiti* catalogue (1978). Both show examples of these stigmatized works in combination.

Epilogue 2008

1. While it is less pronounced today, there has long been a geographical divide in the tattoo world. The West Coast, and San Francisco in particular, is arguably the center of artistic tattooing in the United States. It is the home of some of the most prominent tattoo artists and tattoo collectors in the world. From the San Francisco perspective, East Coast tattooing has always been derivative and unsophisticated.

2. Needles come in three basic formats: rounds, flats, and magnums. Tattoo needles are not hypodermic; rather they hold pigment in the spaces between the points in clusters arranged either in circles ("rounds"), flat rows ("flats"), or staggered rows ("magnums").

3. The pain a recipient experiences is inversely related to the number of needles an artist uses. The outline is substantially more painful than shading, and magnums are substantially less painful than round configurations. Some speculate that this is because magnums spread the sensation out, making it more diffuse and therefore less intense. Also, magnums cover more space with a single pass of the needle and, as a consequence, cause less damage to the skin.

4. Knowledgeable participants in the tattoo world distinguish between "tattooers" and "tattoo artists" using a variety of criteria. The central factor is the amount of custom work the person in question provides. Of course, artistic standards are also important, but they are less easy to

standardize. Tattoo artists specialize in custom-designed tattoos, sometimes actually refusing to use stock designs from commercially available
sheets of tattoo designs ("flash"). Tattooers work less frequently in the
custom realm, sometimes actually preferring to stick with their stock in
trade of "pork chop" tattoos. Well-trained tattoo artists usually start as
tattooers, although the progression from tattooer to artist is far from uni-
versal or assured.

5. The term "collector" is expressly oriented toward artistic sensibilities
and speaks to the tattooee's commitment to the redefinition of tattooing
from a craft to an art form (Becker, 1982).

6. The Japanese "turtle back" design runs from the base of the neck to
the base of the buttocks and often continues down the outside of the
backs of the thighs. Western backpiece aesthetics are somewhat less likely to include the buttocks in the design, although many artists who work
in this scale would consider a backpiece that does not include the buttocks incomplete.

7. As the phrase implies, "sitting for" an artist means undergoing the
process of getting a tattoo. A fair degree of status accrues to the collector
who can "sit well." Sitting well principally involves remaining still and stoically enduring pain. Depending on a variety of factors relating to the
artist's competence, training, and equipment (especially needle configurations and the voltage at which the artist runs his or her machines), backpieces can often take 40 or more hours to complete. Since most people can
only endure somewhere between three and four hours of tattooing, it is
easy to see why backpieces generate such high status in the tattoo world.

8. As a rule, ticklish and/or boney parts of the body hurt the most,
making the ribs an especially difficult region to tattoo. Because the area
between the tops of the buttocks (the gluteal cleft) is so sensitive, backpiece designs often leave it open or untattooed.

9. In the United States, the most experienced artists working in this
scale are probably the New Skool Tattoo Collective, a group of thirteen
artists from California who have recently begun a project called "Full
Coverage" that is designed to turn a book of body-suit designs (Lee, 2004
[2002]) into actual body suits. Perhaps the most experienced Western tattoo artists, however, are in Switzerland (Filip Leu in Lausanne and Mick
Tattoo in Zurich), France (Tin Tin in Paris) and Germany (Luke Atkinson
in Stuttgart), each of whom works exclusively on large-scale work and
specializes in backpieces.

10. Artists of this caliber and renown are often booked for anywhere
from six months to several years in advance.

11. Membership in National Tattoo Association is still limited to 1000
persons, although NTA has added subsidiary categories that come with a
subscription to the newsletter but no voting privileges.

12. Conventions held in arenas have limited access to rest rooms or
places providing brief respites for the artists; they are not catered and the

only food available is expensive and unappetizing; and the size of the arenas is cavernous, making socializing difficult in the best of circumstances. By contrast, conventions held in hotels (as both the National and Tattoo Tour conventions used to be) allow artists the ability to run up to their rooms to use the bathroom or splash water on their faces; they are catered, so artists and clients both have regular access to a variety of food (even if it is hotel food); and their size and scope make socializing a feasible endeavor.

13. For a somewhat more extensive discussion of tattoo publications and conventions, see DeMello, 2000.

14. Of course, the medium was far from new, but in much the same way as Tuchman (1989) discusses the "open field" taken over by Victorian, male, literary romance writers, art students saw artistic possibilities in tattooing that had yet to be explored in the tattoo world. From their perspective, then, tattooing represented a "new" medium since its potential was largely unexplored. See also Becker's (1982) discussion of how artists take over "crafts."

15. A handful of art school-trained tattooists were working when the first edition of Customizing the Body was published. The most notable were Michael Bakaty, Shotsie Gorman, and Ed Hardy.

16. Perhaps the most dramatic example of this phenomenon happened recently in San Francisco where several members of the artists working in Ed Hardy's studio left without notice, only to open up a shop (Black Heart Tattoo) in the same city and right around the corner from another widely respected and well-liked tattoo artist (Coleman, 2006).

17. For discussions of these and other forms of non-mainstream body modification, see Hewitt, 1997; Myers, 1992; Polhemus and Randall, 1996; and Sanders, 2000.

18. Jeffreys's article generated two spirited refutations (see Riley, 2002, and Van Lenning, 2002), both of which criticized Jeffreys's portrayal of women as passive victims of culture, lacking agency or the ability to choose to participate in activities that Jeffreys finds problematic.

19. Participant observation is not especially well-suited for showing the existence of "fads" as it is not longitudinal and traditionally is not based on samples large enough to demonstrate broad cultural movements or patterns. Instead, it is better suited for showing the processes through which people might enact those behaviors that others consider "fads," but this is not what the authors claim to be showing.

20. In the late 1990s, a survey conducted by American Business Information, Inc., indicated that tattooing was one of the six fastest growing businesses in the United States (The Hartford Courant, March 1, 1997, p. F1).

References

Adler, Patricia, and Peter Adler. 1983. "Relationships Between Dealers: The Social Organization of Illicit Drug Transactions." *Sociology and Social Research* 67: 260–278.

Adler, Peter and Patricia Adler. 1987. "The Past and Future of Ethnography." *Journal of Contemporary Ethnography* 16 (April): 4–24.

Agris, Joseph. 1977. "Tattoos in Women." *Plastic and Reconstructive Surgery* 60: 22–37.

Albrecht, Milton, James Barnett, and Mason Griff, eds. 1970. *The Sociology of Art and Literature.* New York: Praeger.

Amaya, Mario. 1972. *Pop Art . . . And After.* New York: Viking.

Anderson, Kirsten, ed. 2004. *Pop Surrealism: The Rise of Underground Art.* San Francisco: Last Gasp.

Anderson, R. R. 1992. "Tattooing Should Be Regulated." *New England Journal of Medicine* 326 (3): 207.

Anscombe, Isabella. 1978. *Not Another Punk Book.* London: Aurum.

Armstrong, Myrna, and C. McConnell. 1994. "Tattooing in Adolescents: More Common than You Think: The Phenomenon and Its Risks." *Journal of School Nursing* 10 (1): 22–29.

Armstrong, Myrna, and Kathleen Pace-Murphy. 1997. Tattooing: Another Risk-Behavior in Adolescents Warranting National Health Attention." *Applied Nursing Research* 10 (4): 181–189.

Assasel, Henry. 1984. *Consumer Behavior and Marketing Action.* Boston: Kent.

Atkinson, Michael. 2003. *Tattooed: The Sociogenesis of a Body Art.* Toronto: University of Toronto Press.

Banks, T. J. 1987. "Art—Semantics or Gender?: Arts versus Crafts." *Hartford Woman* (September), pp. 24ff.

Basirico, Laurence. 1986. "The Art and Craft Fair: A New Institution in an Old Art World. *Qualitative Sociology* 9 (Winter): 339–353.

Battcock, Gregory, ed. 1973. *Idea Art.* New York: Dutton.

"Bear." 1987. "Good Tattoos and How to Get Them." *Outlaw Biker/ Tattoo* (March), p. 83.

Becker, Howard S. 1951. "The Professional Dance Musician and His Audience." *American Journal of Sociology* 57: 136–144.

———. 1963. *Outsider.* New York: Free Press.

————. 1967. "Whose Side Are We On?" *Social Problems* 14 (Winter): 239–247.

————. 1970. *Sociological Work.* Chicago: Aldine.

————. 1974. "Art as Collective Action." *American Sociological Review* 39 (6): 767–776.

————. 1976. "Art Worlds and Social Types." *American Behavioral Scientist* 19: 703–718.

————. 1978. "Arts and Crafts." *American Journal of Sociology* 83: 862–889.

————. 1982. *Art Worlds.* Berkeley: University of California Press.

Becker, Howard, Blanche Geer, Everett Hughes, and Anselm Strauss. 1961. *Boys in White.* Chicago: University of Chicago Press.

Becker, Nickie, and Robert E. Clark. 1979. "Born to Raise Hell: An Ethnography of Tattoo Parlors." Paper presented at the meetings of Southwestern Sociological Association, March 28–31, at Fort Worth, Texas.

Bell, Gerald. 1967. "Self-Confidence, Persuasibility and Cognitive Dissonance Among Automobile Buyers." In *Risk Taking and Information Handling in Consumer Behavior,* ed. Donald Cox, 442–468. Boston: Harvard University Graduate School of Business Administration.

Bell, Quentin. 1976. *On Human Finery.* New York: Schocken.

Ben-Sira, Zeev. 1976. "The Function of the Professional's Affective Behavior in Client Satisfaction: A Revised Approach to Social Interaction Theory." *Journal of Health and Social Behavior* 17: 3–11.

Berscheid, Ellen, E. Walster, and G. Bohrnstedt. 1973. "Body Image, Physical Appearance and Self-Esteem." Paper presented at the annual meeting of the American Sociological Association.

Bertoia, Carl. 1986. "Generating Customer Satisfaction: The Hair Stylist as Interpersonal Tactician." Paper presented at the Conference on Ethnographic Research, May, at University of Waterloo, Canada.

Best, Joel. 1981. "The Social Control of Media Content." *Journal of Popular Culture* 14 (4): 611–617.

Bjorn, Lars. 1981. "The Mass Society and Group Action Theories of Cultural Production: The Case of Stylistic Innovation in Jazz." *Social Forces* 60: 377–394.

Blumer, Herbert. 1969. "Fashion: From Class Differentiation to Collective Selection." *Sociological Quarterly* 10: 275–291.

————. 1969. *Symbolic Interactionism: Perspective and Method.* Berkeley: University of California Press.

Boles, Jacqueline, and Albeno Garbin. 1974. "The Choice of Stripping for a Living." *Sociology of Work and Occupations* 1: 110–123.

Bourdieu, Pierre. 1984. *Distinction: A Social Critique of the Judgement of Taste.* Cambridge, MA: Harvard University Press.

Brachfeld, Ted. 1982. "Tattoos and the Collector." *Tattootime* 1 (Fall): 24–25.

Brain, Dennis. 1979. *The Decorated Body.* New York: Harper and Row.

Briggs, J. 1958. "Tattooing." *Medical Times* 87: 1030–1039.

Brislin, Richard, and Steven Lewis. 1968. "Dating and Physical Attractiveness: A Replication." *Psychological Reports* 22: 976–984.

Bronner, Simon. 1986. "The House on Penn Street: Creativity and Conflict in Folk Art." In *Folk Art and Art Worlds*, ed. J. Vlach and S. Bronner, 123–150. Ann Arbor: UMI Research Press.

Browne, Joy. 1976. "The Used Car Game." In *The Research Experience*, ed. M.P. Golden, 60–70. Itasca, IL: Peacock.

Browne, Ray. 1983. "Popular Culture—New Notes Toward a Definition." In *The Popular Culture Reader*, 3rd ed., ed. C. Geist and J. Nachbar, 13–20. Bowling Green, OH: Bowling Green University Popular Press.

Bryan, James. 1966. "Occupational Ideologies and Individual Attitudes of Call Girls." *Social Problems* 13: 441–450.

Burchett, George, and Peter Leighton. 1958. *Memoirs of a Tattooist*. London: Oldbourne.

Burma, John. 1965. "Self Tattooing Among Delinquents: A Research Note." In *Dress, Adornment and the Social Order*, ed. M. E. Roach and J. B. Eicher, 271–279. New York: Wiley.

Burns, Elizabeth. 1972. *Theatricality*. New York: Harper and Row.

Caplan, Jane, ed. 2000. *Written on the Body: The Tattoo in European and American History*. Princeton, NJ: Princeton University Press.

Carroll, Lynne, and Roxanne Anderson. 2002. "Body Piercing, Tattooing, Self Esteem, and Body Investment in Adolescent Girls." *Adolescence* 37 (147): 627–638.

Castleman, Craig. 1982. *Getting Up*. Cambridge: MIT Press.

Ceniceros, Salvador. 1998. "Tattooing, Body Piercing, and Russian Roulette." *Journal of Nervous and Mental Disease* 186 (8): 503–504.

Charles, Ann, and Roger DeAnfrasio. 1970. *The History of Hair*. New York: Bonanza.

Christopherson, Richard. 1974a. "Making Art with Machines: Photography's Institutional Inadequacies." *Urban Life and Culture* 3 (April): 3–34.

———. 1974b. "From Folk Art to Fine Art: A Transformation in the Meaning of Photographic Work." *Urban Life and Culture* 3: 179–204.

Cohen, Sidney. 1973. "Mods and Rockers: The Inventory as Manufactured News." In *The Manufacture of News: A Reader*, ed. S. Cohen and J. Young, 226–241. Beverly Hills, CA: Sage.

Coleman, Tim. 2006. "Blackheart Tattoo Set the Record Straight." *Skin & Ink* 13 (March): 52–61.

Cooley, Charles H. 1964 [1902]. *Human Nature and the Social Order*. New York: Schocken.

Crane, Diana. 1987. *The Transformation of the Avant-Garde: The New York Art World, 1940–1985*. Chicago: University of Chicago Press.

Csikszentmihalyi, Mihaly, and Eugene Rochberg-Halton. 1981. *The Meaning of Things: Domestic Symbols and the Self*. Cambridge: Cambridge University Press.

Cummings, William, and M. Venkatesan. 1975. "Cognitive Dissonance and Consumer Behavior: A Review of the Evidence." In *Advances in Consumer Research*, vol. II, ed. M. Schlueger, 21–31. Chicago: Association for Consumer Research.

Cunningham, Scott. 1967. "Perceived Risk and Brand Loyalty." In *Risk-Taking and Information Handling in Consumer Behavior*, ed. D. Cox, 507–523. Boston: Harvard Graduate School of Business Administration.

Danto, Arthur. 1964. "The Artworld." *The Journal of Philosophy* 61: 571–585.

DeMello, Margo. 1993. "The Convict Body: Tattooing Among the American Male Prisoners." *Anthropology Today* 9 (6): 10–13.

———. 2000. *Bodies of Inscription: A Cultural History of the Modern Tattoo Community*. Durham, NC: Duke University Press.

Desocio, Lois. 2007. "Indelible Love: My Son's Tattoos and Me." *Newsweek*, July 16, p. 16.

Dickie, George. 1971. *Aesthetics: An Introduction*. New York: Pegasus.

———. 1974. *Art and the Aesthetic: An Institutional Analysis*. Ithaca, NY: Cornell University Press.

DiMaggio, Paul. 1977. "Market Structure, The Creative Process, and Popular Culture: Toward an Organizational Reinterpretation of Mass-Culture Theory." *Journal of Popular Culture* 11 (2): 436–452.

———. 1987. "Classification in Art." *American Sociological Review* 52: 440–455.

Douglas, Mary, and Baron Isherwood. 1979. *The World of Goods: Towards an Anthropology of Consumption*. New York: Norton.

Dube, Philippe. 1985. *Tattoo-Tatoue*. Montreal: Jean Basile.

Durkheim, Emile. 1966 [1938]. *Rules of Sociological Method*. New York: MacMillan.

Ebensten, Hans. 1953. *Pierced Hearts and True Love*. London: Derek Verschoyle.

Ebin, Victoria. 1979. *The Body Decorated*. London: Thames and Hudson.

Edgerton, Robert, and Harvey Dingman. 1963. "Tattooing and Identity." *International Journal of Social Psychiatry* 9: 143–153.

Eldridge, C. J. 1981. *Early Tattoo Attractions*. Berkeley: Tattoo Archive.

———. 1982. *The History of the Tattoo Machine*. Berkeley: Tattoo Archive.

———. 1986. "The History of Tattoo Suppliers." *Tattoo* (Winter): 58–63.

Elias, Norbert. 1991. *The Society of Individuals*. Oxford: Basil Blackwell.

———. 1994. *The Civilizing Process*. New York: Pantheon.

Emerson, Joan. 1970. "Behavior in Private Places: Sustaining Definitions of Reality in a Gynecological Examination." In *Patterns of Communicative Behavior*, ed. H. Freitzel, 74–97. (Recent Sociology, No. 2.) New York: MacMillan.

Emerson, Robert. 1987. "Four Ways to Improve the Craft of Fieldwork." *Journal of Contemporary Ethnography* 16 (April): 69–89.

Farina, A., E. Fischer, S. Sherman, W. Smith, T. Groh, and P. Nermin. 1977. "Physical Attractiveness and Mental Illness." *Journal of Abnormal Psychology* 86: 510–517.

Faris, James. 1972. *Nuba Personal Art*. London: Duckworth.

Farren, Mick. 1985. *The Black Leather Jacket*. New York: Abbeville.

Faulkner, Robert. 1983. *Music on Demand: Composers and Careers in the Hollywood Film Industry*. New Brunswick, NJ: Transaction.

Featherstone, Mike, ed. 2000. *Body Modification*. Thousand Oaks, CA: Sage.

Feldman, Saul. 1975. "The Presentation of Shortness in Everyday Life." In *Life Styles*, ed. S. Feldman and G. Thielbar, 437–442. Boston: Little, Brown.

Fellman, Sandi. 1986. *The Japanese Tattoo*. New York: Abbeville.

Fellowes, C. H. 1971. *The Tattoo Book*. Princeton, NJ: Pyne.

Ferguson-Rayport, Shirley, Richard Griffith, and Erwin Straus. 1955. "The Psychiatric Significance of Tattoos." *Psychiatric Quarterly* 29: 112–131.

Fine, Gary A. 1985. "Occupational Aesthetics: How Trade School Students Learn to Cook." *Urban Life* 14: 3–32.

Finn, Robin. 1984. "The Price of Beauty." *Northeast/The Hartford Courant*, December 16, pp. 10–19.

Fischer, J. L. 1970. "Art Styles as Cultural Cognitive Maps." In *The Sociology of Art and Literature*, ed. M. Albrecht et al., 72–89. New York: Praeger.

Fish, Pat. 1986. *The Big Golden Book of Flash*. Santa Barbara: Common Press.

Fisher, Angela. 1984. "Africa Adorned." *National Geographic* 166 (November): 600–632.

Flugel, J. C. 1969. *The Psychology of Clothes*. New York: International Universities Press.

Fondiller, Harvey. 1984. "Shows We've Seen." *Popular Photography* (February): 51–52.

Fox, James. 1976. "Self-Imposed Stigmata: A Study of Tattooing Among Female Inmates." Ph.D. dissertation, Department of Sociology, State University of New York at Albany.

Freedman, Rita. 1986. *Beauty Bound*. Lexington, MA: Lexington.

Fried, Fred, and Mary Fried. 1978. *America's Forgotten Folk Arts*. New York: Pantheon.

Gans, Herbert. 1971. "The Uses of Power." *Social Policy* 2: 20–24.

———. 1974. *Popular Culture and High Culture*. New York: Basic Books.

———. 1999. *Popular Culture and High Culture: An Analysis and Evaluation of Taste*. New York: Basic Books.

Gardner. James. 1985. "Graffiti and Other Art Forms." *Commentary* 80 (2): 49–53.

Gell, Alfred. 1993. *Wrapping in Images: Tattooing in Polynesia*. New York: Oxford University Press.

Gitlin, Todd. 1983. *Inside Prime Time*. New York: Pantheon.

Gittleson, N., G. Wallen, and K. Dawson-Butterwork. 1969. "The Tattooed Psychiatric Patient." *British Journal of Psychiatry* 115: 1249–1253.

Goffman, Erving. 1959. *The Presentation of Self in Everyday Life.* Garden City, NY: Doubleday.

———. 1961. *Asylums.* New York: Random House.

———. 1963a. *Stigma.* Englewood Cliffs, NJ: Prentice-Hall.

———. 1963b. *Behvaior in Public Places.* New York: Free Press.

Goldstein, Norman. 1979a. "Laws and Regulations Relating to Tattoos." *Journal of Dermatologic Surgery and Oncology* 5: 913–915.

———. 1979b. "Complication From Tattoos." Journal of Dermatologic Surgery and Oncology 5: 869–878.

———. 1979c. "Psychological Implications of Tattoos." *Journal of Dermatologic Surgery and Oncology* 5: 883–888.

Goldstein, Norman, James Penoff, Norman Price, Roger Ceilley, Leon Goldman, Victor Hay-Roe, and Timothy Miller. 1979. "Techniques of Removal of Tattoos." *Journal of Dermatologic Surgery and Oncology* 5: 901–910.

Gombrich, E. H. 1969. *Art and Illusion.* Princeton, NJ: Princeton University Press.

Goode, Eric. 2002. "Does the Death of the Sociology of Deviance Claim Make Sense?" *The American Sociologist* 33 (3): 107–118.

———. 2003. "The Macguffin that Refuses to Die: An Investigation into the Condition of the Sociology of Deviance." *Deviant Behavior* 24: 507–533.

———. 2005. *Deviant Behavior* (7th edition). Upper Saddle River, NJ: Pearson.

Govenar, Alan. 1977. "The Acquisition of Tattooing Competence: An Introduction." *Folklore Annual of the University Folklore Association* 7 & 8: 43–53.

———. 1983. "Christian Tattoos." *Tattootime* 2 (Winter): 4–11.

Green, Norman. 1982. "The World of New Tattoos." *The Hartford Courant,* January 7, p. B1.

Greenley, James, and Richard Schoenherr. 1981. "Organizational Effects on Client Satisfaction With Humaneness of Service." *Journal of Health and Social Behavior* 22: 2–18.

Griff, Milton. 1970. "The Recruitment and Socialization of Artists." In *The Sociology of Art and Literature: A Reader,* ed. M. Albrecht et al., 145–158. New York: Praeger.

Grumet, Gerald. 1983. "Psychodynamic Implications of Tattoos." *Journal of Orthopsychiatry* 53: 482–492.

Guthrie, R. D. 1976. *Body Hot Spots.* New York: Van Nostrand Reinhold.

Haines, William, and Arthur Huffman. 1958. "Tattoos Found in a Prison Environment." *Journal of Social Therapy* 4: 104–113.

Hall, Sarah. 2005. *Electric Michelangelo.* New York: Harper.

Halle, David. 1993. *Inside Culture: Art and Class in the American Home.* Chicago: University of Chicago Press.

227 References

Hambly, W. D. 1974 [1925]. *The History of Tattooing and Its Significance.* Detroit: Gale Research.

Hamburger, Ernest. 1966. "Tattooing as a Psychic Defense Mechanism." *International Journal of Social Psychiatry* 12: 60–62.

Hardy, D. E. 1982a. "The Name Game." *Tattootime* 1 (Fall): 50–54.

———. 1982. "The Mark of the Professional." *Tattootime* 1: 46–49.

———. 1983. "Inventive Cover Work." *Tattootime* 2: 12–17.

———. 1987a. "Eternal Spiral." *Tattootime* 4: 4–14.

———. 1987b. "Remains to be Seen." *Tattootime* 4: 74–78.

Hatfield, Elaine, and Susan Sprecher. 1986. *Mirror, Mirror . . . .* Albany: State University of New York Press.

Hauser, Arnold. 1982. *The Sociology of Art.* Chicago: University of Chicago Press.

Hawkes, Daina, Charlene Y. Senn, and Chantal Thorn. 2004. "Factors that Influence Attitudes Towards Women with Tattoos." *Sex Roles* 50 (9/10): 593–604.

Hawkins, Roger, and John Popplestone. 1964. "The Tattoo as an Exoskeletal Defense." *Perceptual and Motor Skills* 19: 500.

Heller, Nancy. 1987. *Women Artists: An Illustrated History.* New York: Abbeville.

Hendershott, Anne. 2002. *The Politics of Deviance.* San Francisco: Encounter Books.

Hennessy, Val. 1978. *In the Gutter.* London: Quartet.

Henning, Edward. 1960. "Patronage and Style in the Arts: A Suggestion Concerning their Relations." *Journal of Aesthetics and Art Criticism* 18: 464–471.

Henslin, James. 1968. "Trust and the Cab Driver." In *Sociology and Everyday Life,* ed. M. Truzzi, 138–158. Englewood Cliffs, NJ: Prentice-Hall.

Hewitt, Kim. 1997. *Mutilating the Body: Identities in Blood and Ink.* Bowling Green, OH: Popular Press.

Hill, Amie. 1972. "Tattoo Renaissance." In *Side-Saddle on the Golden Calf,* ed. G. Lewis, 245–249. Pacific Palisades, CA: Goodyear.

Hillier, Bevis. 1971. *The World of Art Deco.* New York: Dutton.

Hirsch, Paul. 1972. "Processing Fads and Fashions: An Organization-Set Analysis of Cultural Industry Systems." *American Journal of Sociology* 77: 639–659.

Hirschi, Travis. 1962. "The Professional Prostitute." *Berkeley Journal of Sociology* 7: 37–48.

Hirschman, Elizabeth. 1981a. "Retailing and the Production of Popular Culture." In *Theory in Retailing: Traditional and Nontraditional Sources,* ed. R. Stampfli and E. Hirschman, 71–83. Chicago: American Marketing Association.

———. 1981b. "Comprehending Symbolic Consumption: Three Theoretical Issues." In *Symbolic Consumer Behavior,* ed. E. Hirschman and M. Holbrook, 4–6. Ann Arbor, MI: Association for Consumer

Research.

Hirschman, Elizabeth, and Morris Holbrook, eds. 1981. *Symbolic Consumer Behavior.* Ann Arbor, MI: Association for Consumer Research.

Hirschman, Elizabeth, and Ronald Stampfl. 1980. "Roles of Retailing in the Diffusion of Popular Culture: Microperspectives." *Journal of Retailing* 56: 16–36.

Holbrook, Morris, and William Moore. 1981. "Cue Configurality in Esthetic Responses." In *Symbolic Consumer Behavior,* ed. E. Hirschman and M. Holbrook, 16–25. Ann Arbor, MI: Association for Consumer Research.

Houghton, S. J., K. Durkin, E. Parry, Y. Turbet, and P. Odgers. 1996. "Amateur Tattooing Practices and Beliefs Among High-School Adolescents." *Journal of Adolescent Health* 19 (6): 420–425.

Hughes, Everett. 1971a. "Good People and Dirty Work." In *The Sociological Eye.* 87–97. Chicago: Aldine.

———. 1971b. "Mistakes at Work." In *The Sociological Eye,* 316–325. Chicago: Aldine.

———. 1971c. "Bastard Institutions." In *The Sociological Eye,* 98–105. Chicago: Aldine.

Irving, John. 2005. *Until I Find You.* New York: Random House.

Irwin, John. 1987. "Reflections on Ethnography." *Journal of Contemporary Ethnography* 16 (April): 41–48.

Irwin, Katherine. 2001. "Legitimating the First Tattoo: Moral Passage Through Informal Interaction." *Symbolic Interaction* 24 (1): 49–73.

———. 2003. "Saints and Sinners: Elite Tattoo Collectors and Tattooists as Positive and Negative Deviants." *Sociological Spectrum* 23: 27–57.

Jacobson, Yehuda, and Diana Luzzatto. 2004. "Israeli Youth Body Adornments: Between Protest and Conformity." *Young* 12 (2): 155–174.

Jacoby, Jack, and L. Kaplan. 1972. "The Components of Perceived Risk." In M. Venkatesan (ed.), *Proceedings,* Third Annual Convention of the Association for Consumer Research, pp. 382–393.

Jamiol, Paul. 1987. "Tattooing at the Peabody Museum." *Tattoo* 8: 32–37.

Janson, H. W. 1964. *The History of Art.* Englewood Cliffs, NJ: Prentice-Hall.

Jeffreys, Sheila. 2000. "'Body Art' and Social Status: Cutting, Tattooing, and Piercing from a Feminist Perspective." *Feminism and Psychology* 10 (4): 409–429.

Jenkins, Emily. *Tongue First: Adventures in Physical Culture.* New York: Holt.

Jensen, Joli. 1984. "An Interpretive Approach to Culture Production." In *Interpreting Television: Current Research Perspectives,* ed. W. Rowland, Jr. and B. Watkins. 98–118. Beverly Hills: Sage.

Jonaitis, Aldorna. 1983. "The Symbolism of Piercing: Tlingit Indian Labrets." Paper presented at the Art of the Body Symposium, January, at University of California, Los Angeles.

Jones, Edward, Amerigo Farina, Albert Hastorf, Hazel Markus, Dale Miller, and Robert Scott. 1984. *Social Stigma: The Psychology of Marked*

Relationships. New York: Freeman.

Jordon, Matt. 2005. *Weirdo Deluxe: The Wild World of Pop Surrealism and Lowbrow Art*. San Francisco: Chronicle Books.

Kander, Joseph, and Harold Kohn. 1943. "A Note on Tattooing Among Selectees." *American Journal of Psychiatry* 100: 326–327.

Kang, Miliann, and Katherine Jones. 2007. "Why Do People Get Tattoos?" *Contexts* 6 (1): 42–47.

Katz, Fred E., and H. W. Martin. 1962. "Career Choice Processes." *Social Forces* 41: 149–154.

Kealy, Edward. 1979. "From Craft to Art: The Case of Sound Mixers and Popular Music." *Sociology of Work and Occupations* 6: 3–29.

Kelly, J., and W. George. 1982. "Strategic Management Issues for the Retailing of Services." *Journal of Retailing* 58: 26–43.

Klofas, John, and Charles Cutshall. 1985. "Unobtrusive Research Methods in Criminal Justice: Using Graffiti in the Reconstruction of Institutional Cultures." *Journal of Research in Criminology and Delinquency* 22: 355–373.

Koch, Jerome, Zuojin Zhu, Julie Cannon, Myrna Armstrong, and Donna Owen. 2005. "College Students, Tattooing, and the Health Belief Model: Extending Social Psychological Perspectives on Youth Culture and Deviance." *Sociological Spectrum* 25: 79–102.

Kriesberg, Louis. 1952. "The Retail Furrier: Concepts of Security and Success." *American Journal of Sociology* 52: 478–485.

Kunzle, David. 1982. *Fashion and Fetishism*. Totowa, NJ: Rowman and Littlefield.

Kurtzburg, Richard, Michael Lewin, Norman Cavior, and Douglas Lipton. 1967. "Psychologic Screening of Inmates Requesting Cosmetic Operations: A Preliminary Report." *Plastic and Reconstructive Surgery* 39: 387–396.

Laba, Martin. 1986. "Making Sense: Expressiveness, Stylization and the Popular Culture Process." *Journal of Popular Culture* 19 (4): 107–117.

Laumann, Anne, and Amy Derick. 2006. "Tattoos and Body Piercings in the United States: A National Data Set." *Journal of the American Academy of Dermatology* 55 (3): 413–421.

Lavell, Sharie, and Carson Lewis. 1982. "The Patient's Experience of Aesthetic Regenerative Facial Surgery: A Composite." *Aesthetic Plastic Surgery* 6: 247–249.

Lee, Adrian. 2004 [2002]. *Expert Tailoring: Suits Made to Fit*. San Francisco, CA: NS Tattoo Collective/Last Gasp.

Lemes, Andrew J. 1978. *Tattoo: Trade Secrets*. Los Angeles: Mimeographed Document.

Levy, Jerome, Margaret Sewell, and Norman Goldstein. 1979. "A Short History of Tattooing." *Journal of Dermatologic Surgery and Oncology* 5 (November): 851–864.

Lewis, David. 1969. *Convention: A Philosophical Study*. Cambridge: Harvard

University Press.

Lewis, George, ed. 1972. *Side-Saddle on the Golden Calf.* Pacific Palisades, CA: Goodyear.

———. 1981. "Taste Cultures and Their Composition: Towards a New Theoretical Perspective." In *Mass Media and Social Change*, ed. E. Katz and T. Szecsko, 201–218. Beverly Hills: Sage.

———. 1986. "Uncertain Truths: The Promotion of Popular Culture." *Journal of Popular Culture* 20 (3): 31–44.

Lofland, John. 1969. *Deviance and Identity.* Englewood Cliffs, NJ: Prentice-Hall.

Lofland, Lynn. 1973. *A World of Strangers.* New York: Basic Books.

Lomax, Alan. 1970. "Song Structure and Social Structure." In *The Sociology of Art and Literature*, ed. M. Albrecht et al., 55–71. New York: Praeger.

London, David, and Albert Della-Bitta. 1984. *Consumer Behavior.* New York: McGraw Hill.

Lorimer, N., and E. Werner. 1992. "Tattoos and High Risk Behavior among Drug Addicts." *Medical Law* 11: 167–174.

Lovelock, Charles. 1984. *Services Marketing.* Englewood Cliffs. NJ: Prentice-Hall.

Lurie, Alison. 1983. *The Language of Clothes.* New York: Vintage.

Lyon, Eleanor. 1974. "Work and Play: Resource Constraints in a Small Theater." *Urban Life* 3: 71–97.

Maines, Rachel. 1985. "Evolution of the Potholder: From Technology to Popular Art." *Journal of Popular Culture* 19 (1): 3–33.

Manfredi, John. 1982. *The Social Limits of Art.* Amherst: University of Massachusetts Press.

Manning, Peter. 1982. "Qualitative Methods." In *A Handbook of Social Science Methods*, vol. 2, ed. R. Smith and P. Manning, 1–28. Cambridge, MA: Ballinger.

Martorella, Rosanne. 1982. *The Sociology of Opera.* South Hadley, MA: Bergin.

Mascia-Lees, Frances E., and Patricia Sharpe, eds. 1992. *Tattoo, Torture, Mutilation, and Adornment: The Denaturalization of the Body in Culture and Text.* Albany, NY: SUNY Press.

Matza, David. 1969. *Becoming Deviant.* Englewood Cliffs, NJ: Prentice-Hall.

McCall, Michal. 1977. "Art Without a Market: Creating Artistic Value in a Provincial Art World." *Symbolic Interaction* 1: 32–43.

Mcgregor, Francis. 1974. *Transformation and Identity.* New York: Quadrangle.

Mcgregor, Francis, Theodora Abel, Albert Bryt, Edith Lauer, and Serena Weissmann. 1953. *Facial Deformities and Plastic Surgery.* Springfield, IL: Thomas.

McKinstry, W. 1974. "The Pulp Voyeur: A Peek of Pornography in Public Places." In *Deviance: Field Studies and Self-Disclosures*, ed. Jerry

Jacobs. 30–40. Palo Alto, CA: National Press.

Measly, L. 1972. "The Psychiatric and Social Relevance of Tattoos in Royal Navy Detainees." *British Journal of Criminology* 12: 182–186.

Mennerick, Lewis. 1974. "Client Typologies: A Method of Coping with Conflict in the Service Worker-Client Relationship." *Sociology of Work and Occupations* 1: 396–418.

Merton, Robert. 1968. *Social Theory and Social Structure.* New York: MacMillan.

Meyer, Ursula. 1972. *Conceptual Art.* New York: Dutton.

Miles, Matthew, and A. M. Huberman. 1984. *Qualitative Data Analysis.* Beverly Hills. CA: Sage.

Monaco, James. 1978. *Media Culture.* New York: Delta.

Morse, Albert. 1977. *The Tattooists.* San Francisco: Albert Morse.

Mosher, Donald, Wayne Oliver, and Jeffery Dolgan. 1967. "Body Image in Tattooed Prisoners." *Journal of Clinical Psychology* 23: 31–32.

Mukerji, Chandra. 1978. "Artwork: Collection and Contemporary Culture." *American Journal of Sociology* 84: 348–365.

Myers, James. 1992. "Nonmainstream Body Modification: Genital Piercing, Branding, Burning and Cutting." *Journal of Contemporary Ethnography* 21 (3): 267–306.

Napoleon, T., L. Chassin, and R. D. Young. 1980. "A Replication and Extension of Physical Attractiveness and Mental Illness." *Journal of Abnormal Psychology* 89: 250–253.

Neapolitan, Jerome. 1986. "Art, Craft and Art/Craft Segments Among Craft Media Workers." *Work and Occupations* 13 (May): 203–216.

Needelman, Burt, and Norman Weiner. 1977. "Appearance and Moral Status in the Arts." Paper presented at the annual meeting of the Popular Culture Association in Baltimore.

Needleman, Carla. 1979. *The Work of Craft.* New York: Knopf.

Negrin, Llewellyn. 2000. "Some Thoughts on 'Primitive' Body Decoration." *Postcolonial Studies* 3 (3): 331–5.

Newman, Gustave. 1982. "The Implications of Tattooing in Prisoners." *Journal of Clinical Psychiatry* 43: 231–234.

Nicosia, Franco, and Robert Mayer. 1976. "Toward a Sociology of Consumption." *Journal of Consumer Research* 3: 65–75.

Nye, Russel. 1972. "Notes on Popular Culture." In *Side-Saddle on the Golden Calf,* ed. G. Lewis. 13–19. Pacific Palisades, CA: Goodyear.

Oettermann, Stephan. 1985. "An Art as Old as Humanity." Introduction to *Tattoo,* by S. Richter, 11–17. London: Quartet.

Olguin, B. V. 1997. "Tattoos, Abjection, and the Political Unconscious: Toward a Semiotics of the Pinto Visual Vernacular." *Cultural Critique* 37: 159–213.

Orten, James, and William Bell. 1974. "Personal Graffiti: The Rogue's Tattoo." Report of research in *Psychology Today* (January): 26, 90.

Paine, Jocelyn. 1979. "Skin Deep: A Brief History of Tattooing." *Mankind*

6 (May): 18 ff.

Parry, Albert. 1971 [1933]. *Tattoo: Secrets of a Strange Art Practiced by the Natives of the United States*. New York: Collier.

Pearlstein, Howard. 1978. "Handwriting on the Wall." In *Aesthetics of Graffiti*. San Francisco: Museum of Modern Art, 5–8.

Pellegrini, Aldo. 1966. *New Tendencies in Art*. New York: Crown.

Peterson, Richard. 1976. "The Production of Culture: A Prolegomenon." *American Behavioral Scientist* 19 (July): 669–684.

———. 1982. "Five Constraints on the Production of Culture: Law, Technology, Market, Organizational Structure and Occupational Careers." *Journal of Popular Culture* 16 (2): 143–153.

———. 1983. "Patterns of Cultural Choice: A Prolegomenon." *American Behavioral Scientist* 26: 422–438.

Peterson, Richard, and David Berger. 1975. "Cycles in Symbolic Production: The Case of Popular Music." *American Sociological Review* 40: 158–173.

Pfuhl, Edward. 1986. *The Deviance Process*. 2nd ed. Belmont, CA: Wadsworth.

Phillips, Susan A. 2001. "Gallo's Body: Decoration and Damnation in the Life of a Chicano Gang Member." *Ethnography* 2 (3): 357–388.

Pitts, Victoria. 2003. *In the Flesh: The Cultural Politics of Body Modification*. New York: Palgrave/MacMillan.

Polhemus, Ted, and Randall Housk. 1996. *The Customized Body*. London: Serpent's Tale.

Pollack, Otakar, and Elisabeth McKenna. 1945. "Tattooed Psychotic Patients." *American Journal of Psychiatry* 101: 673–674.

Popplestone, John. 1963. "A Syllabus of Exoskeletal Defenses." *Psychological Record* 13: 15–25.

Post, Richard. 1968. "The Relationship of Tattoos to Personality Disorder." *Journal of Criminal Law, Criminology and Police Science* 59: 516–524.

Pritchard, Stephen. 1999. "Traces of Authority: Anthropology and the Maori Tattoo's 'Proper' Time." *Communal/Plural* 7 (2): 177–194.

———. 2000. "Essence, Identity, Signature: Tattoos and Cultural Property." *Social Semiotics* 10 (3): 331–346.

———. 2001. "An Essential Marking: Maori Tattooing and the Properties of Identity." *Theory, Culture, and Society* 18 (4): 27–45.

Prueitt, Melvin. 1984. *Art and the Computer*. New York: McGraw-Hill.

Read, Madlen. 2006. "Workers' Body Art Piercing Dress Codes." *The Hartford Courant*, October 25, p. E2.

Reuel, Peter. 2006. "Ink Goes Mainstream: One-in-Four Chance Adult Has Tattoo." *The Boston Herald*, Sunday, June 18: 6.

Richie, Donald. 1973. "The Japanese Art of Tattooing." *Natural History* 82 (December): 50–59.

Richie, Donald, and Ian Buruma. 1980. *The Japanese Tattoo*. New York: Weatherhill.

Richter, Hans. 1965. *Dada: Art and Anti-Art*. New York: Oxford University Press.

Richter, Stefan. 1985. *Tattoo.* London: Quartet.

Riley, Sarah. 2002. "A Feminist Construction of Body Art as a Harmful Cultural Practice: A Response to Jeffreys." *Feminism and Psychology* 12 (4): 540–545.

Roberts, Allen F. 1988. "Tabwa Tegumentary Inscription." In *Marks of Civilization*, ed. Arnold Rubin, 41–56. Los Angeles: UCLA Museum of Cultural History.

Roebuck, Julian, and Wolfgang Frese. 1976. "The After-Hours Club: An Illegal Social Organization and Its Client System." *Urban Life* 5: 131–164.

Rondinella, Gippi. 1985. *The Sign Upon Cain: An Overview of the Controversial Art of Tattooing.* Terni, Italy: Alterocca Editore.

Roselius, Ted. 1971. "Consumer Rankings of Risk Reduction Methods." *Journal of Marketing* 35: 56–61.

Rosenberg, Bernard, and Norris Fliegel. 1970. "The Artist and His Publics: The Ambiguity of Success." In *The Sociology of Art and Literature*, ed. M. Albrecht, et al., 499–517. New York: Praeger.

Rosenberg, Harold. 1972. *The De-Definition of Art.* New York: Collier.

Rosenblatt, Daniel. 1997. "The Anti-Social Skin: Structure, Resistance, and 'Modern Primitive' Adornment in the United States." *Cultural Anthropology* 12 (3): 287–334.

Rosenblum, Barbara. 1978. *Photographers at Work: A Sociology of Photographic Styles.* New York: Holmes and Meier.

Rosenkranz, Patrick. 2006. *You Call This Art?!!: A Bigtime Retrospective of Years of Hard Work by Greg Irons.* Seattle: Fantagraphics.

Ross, Ivan. 1975. "Perceived Risk and Consumer Behavior: A Critical Review." In *Advances in Consumer Research*, vol. 2, ed. M. Schlueger, 1–19. Chicago: Association for Consumer Research.

Ross, Robert, and Hugh McKay. 1979. *Self-Mutilation.* Lexington, MA: Heath.

Rubin, Arnold. 1983. "Prologue to a History of the Tattoo Renaissance." Paper presented at the Art of the Body Symposium, January, at University of California, Los Angeles.

Rubin, Arnold, ed. 1988. *Marks of Civilization.* Los Angeles: UCLA Museum of Cultural History.

Rubington, Earl, and Martin Weinberg, eds. 2002. *Deviance: The Interactionist Perspective* (8th edition). Boston: Allyn and Bacon.

Sagarin, Edward. 1979. "Voluntary Associations Among Social Deviants." In *Deviant Behavior*, ed. D. Kelly, 448–463. New York: St. Martin's.

San Francisco Museum of Modern Art. 1978. *Aesthetics of Graffiti: April 28–July 2.* San Francisco: Museum of Modern Art.

Sanders, Clinton R. 1974. "Psyching Out the Crowd: Folk Performers and Their Audiences." *Urban Life and Culture* 3: 264–282.

———. 1982. "Structural and Interactional Features of Popular Culture Production: An Introduction to the Production of Culture Perspective." *Journal of Popular Culture* 16 (2): 66–74.

———. 1986. "Tattooing as Fine Art and Client Work: The Art/Work of

Carl (Shotsie) Gorman." *Appearance* 12: 12–13.

———. 1987. "Psychos and Outlaws: Scientific Images of Tattooed Persons." *Tattootime* 4: 64–68.

———. 1990. "'A Lot of People Like It': The Relationship Between Deviance and Popular Culture." In *Marginal Conventions: Popular Culture, Mass Media, and Social Deviance,* ed. Clinton Sanders, 3–13. Bowling Green, OH: Popular Press.

———. 1991. "Memorial Decoration: Women, Tattooing, and the Meanings of Body Alteration," *Michigan Quarterly Review* 30 (1): 146–157.

———. 1994. "Tattoo You: Tattoos as Self Extensions and Identity Markers." In *Doing Everyday Life: Ethnography as Lived Experience,* eds. Mary Lou Dietz, William Shaffir, and Robert Prus, 203–212. Mississauga, Ontario: Copp Clark Longman.

———. 2000. "Tattooing and Body Piercing." In *Encyclopedia of Criminology and Deviant Behavior (Volume Four: Self Destructive Behavior and Disvalued Identity),* eds. Charles Faupel and Paul Roman, 531–534. Philadelphia: Taylor and Francis.

———. 2001. "Tattoos and Tattooing." In *The Guide to United States Popular Culture,* eds. Ray Browne and Pat Browne, 806–807. Bowling Green, OH: Popular Press.

Sass, Louis. 1986. "Anthropology's Native Problems." *Harper's Magazine* (May): 49–57.

Schroder, David. 1973. *Engagement in the Mirror: Hairdressers and Their Work.* Ph.D dissertation, Department of Sociology, Northwestern University.

Schur, Edwin. 1971. *Labeling Deviant Behavior.* New York: Harper and Row.

Schwartz, Dona. 1986. "Camera Clubs and Fine Art Photography: The Social Construction of an Elite Code." *Urban Life* 15 (July): 165–196.

Scutt, R. W. B., and C. Gotch. 1974. *Art, Sex, and Symbol: The Mystery of Tattooing.* New York: A. S. Barnes.

Shover, Neal. 1975. "Tarnished Goods and Services in the Market Place." *Urban Life and Culture* 3: 471–488.

Simmons, D. R. 1986. *Ta Moko: The Art of Maori Tattoo.* Auckland: Reed Methuen.

Sinha, Anita. 1979. "Control in Craft Work: The Case of Production Potters." *Qualitative Sociology* 2: 3–25.

Sirgy, M. J. 1982. "Self-Concept in Consumer Behavior: A Critical Review." *Journal of Consumer Research* 9: 287–300.

Solomon, Michael. 1983. "The Role of Products as Social Stimuli: A Symbolic Interactionist Perspective." *Journal of Consumer Research* 10: 319–329.

Spector, Malcolm, and John Kitsuse. 1977. *Constructing Social Problems.* Menlo Park, CA: Cummings.

Spiggle, Susan, and Clinton Sanders. 1983. "The Construction of Consumer Typologies: Scientific and Ethnomethods." In *Advances in Consumer Research,* vol. 11, ed. T. Kinnear, 337–342. Provo, UT:

Association for Consumer Research.

St. Clair, Leonard, and Alan Govenar. 1981. *Stoney Knows How: Life as a Tattoo Artist.* Lexington: University of Kentucky Press.

Stone, Gregory. 1970. "Appearance and the Self." In *Social Psychology Through Symbolic Interaction,* ed. G. Stone and H. Faberman, 394–414. Waltham, MA: Xerox.

Sudnow, David. 1965. "Normal Crimes." *Social Problems* 12: 255–275.

Sumner, Colin. 1994. *The Sociology of Deviance: An Obituary.* Buckingham, UK: Open University Press.

Sykes, Gresham. 1966. *The Society of Captives.* New York: Atheneum.

———. 1977. "Techniques of Data Collection and Reduction in Systematic Field Observation." *Behavior Research Methods and Instrumentation* 9 (5): 407–417.

Taylor, A. J. W. 1970. "Tattooing Among Male and Female Offenders of Different Ages in Different Types of Institutions." *Genetic Psychology Monographs* 81: 81–119.

Terkel, Studs. 1972. *Working.* New York: Random House.

Thevoz, Michel. 1984. *The Painted Body.* New York: Rizzoli.

Thomas, Nicholas, Anna Cole, and Bronwen Douglas, eds. 2005. *Tattoo: Bodies, Art, and Exchange in the Pacific and the West.* Durham, NC: Duke University Press.

Trice, Harrison, and Paul Roman. 1979. "Delabeling, Relabeling and Alcoholics Anonymous." In *Deviant Behavior,* ed. D. Kelly, 693–703. New York: St. Martin's.

Tuchman, Gaye. 1983. "Consciousness Industries and the Production of Culture." *Journal of Communication* 33 (3): 330–341.

———. 1989. *Edging Women Out: Victorian Novelists, Publishers, and Social Change.* New Haven, CT: Yale University Press.

Tucker, Marcia. 1976. "Pssst! Wanna See My Tattoo. . . ." *Ms.* (April): 29–33.

———. 1981. "Tattoo: The State of the Art." *Artforum* (May): 42–47.

Turner, Bryan S. 1999. "The Possibility of Primitiveness: Towards a Sociology of Body Marks in Cool Societies." *Body and Society* 5 (2–3): 39–50.

Vail, D. Angus. 1999a. "Tattoos are Like Potato Chips . . . You Can't Have Just One: The Process of Becoming and Being a Collector." *Deviant Behavior* 20 (3): 261–276.

———. 1999b. "The Commodification of Time in Two Art Worlds." *Symbolic Interaction* 22 (4): 325–344.

———. 2000. "Slingin' Ink or Scratching Skin: Producing Culture and Claiming Legitimacy Among Fine Art Tattooers." In *Unusual Occupations and Unusually Organized Occupations: Volume 11 of Current Research on Occupations and Professions,* eds. Helena Z. Lopata and Kevin D. Henson, 55–73. Greenwich, CT: JAI Press.

———. 2001. "Researching from Afar: Distance, Ethnography, and Testing the Edge." *Journal of Contemporary Ethnography* 30 (6): 704–725.

Vale, V., and A. Juno, eds. 2005 [1989]. *Modern Primitives: An*

Investigation of Contemporary Adornment and Ritual. San Francisco: RE/Search.

Van Gennep, Arnold. 1960. *The Rites of Passage.* Chicago: University of Chicago Press.

Van Lenning, Alkeline. 2002. "'The System Made Me Do It?' A Response to Jeffreys." *Feminism and Psychology* 12 (4): 546–552.

Vlach, John, and Simon Bronner, eds. 1986. *Folk Art and Art Worlds.* Ann Arbor: UMI Research Press.

Vlahos, Olivia. 1979. *Body: The Ultimate Symbol.* New York: Lippincott.

Vogel, Susan. 1983. "The Mark of Civilization: Scarification among the Baule." Paper presented at the Art of the Body Symposium, at University of California, Los Angeles.

Wallendorf, Melanie, George Zinkman, and Lydia Zinkman. 1981. "Cognitive Complexity and Aesthetic Preference." In *Symbolic Consumer Behavior,* ed. E. Hirschman and M. Holbrook, 52–59. Ann Arbor, MI: Association for Consumer Research.

Walster, E., V. Aronson, D. Abrahams, and L. Rottmann. 1966. "The Importance of Physical Attractiveness in Dating Behavior." *Journal of Personality and Social Psychology* 4: 508–516.

Ward, Ed. 1986. "Tattoo You." *New Age Journal,* (July/August): 52, 64.

Watson, Bruce. 1968. "On the Nature of Art Publics." *International Social Science Journal* 20 (4): 667–680.

Watson, J. M. 1984. "Outlaw Motorcyclists: An Outgrowth of Lower Class Cultural Concerns." In *Deviant Behavior,* 2nd ed., ed. D. Kelly, 109–124. New York: St. Martin's.

Webb, Spider. 1979. *Pushing Ink: The Fine Art of Tattooing.* New York: Simon and Schuster.

Werner, Oswald, and G. M. Schoepfle. 1987. *Systematic Fieldwork.* Newbury Park, CA: Sage.

Wessel, Harry. 2007. "Fighting the Tattoo Taboo." *The Hartford Courant,* July 9, p. C10.

Wilson, James. 1970. *Varieties of Police Behavior.* New York: Atheneum.

Wilson, Robert. 1986. *Experiencing Creativity: On the Social Psychology of Art.* New Brunswick, NJ: Transaction.

Wolff, Janet. 1983. *Aesthetics and the Sociology of Art.* London: Allen and Unwin.

Wroblewski, Chris. 1981. *Skin Show: The Art and Craft of Tattoo.* New York: Dragon's Dream.

———. 1985. *Tattoo Art.* Wein: Christian Brandstatter.

———. 1987. *Tattoo: Pigments of the Imagination.* New York: Alfred Van Der Marck Editions.

Wrong, Dennis. 1961. "The Oversocialized Conception of Man in Modern Sociology." *American Sociological Review* 26: 183–193.

Yamamoto, Joe, William Seeman, and Boyd Lester. 1963. "The Tattooed Man." *Journal of Nervous and Mental Disease* 136: 365–367.

Young, T. R. 1981. "Sociology and Human Knowledge: Scientific vs. Folk Methods." *American Sociologist* 16: 119–124.

Zarum, Harvey. 1983. "Surgical Body Contouring: Motivations, Expectations, and Operative Techniques in Plastic Surgery." Paper presented at the Art of the Body Symposium, January, at University of California, Los Angeles.

Zeis, Milton. 1984 [1952]. *Secrets of the Art of Tattooing.* Berkeley: Tattoo Archive.

Zeithaml, Valerie. 1984. "How Consumer Evaluation Processes Differ Between Goods and Services." In *Services Marketing,* ed. C. Lovelock, 191–199. Englewood Cliffs, NJ: Prentice-Hall.

Zimmerman, Murray. 1979. "Suits for Malpractice Based on Alleged Unsightly Scars Resulting from Removal of Tattoos." *Journal of Dermatologic Surgery and Oncology* 5: 911–912.

Zolberg, Vera. 1990. *Constructing a Sociology of the Arts.* Cambridge: Cambridge University Press.

Zurcher, Louis A. 1977. *The Mutable Self.* Beverly Hills, CA: Sage.

Index

243 Index